# SCHOFIELD

Lieutenant-General John M. Schofield, U.S.A.,
as a Major General

# SCHOFIELD
## Union General in the Civil War and Reconstruction

James L. McDonough

FLORIDA STATE UNIVERSITY PRESS
TALLAHASSEE/1972

*A Florida State University Press Book*

Manufactured for the publisher by the
E. O. Painter Printing Company, Inc.
DeLeon Springs, Florida

# Preface

SINCE THE Civil War Centennial concluded, I have noticed that several new publications about the conflict have been greeted by some reviewers with feigned unbelief — "Not another book on the Civil War!" Some of these reviewers had long since published their own books and articles on the subject. One suspects that in some cases the additional competition and new interpretations were not welcome. In such instances a horrified remark about the proliferation of Civil War works may be readily dismissed.

No knowledgeable person should deny, however, that some books have been published on minor, even trivial, personalities and events of the war. John M. Schofield, while not ranking with generals such as Grant and Sherman, was a reasonably important and competent Union officer. Anyone who would make a serious study of the war in Missouri, the Spring Hill–Franklin–Nashville Campaign, or Reconstruction in Virginia, must deal with Schofield. He was also fairly important in the Atlanta campaign when it is approached from the Union point of view. And yet, while some military and political leaders of less consequence have been studied extensively and figures of approximately equal rank, particularly Confederates, have occasionally had two or more works about them published, it is a curious fact that there has been no study of Schofield. This may be due, in part at least, to the fact that Schofield, in contrast to so many figures of his era, did not develop characteristics which were notably dashing, colorful, rash, eccentric, or immoral.

Students of the Civil War have had to rely upon Schofield's autobiography—*Forty Six Years In The Army*—for information about him. To evaluate the man solely, or in the main, on the basis of what he himself said, or on the basis of what students of Hood, Sherman, Thomas, etc., have said about him, is not in the best interests of objectivity. There has long been a need for a study of Schofield's career in the Civil War and Reconstruction. The author hopes this volume will satisfactorily fill that void. I have not attempted to cover Schofield's career after he was relieved of duty as military director of Reconstruction in Virginia. Viewing the Civil War and Reconstruction as the most significant events in United States history in the nineteenth century, and perhaps the most important in all U.S. history, I can only think of Schofield's later career as anticlimactic. His brief term as Secretary of War was uneventful and came about because of the necessity of filling the position for the remainder of President Johnson's term in office with a man acceptable both to Johnson and the more moderate Republicans who wanted to vote for acquital of the President at the impeachment trial. While Schofield later held several prominent military posts and finally became general-in-chief of the Army, most of his duties were of a routine nature, and he retired shortly before the Spanish-American War began.

The historian, if he is a historian, is dependent upon his sources. I have been handicapped in portraying Schofield the man by the very limited amount of his private correspondence which has been preserved. For example, the only letters of Schofield to his wife which were available to me were those written from Europe during his diplomatic visit to France in 1866. I could locate only a few letters to members of his family or close friends. Such correspondence, if available, might have been a great help in determining and presenting his personality.

I am indebted to many people who contributed to this work. The late Dr. W. T. Jordan, Professor of History, Florida State University, made helpful suggestions for improving the manuscript and was always a source of encouragement to me. Dr. James P. Jones, Associate Professor of History, Florida State University, who first suggested Schofield as a possible dissertation topic, was helpful in guiding me to the necessary materials, as well as in reading portions of the manuscript and making corrections. Dr. D. D. Horward, Associate Professor of History, Florida State University, made constructive criticisms when part of this study was in an earlier form as a dissertation. Dr. William T. Alderson, Executive Director of the American Association for State and Local History, was gracious to read an earlier draft of the manuscript and offer beneficial suggestions. Dr. James Preu, former Director of the Florida State University Press, has assisted me in preparing this manuscript for publication.

I would like to thank James W. Goodrich, associate editor of the *Missouri Historical Review,* for granting permission to publish in Chapter III part of an article which first appeared in the spring issue, 1970, of the *Review.* I would also like to express my gratitude to Robert M. McBride, editor of the *Tennessee Historical Quarterly,* for permission to publish in Chapter VII part of an article which first appeared in the summer issue, 1969, of the *Quarterly.* John T. Hubbell, editor of *Civil War History,* kindly granted permission to publish in Chapter X part of an article which originally appeared in his journal in the fall issue, 1969.

I am particularly grateful to Dr. Alderson for granting permission to quote from his dissertation, which I found especially helpful in the preparation of Chapter X. Several other works which were of assistance in writing this book are acknowledged by means of footnotes.

The staffs of the following libraries helped in locating materials and in making them available to me: the Library of Florida State University, Tallahassee, Florida; the Library of Congress, Washington, D.C.; the United States Military Academy Library, West Point, New York; the Illinois State Historical Library, Springfield, Illinois; the Crisman Memorial Library of David Lipscomb College, Nashville, Tennessee; the Tennessee State Library, Nashville, Tennessee; and the Joint University Libraries, Nashville, Tennessee.

My wife Nancy made an inestimable contribution, assisting in the research in Washington at the Library of Congress and typing one entire draft of the manuscript. There are others, too numerous to name, who assisted me in this study and I am grateful to them all.

JAMES L. McDONOUGH

# Contents

# List of Maps

# I. The Prelude

ON A FALL day in Washington a slightly stout, gray-haired man of medium height with Burnside whiskers walked from his office at the headquarters of the Army for the last time.[1] The year was 1895 and the General-in-Chief of the United States Army was retiring. He had made an enviable record. He was only the fifth man since Washington to hold the rank of Lieutenant General, following Scott, Grant, Sherman, and Sheridan. Sherman once described him as having more ability than the famed "Rock of Chickamauga," George H. Thomas.[2] John Pope said he "could stand steadier on the bulge of a barrel than any man who ever wore shoulder straps."[3] When a bill was before Congress to revive the grade of lieutenant general for his benefit, a former Confederate General, Senator Eppa Hunton from Virginia, supported him unreservedly. Hunton stated on the Senate floor that as virtual governor of Virginia during reconstruction he had "left behind him none but friends."[4]

1. Description taken from *The Union* (San Diego), June 25, 1891. The Washington *Post*, September 30, 1895.
2. Henry Hitchcock, *Marching With Sherman* (New Haven, 1927), p. 101.
3. David S. Stanley, *Personal Memoirs of Major General David S. Stanley, United States Army* (Cambridge, 1917), p. 214, quoting John Pope. Francis McKinney, *Education in Violence: The Life of George H. Thomas* (Detroit, 1961), pp. 272-73.
4. U. S., *Congressional Record*, 53rd Congress, 3rd Session, 1895, XXVII, 1898.

To the casual observer John McAllister Schofield probably did not present a very military appearance—not even as a young man in his prime. He was a little too short and round-bodied. He did not possess the dash and spirit which characterized some of the more famous Civil War personages. He was "a gentleman of fine address and elegant manners;" a calm, reflective person, who talked well in a terse, graphic way and listened well.[5] A major on Sherman's staff wrote, "One is impressed with the idea that he is in the presence of a statesman rather than a soldier. Perhaps Schofield partakes of the character of both."[6] Schofield was also a man of will and purpose. Beneath his outward calm some could distinguish a certain restlessness. He was an ambitious man.[7]

John Schofield was born on September 29, 1831, in the town of Gerry, Chautauqua County, New York. He was the second old-est of seven children—two girls and five boys.[8] His father, the Reverend James Schofield, was the minister of the Baptist Church in nearby Sinclairville. His mother was Caroline McAllister Scho-field, the daughter of John McAllister, who lived in Gerry.[9] The Schofield family was of old Puritan stock. The grandfather, also a minister named James, had been born in Connecticut, but left that state for New York sometime during the Revolutionary War. John's father had been born in Yates County, New York, in 1801.[10] In addition to preaching, the father supported his family by farm-ing. Schofield, remembering his childhood and youth, later wrote of the "hard work, mainly on the farm . . . which left no time and little inclination for any kind of mischief."[11] Unfortunately, very little material is to be found concerning his childhood. He

5. George W. Nichols, *The Story of the Great March* (New York, 1865), p. 288. *Diary and Letters of Rutherford B. Hayes*, ed. Charles R. Williams, 5 vols. (Columbus, Ohio, 1925) IV, 229.

6. Nichols, *The Great March*, p. 288.

7. E. F. Ware, *The Lyon Campaign in Missouri: A History of the First Iowa Infantry* (Topeka, Kansas, 1907), p. 227. *Daily Missouri Democrat* (St. Louis), October 17, 1862. Freeman Cleaves, *Rock of Chickamauga: Life of General George H. Thomas* (Norman, Oklahoma, 1948), p. 208.

8. The children, in order of birth, were Caroline, John M., George W., Elisha M., Emily M., Franklin P., and Charles B. Schofield. U.S. Bureau of the Census, *Seventh Census of the United States*. 1850. Freeport Township, Stephenson County, Illinois, p. 257.

9. John M. Schofield, *Forty-Six Years in the Army* (New York, 1897), p. 1.

10. *In the Footprints of the Pioneers of Stephenson County, Illinois* (Free-port, 1900), p. 95. Letter from John M. Schofield (hereafter cited as JMS) to a W. B. Schofield, September 26, 1891, Schofield MSS, Library of Congress.

11. Schofield, *Forty-Six Years*, p. 2.

himself said that he always enjoyed the "best possible opportunities for education, in excellent public schools."[12] In view of his record at West Point, this is a reasonable appraisal.

In the summer of 1843, when Schofield was twelve, the family moved to Illinois.[13] After a short stay in Bristol, they built a new home in Freeport, where the father was commissioned by the American Baptist Home Missionary Society to found a church. Freeport was a small town of about forty or fifty houses, featuring a frame courthouse completed in 1840 and a couple of hotels. There were no banks, and farmers left their money with merchants who deposited it in cities with safe deposits. Law enforcement in Freeport was not rigid. Liquor was available at saloons and hotels. Gambling was general, and disorders were relatively frequent in spite of the small population. Otherwise, the arrival of the stage coach from Chicago, which came in three times a week, was perhaps the most exciting event to which the townsfolk looked forward.[14]

Schofield's father, a man of considerable will and energy in addition to his faith, was soon hard at work founding the church. John and his oldest sister Caroline were also active in helping their father as best they could. In December, 1845, twenty-six men and women met in the Schofield kitchen and there organized the First Baptist Church of Freeport.[15] The next year construction of a "meeting house" was begun. John's uncle, Robert C. Schofield, proved to be a financial pillar of the church and it was largely through his contributions that the building was erected and the church maintained.[16]

The "hard work" on the farm continued as Schofield grew into his teens. When he was sixteen, he ventured into "the wilds," as he described it, of northern Wisconsin, helping survey public lands for three months. The next year he taught district school in the little town of Oneco. By this time the rather serious young man thought he wanted to become a lawyer.[17] But, in the spring

12. *Ibid.*, p. 1.
13. *Dictionary of American Biography*, XVI, 453.
14. Addison L. Fulwider, *History of Stephenson County, Illinois*, 2 vols. (Chicago, 1910), I, 76–80, 90.
15. *Ibid.*, p. 427.
16. *Portrait and Biographical Album of Stephenson County, Illinois* (1888), p. 569. *In the Footprints*, p. 75.
17. Schofield, *Forty-Six Years*, p. 2.

of 1849, an unforseen event changed the course of his life. The
Honorable Thomas J. Turner, United States Congressman from
Illinois, presented him with an appointment to West Point. As
one of the public school directors, Turner had been impressed
with Schofield's mathematical ability. And James Turner, brother
of the Congressman, had spoken highly of Schofield's work on the
surveying expedition in Wisconsin. The Congressman urged the
young man to accept the appointment, telling him that the training
at the academy would be good preparation for the study of law.
The father seems to have been a little hesitant, but not much
encouragement was required for the boy. Schofield had saved a
little money and had invested it in a tract of land. Selling this to
pay his expenses, the seventeen-year-old started back to the state
of his birth.[18]

When Schofield entered the military academy on July 1,
1849,[19] the physical plant at West Point left much to be desired.
The stone buildings overlooking the Hudson presented a scattered
and austere appearance. The barracks, not properly insulated,
were drafty and uncomfortable. The small academy hospital was
not adequate. The riding hall was dilapidated. The books in the
library had never been catalogued, and the food served in the mess
hall was generally considered very bad.[20]

The life of the cadet was simple and rigid. None could receive
money or supplies from his parents or anyone else. Tobacco and
playing cards were forbidden. Church attendance was compulsory.
No visiting from room to room was allowed during study hours or
between tattoo and reveille. Cadets were closely confined to the
post and required to undergo daily inspection and continual drilling.[21] To break the monotony many students resorted to bull
sessions after tattoo and visits to Benny Havens' Tavern ("Old
Benny Havens of blessed memory," as Schofield would later de-
scribe the proprietor).[22] Both, of course, were strictly forbidden.

Entering the military academy the same year with Schofield

18. *Ibid.*, pp. 2, 16, 17.
19. G. W. Cullum, *Biographical Register of Officers and Cadets of the
United States Military Academy*, 3 vols. (New York, 1879), II, 338.
20. John P. Dyer, *The Gallant Hood* (Indianapolis and New York, 1950),
p. 27.
21. *Regulations Established for the Organization and Government of the
Military Academy at West Point, New York* (New York, 1839), pp. 25, 26.
22. Schofield, *Forty-Six Years*, p. 6.

were James B. McPherson of Ohio, who would graduate first in his class, and eleven years later lead the Army of the Tennessee until his death before Atlanta; and John B. Hood, a southerner from Kentucky, whose path one day would cross Schofield's in deadly conflict. "Little Phil" Sheridan of Ohio, possibly the greatest cavalry leader produced on the Northern side and the man who would precede Schofield as Commanding General of the Army, had entered the year before, but was set back a year for fighting.[23] Thus he too graduated in the class of '53.

Schofield was assigned to a room in the old South Barracks, which were demolished the next year. His roommates were two fellows from Virginia. They had hardly learned each other's names when one of them said something about the "blank Yankees." Seeing an instant change of expression on Schofield's face the southern cadet added: "*You* are not a *Yankee!*" It seemed that the Southerners considered Illinois a western, not a northern state.[24] Cadets from one part of the country were often suspicious, at first sight, of those from other sections, but upon further acquaintance found them not so bad after all.[25]

After a year spent in studying mathematics, French, and English, Schofield stood eleventh in a class of seventy-four. His best subject was mathematics in which he ranked third. At the completion of his second year he stood sixth in his class.[26] Academic subjects were presenting no problem. Library records of book borrowing show that most of the titles which he checked out through the week had largely to do with coursework. He liked to read on weekends and often picked up something literary or historical. Many Saturdays he checked out a volume of the *Waverly* novels. He read Nares' *General History* and Prescott's *Conquest of Mexico*. And evidently he wished to know more of the six-foot-six-inch, three-hundred-pound commanding general of the Army and Whig nominee for the Presidency in 1852. Twice he checked out Mansfield's *Life of General Scott*.[27]

23. Dyer, *The Gallant Hood*, p. 32.
24. Schofield, *Forty-Six Years*, p. 25.
25. Cleaves, *Rock of Chickamauga*, p. 10.
26. *Official Register of the Officers and Cadets of the U.S. Military Academy* (West Point, 1850–54), 1850, p. 15; 1851, p. 13. Hereafter cited as the *Official Register*.
27. Record of Books borrowed from USMA Library by Cadet John M. Schofield, 1849–53.

By his third year, Schofield's habits underwent a change. His weekend borrowing from the library all but ceased. He was feeling more high spirited and found pleasure in breaking certain of the academy rules. He was then in the old North Barracks with three other cadets. They made a habit of fastening a blanket against the window after "taps" and "burning the midnight oil" over pipes and cards. In his old age he contended that nothing was "either so enjoyable or so beneficial to me as smoking."[28] Once he made a bet that he could go to New York City and back between the two roll calls he had to attend that day. Benny Havens rowed him across the river, and he caught a train to the city. Coming back in the evening he persuaded the conductor to slack the speed enough for him to jump off the rear platform of the train. The Cold Spring ferryman got him back to the point a few minutes before the evening parade.[29]

Some of this youthful exuberance may have laid the background for more serious trouble. It began on June 18, 1852, when the members of the class of 1856 were candidates for admission. Schofield was placed over a section of these candidates as an instructor in mathematics to help prepare them for their entrance examinations. As a result of some "youthful deviltry" which occurred during the course of instruction, Schofield was dismissed from the Academy. From the correspondence between West Point and the chief engineer of the Army, it is evident that Schofield permitted four or five older cadets to enter his section room and that these cadets compelled some of the candidates to answer indecent questions and draw obscene figures on the blackboard. Commandant Bradford R. Alden concluded from his investigation that Schofield "permitted these vulgar and most unworthy persons [or countenanced their act by not observing it] to abuse and attempt to corrupt the boys. . . ." If Schofield did not know what the candidates were compelled to do (and the testimony of the candidates is inconclusive on this point), he was at fault, Alden contended, in allowing the older cadets to enter his section "in open defiance of the superintendent's orders."[30]

Schofield maintained his innocence in an official explanation

28. Schofield, *Forty-Six Years*, p. 5.
29. *Ibid.*, p. 7.
30. Report of Commandant Bradford R. Alden, enclosed with letter of Superintendent Henry Brewerton to General Joseph G. Totten, July 8, 1852, Letter Sent File, 175, West Point Library.

dated June 30, 1852. The testimony of the candidates, he said, demonstrated that he "could not in all probability have had any knowledge of such transactions." Moreover, he added, it had been "the universal custom," so far as he could learn, "for instructors of the candidates to allow cadets to enter their section rooms at pleasure. . . ."[31] Recalling the events some years later, Schofield gave substantially the same account. He wrote that on the last day of instruction when all were prepared except two, "who seemed hopelessly deficient," he gave them instruction at the blackboard for fifteen or twenty minutes longer. Meanwhile, several of his classmates came in and began talking to the other candidates. Schofield said he did not find this disturbing and made no effort to put a stop to it. In fact, he claimed, he never knew the nature of what the others were doing. Later one of the candidates, who failed the exam, wrote his parents of the "deviltry" the others had engaged in which the instructor had failed to correct.[32] Schofield's plea that he was totally innocent appears a bit contrived.

Whatever transpired, the result nearly ended his days at the academy. The Secretary of War had recommended his dismissal. Schofield went to Washington to see what could be done to change the decision by personal appeal. Nothing was obtained through his Congressman or by an interview with the Secretary. Finally he persuaded Senator Stephen A. Douglas to present his appeal. Only then did the Secretary of War recommend that the decision be reconsidered, and the matter was referred to a court of inquiry.[33] It was about six months before the case was finally cleared up.

In the meantime, Schofield entered upon his last year at the Academy, rooming with James B. McPherson and LaRhett L. Livingston in a tower room and trying to obey all the regulations, so he said, except the one about smoking.[34] There was a new superintendent at the Point. In September, 1852, Lieutenant Colonel Robert E. Lee, having recovered from wounds received in the Mexican War, began the direction of Academy affairs.[35] Like nearly every cadet,[36] Schofield was impressed: Lee was the "personification

31. *Ibid.*, Schofield's explanation was enclosed with the report.
32. Schofield, *Forty-Six Years*, pp. 10–12.
33. *Ibid.*
34. *Ibid.*, p. 12.
35. Douglas S. Freeman, *Robert E. Lee: A Biography*, 4 vols. (New York, 1934–35), I, 319.
36. Wharton J. Green, *Recollections and Reflections* (1906), pp. 87, 88.

of dignity, justice and kindness . . . the ideal . . . commanding officer."[37]

There was also a new artillery instructor who received additional duty as cavalry instructor. During cavalry exercises, after the command to trot had been given and the cadets began to anticipate a gallop, the voice of George H. Thomas would check them with the order "slow trot!" The life of "old Slow Trot," as cadets dubbed him, would be closely and eventually unhappily interwoven with that of Schofield.[38] Even then an event was transpiring which Schofield would resent. The court of inquiry, concerning the alleged blackboard obscenities, led to a court martial on which Thomas was one of two out of thirteen who declined to vote for remission of the dismissal sentence. Schofield said he did not learn this fact until 1868 when he became Secretary of War.[39]

During his senior year, Schofield (in spite of all his alleged efforts to observe regulations) received more demerits than ever—196; 200 would have resulted in dismissal.[40] One of his classmates, John Bell Hood, received a like number. Hood was discouraged and discussed his situation with Schofield. He had been publicly reprimanded by Colonel Lee and broken to the ranks, apparently for slipping away to Benny Havens' for a Christmas celebration. His grades were poor, and he seemed about ready to give up.[41] Schofield, whose own situation must have enabled him to be understanding, encouraged Hood to stay.[42] It may only be speculated how much effect Schofield had on his classmate. At any rate Hood stayed.

Information about how Schofield's classmates generally regarded him is almost nonexistent. Wharton J. Green, a cadet in the class below, would one day praise him as "truly . . . 'a soldier in war, a citizen in peace, a gentleman always.' "[43] He made this statement in comparing Schofield with Sheridan and Sherman, both of whom he placed in a secondary position to Schofield. The term "gentle-

37. Schofield, *Forty-Six Years*, p. 15.
38. Cleaves, *Rock of Chickamauga*, pp. 48, 49.
39. Schofield, *Forty-Six Years*, p. 241.
40. The offenses for which he was most frequently demerited were smoking, being late, and inattention at cavalry drills. *Delinquency Record of Cadet John M. Schofield*, West Point Library.
41. Dyer, *The Gallant Hood*, p. 32.
42. Schofield, *Forty-Six Years*, p. 138.
43. Green, *Recollections*, p. 94

man" seemed to come to the mind of several people when they described Schofield.

In the Class of 1853, Schofield graduated first in infantry tactics and seventh overall.[44] His graduating leave was used to visit his family in Illinois. His first monthly check in the amount of $65.50 seemed like a small fortune, and his father thought it was enough to ruin a boy. But when Schofield offered to lend $50.00 of it to pay a debt on a "meeting house," the father's confidence in his son was restored.[45] Graduating leave having expired, Schofield, breveted second lieutenant, was assigned to duty at Fort Moultrie, South Carolina.[46]

He landed at Charleston on his twenty-second birthday, September 29, 1853, and thought the southern society was of "the most charming character." Schofield always seemed to like the South and after retiring he spent his winters in St. Augustine. But he had only a little over two months to enjoy Charleston before he was ordered to Fort Capron, Indian River, Florida. After a twenty-five-day journey by boat and mule, the New Year found Schofield at the fort, reunited with one of his roommates of the previous year, LaRhett L. Livingston. Here he met and eventually formed a warm relationship with First Lieutenant Ambrose P. Hill, later Lieutenant General in the Confederate Army.[47] When Hill was killed in the Civil War, Schofield was deeply moved upon receiving the news.

Schofield wrote that "life at Fort Capron was not by any means monotonous." There was opportunity for sailing, fishing and shooting. But Schofield, always of a scholarly turn of mind, spent much of his time reading law books, learning portions of Blackstone by heart. And then, as he phrased it, "for want of anything better . . . read the entire code of the State of Florida."[48]

About mid-winter of 1854–55, Schofield was entrusted with the task of constructing a new post at Fort Jupiter and building a blockhouse on the bank of Lake Okeechobee. Within a few weeks after beginning this task, he, along with many others, was down with malaria. While recovering at Fort Capron, orders came promoting

44. *Official Register*, 1853, p. 7.
45. Schofield, *Forty-Six Years*, pp. 16, 17.
46. Cullum, *Biographical Register*, II, 338. Confirmation as Second Lieutenant came on August 31, 1853.
47. Schofield, *Forty-Six Years*, p. 19.
48. *Ibid.*, pp. 20, 22.

him to first lieutenant and detailing him for duty at West Point.[49] A. P. Hill had also been having difficulty with malaria and had a relapse at the fort. When he was sufficiently recovered, the two left Florida together. Then Schofield came down with the fever again at Savannah. Finally he accompanied Hill to his home at Culpepper Court House in Virginia, where he stayed several days until his recovery was complete, but not until his weight had dropped to 120 pounds.[50]

In December, 1855, Schofield reported for duty at West Point as an instructor in philosophy.[51] For the next four and one-half years he continued to work under the direction of Professor W. H. C. Bartlett, chairman of the department and one of the most highly esteemed men at the academy.[52] Professor Bartlett also had a daughter who attracted Schofield's interest. Romance blossomed and in the month for weddings, June, 1857, he married Miss Harriet Bartlett. Five children were eventually born, three of whom—two sons and one daughter—grew to maturity.[53]

By the summer of 1860, his tour of duty at West Point completed, Schofield was convinced that his chances for promotion were very slight. And his interests were tending in another direction. He was working on a book in physics which he hoped to be able to publish. He secured a leave of absence from the army for a year and took a position as professor of physics at Washington University in Saint Louis. As autumn wore into winter and the Civil War approached, Schofield was working, between his teaching duties, to revise his book on physics and get it ready for a publisher. He was not unaware, however, of the impending tragedy. When it became possible that military force would be required to prevent disunion, the twenty-nine-year-old wrote General Scott that he would relinquish his leave of absence and return to duty whenever his services should be required.[54] There was never any doubt about where Schofield's sympathy lay. He felt that the Union must be preserved. There is no evidence that he was particularly concerned about the issue of slavery.

49. Cullum, *Biographical Register*, II, 338.
50. Schofield, *Forty-Six Years*, pp. 25, 26, 28.
51. Cullum, *Biographical Register*, II, 338.
52. Morris Schaff, *The Spirit of Old West Point* (Boston and New York, 1907), pp. 273, 274.
53. Schofield, *Forty-Six Years*, p. 28.
54. *Ibid.*, pp. 28, 31, 32.

# II. The Professor Goes to War

SECESSION breathed hot in Missouri in 1861. At Jefferson City, Claiborne F. Jackson, in full sympathy with the southern fire-eaters, had been inaugurated as governor on the last day of the old year.[1] While Lincoln, as yet without authority, remained silent, and Buchanan said there was no right for a state to secede nor for the President to make war upon a state, Missouri's new governor spoke of "standing by" the state which had declared herself separated from the Union. Jackson also recommended a convention to consider secession.[2] As the national situation steadily became more tense, he and his advisors were shaping political affairs so as to take Missouri out of the Union should other southern states follow South Carolina's example.[3]

A majority of the state legislature favored the Union and served as a partial check on the governor's designs. But Jackson had all the machinery of the state under his control. And, as commander-in-chief of the militia, he worked to mold that body in the interest of the southern cause. Soon camps of instruction, officered by men of the governor's choosing, began functioning in various parts of the state. Jackson strove to cloak his actions with legitimacy, and the

1. Jay Monaghan, *Civil War on the Western Border, 1854–1865* (Boston, 1955), p. 123.
2. J. G. Randall and David Donald, *The Civil War and Reconstruction* (Boston, 1961), p. 154.
3. Benjamin P. Thomas, *Abraham Lincoln* (New York, 1952), p. 236. Wiley Britton, *The Civil War on the Border* (New York, 1899), p. 1.

militia organization was publicized as solely for home protection.[4] One major problem confronted the governor—the militia groups were not adequately armed. There were two places in Missouri where large quantities of ordinance stores, such as arms, ammunition, and equipment, were kept: the Federal arsenals at Liberty and St. Louis. Farther south, Federal forts and arsenals were being taken over by seceding states. Why not in Missouri?

Unionist forces in Missouri were striving to keep abreast of the governor's plans. In St. Louis, chief point of interest in the state and center of Union strength, prominent loyal men were advising Washington of the situation. The most notable among these was Frank P. Blair. About the middle of February, the national administration became apprehensive that the secessionists were intending to seize the largest of the two arsenals—the one at St. Louis. General William S. Harney, commanding the Western Department, was so advised. Harney found this difficult to believe. But rumor was on the lips of many that the southerners were planning to seize all of the government property in the city.[5]

Meanwhile, Governor Jackson was exerting every effort to have secessionists elected to the convention, which had been scheduled for early March, to consider the question of withdrawing Missouri from the United States. Blair was leading the effort to select pro-Union men. Blair was also working to perfect loyal military organizations—"home guards," as they were known. In this he had the help of Captain Nathaniel Lyon, lately arrived from Fort Riley, Kansas. Many citizens of St. Louis, largely German, were organized into companies and began carrying on secret night drills in halls where sawdust was sprinkled to muffle the tramping feet.[6] Blair served as colonel of one regiment. March came, and, despite the governor's efforts, only 19 per cent of the "secession" convention voted for secession and that not immediate.[7] When Lincoln became President, Blair's brother Montgomery was sworn in as Postmaster General. With new influence and authority in Washington, Blair and Lyon busied themselves implementing plans to counter Governor Jackson and his supporters. Lyon, whose loyalty and energy were unquestioned, had immediate command of the St. Louis

4. Monaghan, *Civil War*, p. 123. Britton, *The Civil War*, pp. 1, 2.

5. Britton, *The Civil War*, p. 3.

6. William T. Sherman, *Memoirs of General W. T. Sherman*, 2 vols. (New York, 1875), I, 169. Monaghan, *Civil War*, pp. 124–25.

7. Monaghan, *Civil War*, p. 125.

arsenals. But neither the pro-Union nor the secession forces were yet willing to avow their intentions openly.

Schofield, although he had been in St. Louis less than a year, had become fairly well known by this time. His work at Washington University had brought him into contact with many Union men.[8] Prior to the firing on Fort Sumter, however, his duties at the university had continued to occupy his primary attention. Then, on April 15, Lincoln called for 75,000 enlistees for three months. Secretary of War Simon Cameron requested that four regiments be raised in Missouri, and detailed Schofield to muster in troops. According to instructions for mustering in, Schofield wired Governor Jackson and offered his services as mustering officer. But now pro-Union and secession factions were unmasking. The only reply Schofield received from the governor was his statement in the press: Missouri would not furnish a single man "to subjugate her sister states of the South." And the governor ordered a special session of the legislature to convene at Jefferson City on May 2.[9] Doubtless the governor hoped this meeting would be an instrument of secession.

After reading Jackson's answer in the press, Schofield next conferred with the department commander, General Harney. The general said he had no authority to swear in troops without direct orders from Washington. Schofield urged upon him the necessity of protecting the arsenal in the city and reminded him of the rumors that the governor planned to seize it. Harney was still not moved. "Why, the state has not yet passed an ordinance of secession," he said.[10] The general's attitude was not what Schofield had expected. Nor had it been what Blair and other strong Unionists felt the situation required. Blair would soon be in contact with Washington maneuvering to have Harney replaced.[11]

After his disheartening interview with the commanding general, Schofield caught a horsecar that took him to the arsenal, where, for the first time, he met Captain Lyon.[12] Lyon was not surprised

8. James Peckham, *General Nathaniel Lyon and Missouri in 1861* (New York, 1866), p. 109. Schofield, *Forty-Six Years*, pp. 36, 31.

9. Peckham, *General Lyon*, pp. 107–8. Schofield, *Forty-Six Years*, p. 32.

10. Schofield, *Forty-Six Years*, p. 33.

11. Britton, *The Civil War*, pp. 5, 6. Hans Christian Adamson, *Rebellion in Missouri: 1861; Nathaniel Lyon and His Army of the West* (Philadelphia and New York, 1961), p. 27.

12. Adamson, *Rebellion in Missouri*, p. 18.

to hear Schofield's report of the department commander's attitude. He told Schofield of his own experience. There had been an effort to assign him to a board of inquiry at Fort Leavenworth. Such proceedings frequently dragged on for weeks. It seemed like a plot to sidetrack a strong Union man. Lyon was certain someone in Harney's headquarters was responsible. Fortunately, the orders had been canceled by the adjutant general in Washington.

Since Harney had refused permission, Lyon, of course, could not enroll volunteers without subjecting himself to serious consequences. But Lyon was sure that, regardless of Harney or the governor, steps would be taken in a very few days to raise Union regiments in St. Louis. Schofield's services would then be needed. When Schofield left Lyon's company, he was convinced that Lyon was a man who intended to defend the interests of the national government—a welcome change from his most recent experiences.[13]

Schofield did not have long to wait. On Sunday morning, April 21, he was called out of church by a delegation from Blair.[14] Four days earlier Blair had telegraphed the Secretary of War informing him that Governor Jackson would not raise troops and requesting that Captain Lyon be ordered to meet the secretary's request. Now Blair had a reply. Cameron had given authority for the enrollment of four regiments. Soon Schofield was on his way to the arsenal to act as mustering officer. There he met Lyon, who reluctantly reminded him that there was no authority to arm and equip the men once they were enrolled. General Harney had explicitly ordered that no arms should be issued. Lyon suggested that Schofield and Blair should call on the department commander and present the latest developments. Perhaps he would change his orders.[15]

In company with Blair, Schofield called upon the general once more. The conference was to no avail. As long as Harney commanded the department, no troops were going to be mustered in. Blair returned to his home and prepared a telegram which was dispatched from the east side of the river in order to avoid betrayal in the St. Louis telegraph office. Intended for the Secretary of War, it read in part: "Harney should be superseded immediately by putting another commander in this district. . . . The object of

13. *Ibid.*, pp. 18–21. Schofield, *Forty-Six Years*, pp. 33, 35.
14. Peckham, *General Lyon*, p. 109.
15. *Ibid.* Adamson, *Rebellion in Missouri*, pp. 27, 29, 30.

the secessionists is to seize the arsenal here . . . and he refuses the means of defending it. We have plenty of men, but no arms."[16]

When Lyon heard of Blair and Schofield's futile effort to sway Harney, he was convinced that the time for action was at hand. Lyon stated that he would be responsible for the enrollment of volunteers regardless of the department commander's wrath.[17] Plans were made for the loyal secret organizations to enter the arsenal individually that night. Each member was furnished with a pass to gain admittance, and in a short while Schofield was distributing arms and ammunition to the men as they arrived. The work went on all night and the following day.[18] About midnight a welcome telegram arrived from Washington. It was addressed to Lyon, and it read: "General Harney has this date been relieved from his command."[19] The direction of military affairs at St. Louis was thus left in the hands of Lyon, with orders to muster in and arm four regiments of volunteers. Once enough arms were distributed that the successful defense of the arsenal seemed assured, Schofield began the more time-consuming work of enrolling the men, organizing them into companies and supervising the election of officers. Before the night of April 21 was over, seven hundred men entered the arsenal. Some six hundred were received on April 22, seven hundred on the following day. By the middle of the week over two thousand had been received, sworn in, and armed. Day by day, volunteers by the hundreds streamed in.[20]

Meanwhile, the government arsenal at Liberty had already been taken by secessionist forces. And Governor Jackson was negotiating with Confederate authorities at Montgomery, Alabama, for arms and ammunition to capture the St. Louis arsenal.[21] His plan was to call out a militia brigade, ostensibly for training purposes, which would be encamped at Lindell Grove in St. Louis, only a few miles from the arsenal. At the proper moment it would be in excellent position to swoop down upon the Federal force. On May 2, a special session of the legislature convened at Jefferson

16. Peckham, *General Lyon*, pp. 109, 110.
17. Adamson, *Rebellion in Missouri*, p. 31.
18. Schofield, *Forty-Six Years*, p. 34.
19. Adamson, *Rebellion in Missouri*, p. 31. Harney soon left for Washington to present his side of the matter and was re-instated on May 11, but finally relieved on May 30.
20. *Ibid.*, p. 32.
21. Britton, *The Civil War*, p. 6.

City. But it passed no important measures for several days. On the
third, a brigade of state militia, acting under Jackson's directions,
went into camp at St. Louis.[22] The brigade commander, General
Daniel M. Frost, stated in a communiqué to Lyon that the troops
intended no hostility toward the United States. But all his actions
and preparations indicated the contrary. Even the principal avenue
of the camp was named "Davis," and another "Beauregard." The
Union leaders knew that supplies of arms and ammunition, most
of them from United States arsenals in seceded states, were being
received by "Camp Jackson" as the site was called. It was rumored
that other militia would soon reinforce the camp. On the night
of May 8 a steamer arrived from Baton Rouge with a large load of
heavy boxes marked "marble" which turned out to be mortar and
siege guns. If there ever had been any doubt of the intention at
Camp Jackson, it was dispelled when Union spies reported this
information.[23]

A consultation was held among the Union leaders, and the
decision reached to march out and take Camp Jackson without
delay. Action seemed all the more imperative when Lyon revealed
that he had word from the adjutant general's office in Washington
that Harney had been reinstated as commanding general of the
department. He was expected back on May 11. If Camp Jackson
were to be taken at all, it had to be taken at once. On May 9,
Schofield, together with Lyon, Blair, Chester Harding, and Captains
James Totten and Thomas W. Sweeney, worked far into the night
drawing up the plans for the next day's action. Orders were to be
issued for the various Union units to march on parallel streets and
reach Lindell Grove promptly at 2:30 P.M. Each man would carry
forty rounds of ammunition, and two batteries of artillery would
be prepared to fire grape and canister. Lyon expected Frost to
surrender, but if he did not, the Union force was prepared to
enforce its demand.[24]

The first column to march on May 10 was headed by Lyon.
As he moved out, Schofield, along with Harding, both serving as
Lyon's adjutants, rode closely behind. There were no bands playing
or drums rolling. Nevertheless, streets, doorways, windows, and
even housetops filled with people watching the four regiments

22. Monaghan, *Civil War*, p. 130.
23. Britton, *The Civil War*, p. 7. Monaghan, *Civil War*, p. 131.
24. Adamson, *Rebellion in Missouri*, pp. 51, 53, 54.

composed largely of the German element as they marched through the streets.[25] Soon a large group was following. Among the observers were William T. Sherman with his small son and Ulysses S. Grant, then only faces in the crowd.[26]

At the appointed time the regiments deployed in battle line around the camp. Lyon turned to Schofield and handed him a letter which he had penned during the early morning. It called upon General Frost to surrender, and Schofield was instructed to deliver it to the general in person. Frost had not expected any opposition for several days and was not prepared to meet such a challenge as Lyon's force posed. Schofield soon returned at a rapid trot and handed Lyon the surrender note. The next step was to take charge of the prisoners, march them back to the arsenal, and take possession of the pile of war materials in the nearby woods. Lyon swung to the ground from his horse and was immediately kicked in the stomach by the hind leg of an aide's mount. The little man slumped to the ground, and a regimental surgeon rushed to his aid.[27]

There was no time to wait for Lyon to recover. An aide-de-camp from Frost had arrived, inquiring for Lyon, to ask if the surrendering officers would be allowed to retain their sidearms. Schofield consulted with Sweeney. It was no occasion for the enemy to know Lyon was unconscious. Reply was given that Sweeney had been authorized to receive communications from Frost and to act upon them. The officers would be allowed to retain their sidearms; all public property, such as arms, ammunition, and military equipment would be confiscated by the United States.[28]

The minor crisis had been met, and after about thirty minutes Lyon resumed command. A Union regiment was formed in single file on opposite sides of the street, and the disarmed prisoners— about a thousand—marched in between. The rest of the troops followed, and the long column started for the arsenal. By this time many of the violent secessionists had seized rifles, shot-guns, pistols, or whatever weapons they could lay their hands on. They made up a part of the huge mob—many of them women and

25. Monaghan, *Civil War,* p. 131.
26. Ulysses S. Grant, *Personal Memoirs of U. S. Grant,* 2 vols. (New York, 1885), I, 236, 237. Sherman, *Memoirs,* I, 36.
27. Adamson, *Rebellion in Missouri,* pp. 60, 61. Monaghan, *Civil War,* p. 131. Schofield, *Forty-Six Years,* p. 36.
28. Adamson, *Rebellion in Missouri,* pp. 60, 61. Schofield, *Forty-Six Years,* pp. 36, 37.

children—which clustered about the marching soldiers. Curses and shouts were heard—"Hurrah for Jeff Davis" and "Damn the Dutch." Rocks, stones, and even bricks began to be hurled at the soldiers. Suddenly several discharges of small arms were heard near the head of the column, and men, women, and children were seen fleeing in terror. Then volley after volley of musketry was heard from the extreme rear ranks. The latter left some twenty-five persons killed and wounded. As always in such an outbreak, accounts vary. Most reports indicate that in the midst of the jeers and rock pelting, a drunken man tried to push through the Union line to the captives. A rank closer shoved him back down an embankment. The man turned and fired, wounding an officer. The soldiers opened fire.[29]

When the column reached the arsenal, the prisoners were packed into cramped quarters for the night and promised a parole the next morning. That night in Jefferson City, the halls of the Capitol were filled by excited men, many of whom were now ready for secession. Notified of the capture of Camp Jackson and the "massacre" following, they were both indignant and scared. Rumors said "the Germans" were coming up the Missouri to take the capital. As the special session of the legislature proceeded to "business," nearly every individual was armed. Guns were leaning against desks and chairs. Many members had pistols and bowie knives fastened to their belts. They passed a special military bill, gave Governor Jackson dictatorial power, and authorized the borrowing of $1 million from banks and the raising of another million by bonds to support a state army.[30]

As expected, General Harney arrived in St. Louis the next day—May 11. He was upset by Lyon's action and worked to appease the governor and the offended citizens of St. Louis. There was talk of ordering the German regiments out of the city. The Union leaders feared the advantage gained was about to be lost. Blair sent a delegation to Washington to explain the situation to Lincoln. Harney's friends also sent a delegation.[31] The harassed President wanted peace in Missouri, but even more he wanted to hold Missouri in the Union. He gave no immediate decision. Then on May 20 Lincoln sent Blair a letter with an order relieving Harney

29. Britton, *The Civil War*, pp. 10, 11. Monaghan, *Civil War*, pp. 132, 133. Adamson, *Rebellion in Missouri*, pp. 62, 63. Sherman, *Memoirs*, I, 174.

30. Peckham, *General Lyon*, p. 168. Monaghan, *Civil War*, p. 132.

31. William E. Parrish, "General Nathaniel Lyon: A Portrait," *Missouri Historical Review* (October, 1954), p. 13.

of department command and a commission for Lyon as a brigadier general. The letter advised Blair to use the papers at his discretion. Holding the trump card, Blair bided his time. On May 21 General Harney announced that he had concluded a truce with Governor Jackson. Harney agreed to recognize Missouri's neutrality and stated that he would use the army to enforce state laws. On May 30 the department commander began moving the German regiments out of St. Louis. The same day Blair sent him the President's order relieving him of command.[32]

During the days following the capture of Camp Jackson, Schofield's time had been largely consumed with perfecting the organization of Union volunteers. On June 4 he turned over to the adjutant general the muster rolls of five regiments of infantry, four rifle battalions and one artillery battalion.[33] The officers of the First Missouri Volunteer Infantry wanted Schofield to serve as major of the regiment. He accepted the position, and when time could be spared from his mustering duties he instructed the officers of the regiment in tactics and military administration.[34] His work as mustering officer was not completed until June 24 when he made a full report of the discharge of his duties. The next day General Lyon ordered Schofield to report at Boonville to serve as his adjutant general.[35]

After the second and final departure of Harney, Lyon had moved on Jefferson City in force, occupying the capital on June 15. There was no opposition. The governor and the legislature had fled. Lyon left three companies in the capital and moved on up the river past Boonville, where the governor had decided to make his stand. There on June 17 he engaged and routed an inferior and untrained force under Governor Jackson's nephew, Colonel John S. Marmaduke.[36]

When Schofield arrived at Boonville on June 26, preparations

32. Monaghan, *Civil War*, p. 134.

33. Schofield, *Forty-Six Years*, p. 34.

34. *Annual Report of the Adjutant General of the State of Missouri, for the year 1863.* Paper C. Roster and History of Regiments, etc., Missouri State Militia, Accompanying Adjutant General's Report for 1863, pp. 120, 121. Schofield, *Forty-Six Years*, p. 35.

35. Schofield, *Forty-Six Years*, p. 37.

36. Monaghan, *Civil War*, pp. 140, 141. Marmaduke advised against the engagement but the governor insisted. The Union loss was two killed and nine wounded; the Confederate loss, ten killed and some twenty wounded. Britton, *The Civil War*, p. 36.

were under way to push operations into southwestern Missouri as
rapidly as possible. There the Confederates were reported gather-
ing in large numbers and preparing for a determined advance.
Lyon planned to effect a junction with the forces under Colonel
Franz Sigel, about 1,500 infantry, and Major Samuel D. Sturgis,
about the same number of cavalry. The former would march from
St. Louis and the latter from Kansas City. Then Lyon hoped to
push forward and attack while still superior in numbers to the
enemy. On July 3 Schofield accompanied Lyon as the command,
2,000 strong, headed for Springfield. Major Sturgis' troopers joined
up the next day. Springfield was reached on July 13, and there
Sigel's command, which had already arrived, joined with Lyon's.[37]
It was about this time that a private in the First Iowa remembered
seeing Schofield for the first time. Eugene F. Ware said he was "a
handsome young man and . . . full of steam, just like Lyon.
Lyon was a sleepless man, and so was Schofield. The latter finally
got in command of the entire army of the United States . . . and
well deserved it."[38]

Operations went badly for the Federals during the remaining
hot July days. The quartermaster goods and supplies Lyon had
depended on for continuation of his forced march were all piled
up at Rolla, 125 miles back. By the last of the month many of
the men ate nothing but coffee, cornmeal, and whatever they could
find in the country. Some had no shoes and the enlistment time
had expired for many. Lyon kept wiring the new department commander, John C. Frémont, for reinforcements. None came. On
top of it all, word was received of the Union defeat at Bull Run.[39]

Reliable information about the increase of the enemy's force
continued to come in daily. Lyon determined to act. On the first
of August, having received information of an advance of the
enemy, he moved out from Springfield down the Cassville Road.
The Confederates were coming from the southwest by two or three
different roads. Lyon hoped to attack the largest and most advanced column, and if successful, strike the others in detail.[40] On

37. R. I. Holcombe and F. W. Adams, *An Account of the Battle of Wilson's
Creek, or Oak Hills, Compiled and Written from Authentic Sources* (Springfield, Missouri, 1883), p. 8.
38. Ware, *First Iowa Infantry*, p. 227.
39. *Ibid.*, p. 256. Monaghan, *Civil War*, p. 160. Schofield, *Forty-Six Years*, p.
38.
40. Clarence C. Buel and Robert U. Johnson, eds., *Battles and Leaders of the*

August 2 his advance brought on a lively skirmish at Dug Springs. The next day there was a similar affair at McCullah's farm; but it was evident that the enemy was not going to be drawn into a general engagement—at least not yet. The Confederates kept retiring and Lyon was convinced he was purposely being drawn from his base. On August 5 he returned to Springfield.

Conditions there were no better—no supplies from Rolla and no encouragement from Frémont. On August 8 Lyon called a council of his officers at his headquarters. He proposed a quick attack, which, if it did not succeed in conquering, would at least disorganize the enemy and make retreat to Rolla safer. Sweeney favored an attack and so did a couple of regimental officers. But the majority counseled a retreat.[41] The next day a letter from Frémont arrived: If Lyon was not strong enough to maintain his position at Springfield, he should fall back toward Rolla until reinforcements should arrive. Schofield prepared Lyon's answer. The general had decided to hold his ground as long as possible.[42] In fact, as Schofield soon learned, Lyon had decided to fight. A force under Sigel, about 1,200 strong, was to attack the enemy from the east while Lyon, with the main body, a little less than 4,000 strong, would attack from the west. The two columns were to advance by widely separated roads, and strike the Confederates at the same time—dawn on the tenth.[43]

Schofield, his West Point training coming readily to mind, could hardly believe it—divide the command in the presence of the enemy when outnumbered more than two to one already? "Is Sigel willing to undertake this?" Schofield asked. Lyon replied, "Yes, it is his plan."[44] Sigel had privately gained Lyon's ear and convinced him to try this rash maneuver. Schofield said nothing more. Doubtless Lyon knew what he thought. He had previously spoken in favor of retreat. Schofield later wrote that Lyon was obsessed with the feeling that he must fight before retreating and despondent with the belief that he was being sacrificed to the ambition of another: Frémont.[45]

*Civil War*, 4 vols. (New York, 1887–88), I, 290. Hereafter cited as *Battles and Leaders*.

41. Monaghan, *Civil War*, p. 163.
42. Schofield, *Forty-Six Years*, pp. 40, 41.
43. Monaghan, *Civil War*, p. 164.
44. Schofield, *Forty-Six Years*, p. 42.
45. *Ibid.*, p. 43.

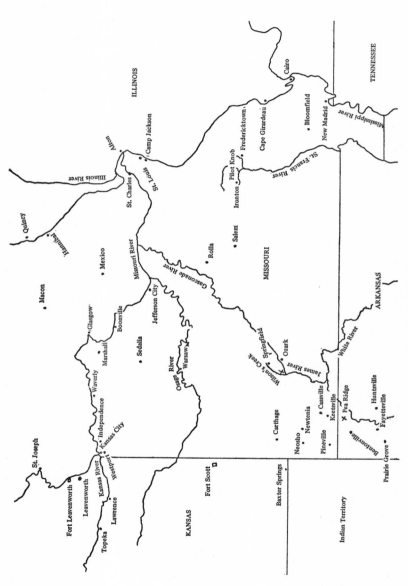

THE MISSOURI REGION

It was about six o'clock and the clouds were heavy with rain when Schofield swung into the saddle and accompanied Lyon as they rode to the camp west of town.[46] The companies were drawn up in regimental formations and Schofield watched as Lyon rode down the lines, coming to a stop before each company, and making the same speech: "Men, we are going to have a fight. We will march out in a short time. Don't shoot until you get orders. Fire low—don't aim higher than their knees; wait until they get close; don't get scared; it is no part of a soldier's duty to get scared."[47] There was no cheering. One private remarked to another, "How is a man to help being skeered when he is skeered?"[48] Evidently Lyon's little talk on the eve of battle was not what many of the men expected. Later they heard what the one-armed Sweeney told his cavalry: "Stay together boys, and we'll saber hell out of them."[49] Some thought this was more nearly what the occasion called for.

Sigel's flanking column moved out of camp between about six-thirty and seven o'clock, heading down the Springfield Road toward Wilson's Creek. Soon after, Lyon's column started west from Springfield on the Mount Vernon Road. Rain was beginning to fall as Schofield rode along with the general. When the column moved far enough from Springfield to stretch out on the road, Lyon halted his horse on the top of a rise and let the troops march past. Talking, laughter, and even singing could be heard as the soldiers went by in the dim twilight.[50]

About five miles out of town, the column turned south and made its way over neighboring roads and across prairies as best it could for nearly six miles.[51] About midnight scouts reported that the army was within a very few miles of the enemy's camp. Moving forward slowly, they discovered an abandoned picket post.[52] By this time the crimson reflections of the enemy campfires were becoming visible on the low-hanging clouds.[53] The entire column was halted and deployed in columns of companies with sufficient

46. Holcombe and Adams, *Wilson's Creek*, p. 28. Adamson, *Rebellion in Missouri*, p. 214.
47. Ware, *First Iowa Infantry*, p. 312.
48. *Ibid.*
49. Monaghan, *Civil War*, p. 165.
50. Adamson, *Rebellion in Missouri*, pp. 215, 217. Holcombe and Adams, *Wilson's Creek*, p. 29.
51. Holcombe and Adams, *Wilson's Creek*, p. 29.
52. Adamson, *Rebellion in Missouri*, pp. 222, 223.
53. Ware, *First Iowa Infantry*, p. 315.

intervals for each regiment to be brought into battle line. In the darkness and with little or no explanation, many of the men did not understand what was being done. But no one seemed disturbed.

It was still drizzling rain when Schofield finally bivouacked on the morning of August 10. He was between two rows of corn in a field by a road and shared a rubber coat with his commander. Schofield thought Lyon seemed depressed. The little man hardly uttered a word.[54] There was not much rest to be had that morning. At early dawn Schofield mounted his horse and followed Lyon— riding into battle for the first time. The advance was led down the west bank of Wilson's Creek by a battalion of the First United States Infantry with skirmishers thrown out in front. It was followed closely by a battalion of the Second Missouri Volunteers and a battery of the Second United States Artillery. The rest of the troops came on at intervals. In a short time they stumbled upon the first outpost of the enemy and drove them back rapidly.

The element of surprise was lost. The column was halted and deployed for battle. The First United States Infantry was crossed to the east bank of the creek and instructed to keep pace with the advance, thus protecting the left flank. The Second Missouri was deployed on the right as skirmishers and the First Missouri Volunteers brought forward and center to support the battery of artillery. The main body of the army then advanced obliquely across the tongue of land between Wilson's Creek and Skegg's Branch for a mile or more. The rain had ceased, and it was about five o'clock when the Confederates were encountered in force.

The Rebels occupied the crest of a ridge running nearly perpendicular to the Federal line of march. The First Missouri at once charged up the ridge under a brisk fire. The First Kansas advanced up the ridge on the left, and the artillery moved forward into the center position. The Second Missouri protected the right flank, while the Second Kansas and First Iowa brought up the rear and were held in reserve. The Confederates were driven from the ridge by the initial Union charge but rallied near the foot of the slope and on the crest of a ridge to the Federal right which ran parallel to their line of advance. Troops scrambled for cover as best they could and began cracking away at the enemy.[55]

54. *Battles and Leaders*, I, 292. Monaghan, *Civil War*, p. 168. Schofield, *Forty-Six Years*, p. 42.
55. *The War of the Rebellion: A Compilation of the Official Records of the*

In his official report of the battle, Schofield wrote that about this time he heard artillery fire opening from a high point some two miles in front. It was answered by a battery at a still greater distance. The line of fire was in the direction from which Sigel's column was expected to be advancing. Did the firing signal his arrival? After about ten or twelve shots on each side, the noise ceased. Nothing more was heard from that general direction for some three hours. Then a few more shots were heard farther to the right.[56]

Meanwhile, the fighting was also raging east of Wilson's Creek, and the First United States Infantry was pinned down briefly at the entrance to a large cornfield. A light artillery battery supported by infantry was moved up to a hill on the left and opened fire on the enemy, enabling the troops to be drawn off in good order.[57] At the same time the firing on the main line west of the creek was increasing to a continuous roar as the whole Federal line advanced on the Rebel position. But the line was driven back, and a see-saw action began as the troops rallied and pressed forward again only to be forced back once more.

Lyon was at the front, to the left of the artillery, directing the battle. Schofield was moving from point to point carrying the orders of his chief. For the first time he could hear the horrible sounds of men and animals suffering and dying. Private Ware, also in war for the first time, recalled the "blood-curdling" screams and neighing of a horse whose left shoulder was torn off by a shell.[58] If Schofield had any fear or any other emotion, he did not show it. Many were impressed with his coolness, even where the battle raged most fiercely.[59] After several advances the Confederates gave up their position, creating a momentary lull, except on the extreme right. There a superior force was attempting to turn the Union flank. The First Missouri was about to be forced back. Lyon and Schofield together led the Second Kansas to the critical point, and after a fierce engagement, the flank was saved.[60]

Again there was a lull as the Confederates readjusted their

*Union and Confederate Armies*, 129 vols. (Washington, 1880–1901), Serial 1, III, 60, 61, 65, 66, 75, 76. Hereafter cited as *O.R.* Monaghan, *Civil War*, p. 170.

56. *O.R.*, Ser. 1, III, 61.

57. *Battles and Leaders*, I, 292.

58. Ware, *First Iowa Infantry*, p. 318.

59. *O.R.*, Ser. 1, III, 69. *Daily Missouri Democrat* (St. Louis), August 20, 1861.

60. *Battles and Leaders*, I, 292. *O.R.*, Ser. 1, III, 61, 67, 77.

lines, brought up fresh troops, and then made a determined advance along nearly the whole Federal front. About this time both Lyon and Schofield had their horses shot from under them. The general was also wounded in the leg and in the head. With blood trickling down his face, Lyon turned and said to Schofield: "Major, I am afraid the day is lost." But Schofield was not ready to quit and did not believe Lyon should be either. "No, General," he replied, "let us try it again."[61] Schofield then went in search of another mount.

About this time a body of Confederates was observed moving down a hill on the east bank of Wilson's Creek and toward the Federal rear. Schofield formed up eight companies of the First Iowa and led them to the attack in person.[62] As the distance between his troops and the enemy narrowed, Schofield was yelling at his men to "charge!" He wrote later that he had hoped to "try conclusions with the bayonet."[63] But when the enemy opened fire, his own troops halted and began shooting. There was nothing left to do but get out of the line of fire. Schofield passed around the flank and stood in the rear of the line. Here he witnessed a soldier rapidly loading his musket and firing into the air. Schofield grabbed his arm and shook him. The man seemed to be aroused from a trance, and Schofield thought he must have been too brave to run, but too scared to fight.[64]

Schofield then made his way to the right of the Iowa troops, looking for Lyon. Suddenly he saw him. His body was stretched upon the ground—lifeless from a bullet through the left breast. He had gone down while leading a charge on the right of the one Schofield had led. Lyon's orderly was at his side, mourning the general's death. Schofield told the man to stop crying and carry the body to the rear before the word spread along the line that the general was dead. Major Sturgis must assume command. Schofield secured a loose horse, swung on, and rode off to find him.[65]

The engagement continued for some thirty minutes after Lyon's

61. Schofield, *Forty-Six Years*, p. 44. *O.R.*, Ser. 1, III, 62. *Battles and Leaders*, I, 293.

62. *Battles and Leaders*, I, 295.

63. Schofield, *Forty-Six Years*, p. 44. He was awarded the Congressional Medal of Honor for leading this charge. *American Decorations* (Washington, 1927), p. 95.

64. Schofield, *Forty-Six Years*, p. 45.

65. *Battles and Leaders*, I, 296. Schofield, *Forty-Six Years*, pp. 45, 46.

death. Finally the Confederates withdrew and silence reigned across the field. Schofield, having found Sturgis, rode to the edge of a point which afforded a view of a portion of the enemy. They were re-forming for another charge.[66] He rode back as Sturgis was calling together the principal officers of the command and consulting with them about whether or not to retreat. As they were talking, the Rebels appeared again. They pulled a battery upon a hill in front and began for the first time to pour shrapnel and canister into the Federals. Then the Confederates moved forward, and what seemed to some officers to be the fiercest and bloodiest encounter of the day got under way.[67] But the Federal line maintained its position firmly until the enemy once again retired down the ridge.

It was nearly noon. Ammunition was low and Sturgis feared the Federals could not withstand another such assault. Against the advice of at least one officer, Sturgis gave the order to retreat. Undoubtedly many men in the ranks also wanted to stand their ground.[68] About this time a noncommissioned officer from Sigel's column arrived with news that the German's command had been routed and Sigel captured or killed. Actually Sigel was still alive and he was not captured, but his command had been routed.[69] Sturgis was all the more assured that his judgment to retreat was sound. Schofield wrote in his autobiography that the retreat "was undoubtedly an error. . . . It was only necessary to hold our ground and the victory would have been ours."[70] Apparently he did not believe the Confederates would have attempted another attack.

In the battle of Wilson's Creek the Union troops lost 944 killed or wounded out of a total of about 5,400 engaged. The Confederate losses were 1,157 killed and wounded out of some 11,600 engaged.[71] The Army was withdrawn, and the engagement was generally considered a defeat. The retreat continued on past Springfield all the way to Rolla, where the column arrived on August 19.

It must have been about this time that Schofield received a

---

66. Monaghan, *Civil War*, p. 180.
67. *O.R.*, Ser. 1, III, 62, 68.
68. Monaghan, *Civil War*, p. 181. *Battles and Leaders*, I, 297.
69. Monaghan, *Civil War*, pp. 178, 179.
70. Schofield, *Forty-Six Years*, p. 46.
71. Thomas L. Livermore, *Numbers and Losses in the Civil War in America, 1861–1865* (Boston, 1900), p. 78.

letter from Philadelphia, dated August 12, 1861. It was addressed to Professor J. M. Schofield, from the publishing firm of Peck and Bliss. The professor was reminded that some three months had passed since he had been sent a copy of Professor Silliman's *Physics* for examination. The firm was anxious to know his opinion of the book and if they could look for its adoption as a textbook in Washington University.[72] If Schofield answered this letter, there is no record of his reply in his papers. It may be assumed he was not interested in using the textbook in his classes. For better or worse, the professor had gone to war.

72. Letter from Peck and Bliss to JMS, August 12, 1861, Schofield MSS.

# III. "And All for Nothing"

IF SCHOFIELD read his "press clippings" in the St. Louis *Daily Missouri Democrat,* he might have felt a tingle of pride and perhaps a little amusement at the flattering and flamboyant article of August 20, 1861. An "eyewitness" of the Battle of Wilson's Creek wrote: "Pages could be filled with incidents of bravery on the part of our troops and officers," but, of course, the writer continued, all could not be cited. The witness "could not, however, refrain from making mention of Major J. M. Schofield, than whom . . . a braver soldier does not live. In all that bloody fight . . . he was ever in the lead, foremost, coolest." For six hours he had displayed "the utmost . . . bravery."[1]

A study of the engagement at Wilson's Creek does reveal Schofield as a man of courage and calmness under fire.[2] His introduction to fighting so soon in the war, the acclaim he received, his association with a man of Lyon's importance in the early months of the war, and his access to the politically influential Blair family, particularly Frank Blair Jr., as well as his ambition which becomes evident from a study of his papers, probably led Schofield to expect more rapid advancement than his military career in Missouri was to provide. These factors and the drudgery of some of his tasks are important in understanding the growing

1. *Daily Missouri Democrat* (St. Louis), August 20, 1861.
2. *O.R.*, Ser. 1, III, 61, 67, 69, 77. *Battles and Leaders*, I, 292, 293, 295.

29

feeling of disillusionment and dissatisfaction which seemed to almost overwhelm him by the latter part of 1862.

Schofield arrived in St. Louis from Rolla on August 20, with instructions from Major Samuel D. Sturgis to call on the department commander as soon as possible. It seemed like a reasonable assumption that General John C. Frémont, western explorer and unsuccessful Republican presidential nominee, would be interested in his first-hand report of the contest at Wilson's Creek. Schofield first went to the arsenal to pick up a change of clothing. There he met Frank Blair, recently returned from Washington. Schofield, although a major in the volunteers, was only a lieutenant in the regular army and was doubtful that he could get in to see Frémont without considerable delay. Blair thought that he could arrange for a meeting the next day.[3]

Frémont was commanding the Department of the West, comprising Illinois, Missouri, and the territory west to the mountains. He held forth in virtually imperial state at the J. B. Brant mansion on Chouteau Avenue in St. Louis. The news of Wilson's Creek had made the secessionists in the city increasingly restive, and on August 14 Frémont had established martial law in the city and county.[4] The regulations which were set up gave rise to bitter complaints from citizens, many of whom vented their wrath upon Frémont. But "the Pathfinder" did not seem disturbed.

As Schofield and Blair approached the headquarter palace, numerous uniformed sentries stood on guard. Blair had "some magic word" by which the two passed, entering a door into the basement, which had been converted into an armory. Ascending two flights of stairs (the first floor was occupied with lesser executives at their desks), they came upon the commanding general, with one secretary, occupying a suite of rooms extending from the front to the rear of the building.[5] Frémont received both cordially, at once led Schofield over to a large table on which maps were spread, and began to explain at length the plans of the campaign for which he was then preparing (it seemed that Blair had already heard them). Frémont intended to march southwest through Missouri, into northwest Arkansas, and then to the Mississippi, thus turning all the Confederate defenses to below Memphis. After

3. Adamson, *Rebellion in Missouri*, p. 278.
4. *Missouri Republican* (St. Louis), August 14, 1861. *O.R.*, Ser. 1, III, 442.
5. Monaghan, *Civil War*, p. 184.

more than an hour, the detailed explanation ended. Schofield and Blair left through the same basement door by which they had entered. Frémont had never said a word about General Lyon or the Battle at Wilson's Creek. After walking down the street for some distance in silence, Blair said: "Well, what do you think of him?" Schofield replied in strong language—a rare thing for him—to the effect that his opinion of Frémont's wisdom was the same as it always had been! "I have been suspecting that for some time," Blair said.[6]

During the latter part of August and into September, Schofield carried out Frémont's orders to convert the First Missouri Volunteer Infantry into an artillery regiment. He organized eight batteries, using all the field guns he could get, but there was still one company of officers and men which had none. He finally made a trip back East which resulted in obtaining twenty-four new rifled Parrott guns for service in the Western Department.[7]

It was early October when Schofield returned to St. Louis. Frémont was then in central Missouri, having taken eight batteries of Schofield's regiment with him, leaving orders for Schofield to complete the organization and equipment of the regiment when the guns and other supplies arrived from the East.[8] While waiting for the guns, Schofield responded to a call for more artillery from Colonel William P. Carlin, commanding an infantry brigade at Pilot Knob, some eighty miles south of St. Louis. The Rebel cavalry leader, M. Jeff Thompson, raiding in Carlin's rear, had destroyed the railroad bridge over Big River and interfered with communication lines to St. Louis.

Schofield rounded up enough men to form a medium sized company, although they had received no instruction other than how to fire a cannon. Loading the men on a train, along with four smooth-bore bronze guns and some horses which had never been hitched to a cannon, he started south.[9] With this motley crew he took part in the minor engagement at Fredericktown on October 21, helping to deploy the artillery on the Union right and then forming and directing several companies of infantry as the Federals, bayonets glistening in the sun, advanced upon the Confederates.

6. Schofield, *Forty-Six Years*, pp. 48, 49.
7. *Ibid.*, p. 50.
8. *Ibid.*, p. 51.
9. *Ibid.*

The Rebels abandoned their position, reportedly without the Blue line firing a shot. Twice they rallied only to break again as the Union advance came on. At last they gave way in some disorder, evidently convinced that the Federals had too many men and too much cold steel. The next day Schofield returned to St. Louis.[10]

Meanwhile Frémont's status in Missouri had gone from bad to worse. His first serious mistake was in alienating the Blair brothers, Frank and Montgomery, who had been in large measure responsible for placing him in the position of department commander.[11] He might have weathered this storm if he had not presumed upon the patience of the President about the emancipation issue.[12] And it would have helped if he could have gotten along better with Hamilton R. Gamble who headed Missouri's provisional government. On October 11, Simon Cameron, Secretary of War, and Adjutant General Lorenzo Thomas arrived in St. Louis at the President's request to conduct an investigation. Evidences of Frémont's extravagance and irresponsibility were widespread—such as the government paying $6,000 annually in rent for the Brant mansion while the General issued government contracts indiscriminately to recipients indulging largely in graft. "The Pathfinder" was soon relieved of command, and on November 19, the President appointed Major General Henry W. Halleck to reorganize the western theater of war.[13]

10. O.R., Ser. 1, III, 222, 223. Schofield, Forty-Six Years, pp. 52, 53.
11. Thomas L. Snead, The Fight for Missouri from the Election of Lincoln to the Death of Lyon (New York, 1888), pp. 219–20. Peckham, General Lyon, pp. 266–67.
12. Monaghan, Civil War, p. 185. Sceva Bright Laughlin, "Missouri Politics During the Civil War," Missouri Historical Review (October, 1929), p. 89. John G. Nicolay and John Hay, Abraham Lincoln, 10 vols. (New York 1886–90), IV, 422. On August 30, Frémont had issued a proclamation which extended marital law throughout the state and raised the emancipation issue all over the country. The proclamation, issued entirely without authority from Washington, freed all slaves of disloyal persons and ordered that all men bearing arms without authority were to be court-martialed and shot. Two days later Lincoln wrote Frémont not to shoot any man under the proclamation without first having the President's signature and asked him to modify that part dealing with the slaves. The latter had caused serious difficulty in the slaveholding border states. A whole company of Kentucky volunteers had thrown down their arms and disbanded when they heard what Frémont had done. The general defended his position, but told Lincoln to direct him to modify the order if he still objected to it. The President was still opposed and so informed Frémont again on September 11.
13. O.R., Ser. 1, III, 540–49. James G. Blunt, "General Blunt's Account of His Civil War Experiences," Kansas Historical Quarterly, XVIII (May, 1932),

Commanding the new Department of the Mississippi, "Old Brains," as Halleck was known to the soldiers because of his scholarly background and authoritative writings on military science, assigned Schofield, now brigadier general of volunteers effective November 21, 1861, to the command of all the militia of Missouri.[14] From the last of November until about mid-April, 1862, Schofield's main duty was to raise, organize, and discipline this special force which was to be employed only in the defense of the state but paid, equipped, and supplied by the Federal government. This arrangement seems to have been due, in large measure, to Governor Gamble's influence upon President Lincoln.[15]

Soon after Schofield began organizing the state militia, he was called upon to cooperate with General Benjamin M. Prentiss, commanding the District of North Missouri, in ridding the counties north of the Missouri River of secessionists who were organizing widespread uprisings. Bridge burners, particularly, were giving the Federal authorities trouble. On December 22, Halleck issued an order that men disguised as peaceable citizens and caught in the act of burning bridges or destroying railroad or telegraph wires should be shot immediately.[16]

Schofield assisted Prentiss by trying to occupy the important points along the railroad northwest of St. Louis from St. Charles to Mexico, a distance of about one hundred miles; and he organized a system of scouting, hoping to capture the small bands of Rebels which were so annoying.[17] His task was doubly difficult because of some "well mounted and well armed" Union "barbarians," as he called them, who gave him about as much trouble as the Confederates. At Warrenton a Federal battalion of Reserve Corps Cavalry murdered one of the few Union men in the vicinity and plundered and destroyed thousands of dollars worth of property of peaceable citizens—"a burning disgrace to the army and the Union cause," Schofield reported. He finally succeeded in getting five of the most notorious offenders "in irons."[18] Progress was

216. Britton, *The Civil War*, p. 159. Marvin R. Cain, "Edward Bates and Hamilton R. Gamble: A Wartime Partnership," *Missouri Historical Review* (January, 1962), p. 149.
14. *O.R.*, Ser. 1, VIII, 389.
15. Laughlin, "Missouri Politics," p. 96.
16. Britton, *The Civil War*, pp. 163, 192, 193.
17. *O.R.*, Ser. 1, VIII, 479, 482.
18. *Ibid.*, pp. 482, 503.

gradually made in restoring relative quiet to north Missouri as
Schofield placed companies of the state militia in strategic positions
as soon as they were raised and organized.

A prominent topic of conversation among the Federals in Missouri was the military merit of Colonel Franz Sigel, who had re-
signed as commander of the Union force at Rolla. His defenders
said he was cramped and restricted by many of the regular army,
above all, General Samuel R. Curtis, commanding the Southwestern
District, who had formed a "conspiracy" against him. The newspapers frequently mentioned the Sigel case. Schofield probably
saw the St. Louis *Daily Missouri Democrat* of January 21, 1862,
which carried a page-one account from the New York *Times* of
January 17, of a great demonstration for Sigel, staged primarily
by German-Americans at the Cooper Institute in New York. Sigel
was praised as "the twin of Garibaldi," a man who possessed
military ability of the highest order, and Missouri's battlefields
were "ever lasting monuments of his valor and . . . superior
tactics." This was too much for Schofield to endure. As the snow
blanketed St. Louis on February 13, he wrote General Halleck a
long letter about Sigel. Schofield's official report of the Battle of
Wilson's Creek did not present a favorable image of Sigel. Now
Schofield was giving the full story.

He deemed it his "duty" (Schofield often professed his concern with "duty" during these early months of the war) to state
the facts about the merit of Sigel as a commander. When General
Lyon had sent Sigel to Rolla to cut off the retreat of Sterling Price's
rebel force, he had "allowed" one company to be captured, after
which he made a "masterly retreat" before Price's "miserable
rabble." Thus Price and Ben McCulloch were permitted to join
forces. A short time later at Wilson's Creek, when trying to carry
out the flanking operation which he himself had suggested in opposition to the other officers, Sigel "lost his artillery . . . his infantry
and fled alone, or nearly so, to Springfield, arriving there long before the battle was ended." After giving several more examples in
the same vein, Schofield concluded that Sigel "in tactics, great
and small logistics, and discipline," was "greatly deficient." And
it would be "less than his duty" if he did not enter his protest
against the appointment of Sigel to high command.[19] The letter
was signed by nine other officers who expressed their "entire agree-

19. *Ibid.*, pp. 94, 95.

ment" with the facts stated by Schofield. There was doubtless some prejudice against foreigners involved in the Sigel controversy, but his military capacity did seem deficient.

On April 10, 1862, General Halleck, disturbed by the reports of Grant's alleged drunkenness at Shiloh, left his headquarters in St. Louis to take command of the army before Corinth, Mississippi. He gave Schofield instructions to "take care of Missouri." Schofield's command of state militia had then been extended over about three-fourths of the state, especially the north, central, and eastern portions.[20] Several of the guerrilla bands had been broken up or captured. Victory at Pea Ridge had diminished Rebel power in the state. And General Curtis, with a formidable force, was supposedly marching on Little Rock. Missouri was quieter than it had been in some time—the calm before the storm.

On May 6, Halleck, expecting a big battle at Corinth, ordered Schofield to send him "all the infantry within his reach and replace them with cavalry."[21] Schofield sent all the infantry in the state except a small force of reserve corps guarding the Pacific Railroad and the St. Louis and Iron Mountain Railroad, and two volunteer regiments in the central and southwestern districts. Only cavalry was left to guard the long rail lines north of the Missouri River and a portion of the Pacific Railroad.[22] Few of Halleck's subordinates ever responded so swiftly and helpfully.

Meanwhile General Curtis' movement on Little Rock left the southwestern district of Missouri virtually without troops. Small bands of outlaws and Rebel cavalry were soon terrorizing people and playing havoc with Curtis' line of communications with Rolla, destroying several of his trains. Though the district was not under his command, Schofield sent his one remaining infantry regiment with three regiments of cavalry and a battery of artillery to protect the communication lines. On June 5, he received orders from Halleck to move all his available force to the southern border of Missouri and support Curtis, who was repeatedly calling for more troops. Schofield sent him portions of three cavalry regiments. A regiment of Reserve Corps Infantry refused to cross the line into Arkansas. Schofield had done all he could. Curtis wanted more, but no more troops were available.[23]

20. *Ibid.*, p. 7.     21. *Ibid.*, p. 371.
22. *Ibid.*, p. 8.
23. *Ibid.*

At this time, at least in part due to Schofield's advocacy and the pressure on Lincoln from Missouri's members of Congress, Missouri, except for the three southeastern counties, was organized into a military district and placed under Schofield's command. Troops in the southwestern part of the state, however, were still subject to orders from Curtis—a situation which could prove confusing and troublesome. The District of Missouri was divided into five parts, with a total force available in all these commands of about 17,360.[24] As Schofield positioned his command to try to preserve peace in the state, General Curtis shifted his force eastward to Helena, Arkansas, and left Missouri's southern border without protection against raids from across the Arkansas line. To make matters worse, the Rebels were just beginning a determined bid to gain reinforcements in Missouri and eventually to regain possession of the state.

When Schofield learned of this he requested cooperation from Curtis' army—in the form of a diversionary movement on Little Rock—and reinforcements. The diversionary movement was promised but never materialized. Curtis said no reinforcements were available. In the meantime Rebel bands were appearing all over the state. Schofield had to have more troops. On July 22, he issued General Order No. 19, which required every able-bodied man in the state to enroll in the militia, even those who had aided or supported the South.[25] His purpose in enrolling such men was to keep them under surveillance. They were not to be armed or made a part of the fighting force. Eventually some 50,000 were enlisted, about 30,000 of whom were armed as loyal men.[26] By this time guerrilla warfare in Missouri was reaching a new peak of devastation.

24. *Ibid.*, pp. 9, 368.
25. *Missouri Republican* (St. Louis), July 23, 1862.
26. *Ibid.*, August 17, 1862. Marguerite Potter, "Hamilton R. Gamble, Missouri's War Governor," *Missouri Historical Review* (October, 1940), p. 53. The question of what to do with the disloyal among those subject to enrollment was a difficult one to settle. Many loyal people considered it a great injustice if the Rebel sympathizers were excused from a military duty, which their own unfaithfulness had made necessary in the first place. But unfaithful men could not be embodied in small scattered forces such as the militia would often be, where they might well outnumber the loyal men. Thought was given to exempting them with the payment of a fee. But Schofield felt that there was too much difference between what was reasonable for a poor man and a rich man to pay for this to be practicable. Finally it was determined to permit none but those of approved loyalty to bear arms.

Between April 1 and September 20, Schofield's forces confronted the enemy in more than one hundred engagements, ranging from forty or fifty men on each side to a thousand or more. The principal area of trouble was the northeastern division and a large portion of the St. Louis district, especially that part north of the Missouri River. Rebel bands under Joseph C. Porter, John A. Poindexter, and others of lesser note totaled a little more than 5,000. Even after the destruction of Porter's band and the capture of Poindexter, to dispose of the smaller guerrilla bands was a work which took much time. Petty warfare continued for weeks as Schofield attempted to hunt down these groups, many of whom were simply outlaws—rebels before they ever heard of the Confederacy.[27]

As the Rebels north of the Missouri were being beaten back, secessionists intensified their efforts in other portions of the state. A Confederate force led by John T. Hughes captured Independence on August 11, and then, joined by John T. Coffee's cavalry, repulsed a Union force at Lone Jack, some eighteen miles southeast of Independence. Schofield finally united a sufficient command to clear central Missouri of the majority of the insurgents, Coffee being hotly pursued to the Arkansas line.[28]

While Schofield was attempting to put the sword to marauding guerrillas in his front, he was also forced to fend off certain citizens and politicians in his rear. On August 4, a group of prominent citizens of St. Louis, who generally opposed Governor Gamble with whom Schofield enjoyed amicable relations, decided that Schofield was not acting with enough vigor in suppressing the guerrillas.[29] A committee was formed to go to Washington and urge the President to replace Schofield with a man who, in their judgment, would act with more zeal. On August 11, Schofield received a telegram from Halleck who had recently become general-in-chief of the army: "There is a deputation here from Colonel Blair and others asking for your removal on account of ineffi-

27. *O.R.*, Ser. 1, XIII, 12–14.
28. *Ibid.*, pp. 15, 16.
29. His most offensive act seems to have been his failure to execute the act of Congress of July 16, 1862, relative to confiscation of the property of persons engaged in the rebellion. But this law provided for its execution by the judicial department of the government. It gave no authority for military action, and all Schofield could lawfully do was to secure property subject to confiscation, and liable to be removed or otherwise disposed of, and collect evidence for the use of judicial officers.

ciency."[30] Just a few minutes after Schofield received this dispatch, Blair happened to walk into his office. Schofield simply handed him the cable. Reading it Blair replied, according to Schofield, with considerable feeling: "No one is authorized to ask in my name for your removal."[31] Blair sent a wire to Halleck trying to correct the matter. The next day he sent another one and the committee's efforts finally came to naught.

In late September, by order of the President, the War Department directed that the states of Missouri, Kansas, Arkansas, and the Indian Territory be consolidated into the Department of Missouri with General Curtis, senior officer in the area, taking command.[32] With the commanding general of the department once more in St. Louis, Schofield requested to be relieved of all administrative duties as commander of the subordinate District of Missouri in order to take command of troops in the field in the southwestern part of the state. His request was granted, and on September 26, he assumed command of the "Army of the Frontier" —a force of 10,800 men under Generals Francis J. Herron and James Totten. General James G. Blunt's Kansas division of about 4,000 was also placed under Schofield's orders.

Leaving Herron's troops at Springfield, Schofield joined up with Blunt's command at Sarcoxie and attempted to surprise the Rebels, commanded by Colonel Douglas H. Cooper, at Newtonia. At dawn on October 4, Blunt's division emerged from the valley of Shoal Creek into the plain north and west of Newtonia. Totten's division came in from the east. The cavalry clattered through the town in a charge. But the Confederates, since expected reinforcements had not arrived, had evacuated Newtonia, leaving only Joseph O. Shelby's brigade to screen the movement. Shelby annoyed Blunt's advance, skirmished briefly with Schofield, and retreated into the timbered area some three miles out of town, finally following the rest of the Confederates into Arkansas.[33]

Reports had been coming in for some time that the Rebels in Arkansas were planning a vigorous effort to re-enter Missouri. Schofield decided that an invasion of northwestern Arkansas would

30. O.R., Ser. 1, XIII, 552.
31. Schofield, Forty-Six Years, p. 59.
32. O.R., Ser. 1, XIII, 653.
33. Ibid., p. 19. Daily Missouri Democrat (St. Louis), October 17, 1862. John N. Edwards, Shelby and His Men, or War in the West (Cincinnati, 1867), pp. 89–91. Blunt, "Civil War Experiences," pp. 226–27.

be the best possible defense of Missouri. Thus he ordered Herron, with the rest of the troops at Springfield, to move toward Cassville near the Missouri-Arkansas border and join the main column at that point from whence the invasion would begin.

Schofield's advance, heading in the general direction of Huntsville, resulted in several days of hard marching, part of the time over the White River Mountains, some of the roughest territory in the Ozarks, causing the soldiers to mumble and curse.[34] The army pursued a "seeming phantom," wrote a soldier in the 19th Iowa Infantry who was especially bitter. He blamed it all on Schofield whom he referred to as "Granny Schofield."[35] On this march the "Army of the Frontier" was proving the appropriateness of its name.

At Huntsville, Schofield made contact with a small force of the enemy only to learn that it was the Confederate rear guard. The Rebels were again retreating farther south across the Boston Mountains toward Ozark and the Arkansas River. It appeared to be impossible to overtake them. Communication lines were long and the danger of being cut off and ambushed was troubling Schofield. He decided to occupy positions at Cross Hollows, Osage Springs, and Prairie Creek, thus holding a line north of the mountains where corn and wheat could be obtained and wait for a more favorable time to advance.

About this time he came down with what the St. Louis *Daily Missouri Democrat* said was typhoid fever.[36] He had already entered upon his most miserable months of the war—so his letters indicate—and the period of sickness only added to his depression and melancholy. He unburdened his feelings in a long private letter to General-in-Chief Halleck, written from Springfield on November 18, 1862. It was a "bitter pill" he said, to come under the command of General Curtis who "was really the cause of all my troubles, who by leaving the long border between Missouri and Arkansas entirely unprotected and by lying . . . at Helena for months, involved Missouri in a guerrilla warfare, perhaps never before equalled in extent and intensity, and which involved me in almost

34. *Daily Missouri Democrat* (St. Louis), November 1, 1862.

35. Benjamin F. McIntyre, *Federals on the Frontier: The Diary of Benjamin F. McIntyre, 1862–1864,* ed. Nannie M. Tilley (Austin, Texas, 1963), pp. 33, 34, 133.

36. *Daily Missouri Democrat* (St. Louis), November 11, 1862. Schofield, *Forty-Six Years,* p. 62.

endless trouble and came near ruining my reputation as a successful commander." He continued to complain at length about Little Rock not being taken when it had been "threatened for the past eight months by a force amply strong to take it. . . ." He was "sick, tired, and disheartened at this endless idleness" in Arkansas which enabled the Rebels to threaten Missouri continually. He was also disturbed because "my juniors [are] promoted over me for meritorious conduct, while I, the only officer who has tried to do anything in this department, am tied down and condemned to almost obscurity." Schofield "begged" Halleck to transfer him to some other command where he would not be "trameled [sic] by endless sloth and imbecility [sic]," and finally concluded: "Pardon, General, this long letter. I am sick—scarce able to leave my bed. . . . I have broken myself down in the service—and all for nothing."[37] Schofield's ambition was outrunning his opportunities and the "green eyed monster" was troubling him, but there was truth in his complaints about Union operations in Arkansas.

Not long after Schofield recovered from his illness, he became involved in a "discussion" with General Curtis concerning the accuracy of Schofield's report of operations in Missouri and northwestern Arkansas from April 10 to November 20, 1862. Both men were rather petty about the matter, engaging in sarcastically biting charges and replies to each other.[38] By the first of 1863 it was becoming increasingly evident that Schofield and Curtis could not work together. After resuming command of the Army of the Frontier, Schofield learned that General Blunt had made some errors at the recent battle of Prairie Grove. On January 1, 1863, perhaps in part jealous of the promotion which Blunt had received, as well as to set the record straight, Schofield addressed Curtis about the "blunders" of Blunt.[39] Curtis replied with a not too subtle rebuke of Schofield for backbiting a fellow officer.[40] Schofield responded in a shocked and highly insulted tone, declaring that Curtis had received the information which his "duty" had

37. JMS to Henry Halleck, November 18, 1862, Schofield MSS. According to *O.R.*, Ser. 1, XIII, 793, this letter was "Not found."

38. *O.R.*, Ser. 1, XIII, 23–28, 782.

39. Schofield, *Forty-Six Years*, p. 63. *O.R.*, Ser. 1, XXII, part 2, 6.

40. *O.R.*, Ser. 1, XIII, 933. According to Schofield, Curtis also showed the dispatch to Senator James Lane from Kansas, who along with other of Blunt's political friends, presented Schofield before the Senate as being unjustly hostile to gallant officers who had won victories. Schofield, *Forty-Six Years*, p. 63.

compelled him to state, with "expressions of contempt."[41] It was not long before Schofield was again seeking relief through Halleck, requesting to be transferred to another command. "The good of the service" demanded it, he said.[42]

His letters to Halleck at last brought results. On April 1, 1863, he was relieved of command of the Army of the Frontier by General Herron and ordered to join the Army of the Cumberland in Tennessee. Thanking the general-in-chief, Schofield wrote: "I am as willing as anybody to be sacrificed when any good is to be accomplished by it, but do not like to be slaughtered for nothing."[43] As Schofield headed for Tennessee in the spring of 1863, he evidently still felt, as he had written Halleck in November, that his service in Missouri had been "all for nothing."

41. *O.R.*, Ser. 1, XXII, part 2, 12, 13.
42. *Ibid.*, pp. 94, 95.
43. *Ibid.*, p. 208.

# IV. On to Little Rock

"ONE OF THE happiest days of my life," Schofield later wrote, "was when I reported to [General William S.] Rosecrans and [General George H.] Thomas at Murfreesboro, received their cordial welcome, and was assigned to the command of . . . the Fourteenth Corps."[1] For about thirty days in the spring of 1863 he was stationed at Triune, Tennessee, a small town twenty miles west of Murfreesboro. Unfortunately, information about his activities during these days, which he considered one of the most agreeable periods of his military service, is virtually nonexistent.[2] But this pleasant interlude soon came to an abrupt end. On May 13 Schofield was ordered to relieve General Curtis from the command of the Department of the Missouri. In a letter from the general-in-chief dated May 22, Halleck told Schofield that he owed his appointment "entirely to the choice of the President himself." Halleck had not interfered "directly or indirectly," but assured Schofield that he "fully concurred" in the choice and would give him "all possible support and assistance."[3]

Lincoln's first consideration in removing Curtis was to get every

1. Schofield, *Forty-Six Years*, p. 66.
2. He was not engaged in any significant military operation. Consequently the *O.R.* contains only a handful of unimportant references and dispatches concerning his activities in Tennessee. There is nothing in his personal papers which sheds light on this period either.
3. *O.R.*, Ser. 1, XXII, part 2, 292.

man he could for Grant who was then engrossed in his effort to take Vicksburg and open the Mississippi. When Grant had called for more soldiers, Halleck had, for the second time, levied a draft on Curtis' department. Curtis replied that he could not spare any more men. The President then, without further notice, removed Curtis and a few days later sent Schofield a brief but concise statement of the reason, as well as instructions for his own procedure. Governor Gamble had sufficient militia to replace Curtis' troops in Missouri but had refused to cooperate with Curtis whom he considered a "radical." After attempting unsuccessfully to reconcile the difficulty between the two, Lincoln had decided to "break it up somehow," and as he could not remove Gamble, he decided to remove Curtis. Schofield should not, the President advised, undo anything merely because Curtis or Gamble did it. He must use his own judgment and act according to what was best for the public interest. "If both factions, or neither," Lincoln concluded, "shall abuse you, you will, probably, be about right. Beware of being assailed by one and praised by the other."[4]

Schofield arrived in St. Louis on Saturday morning, May 23. A large delegation met him on the east side of the Mississippi River and escorted him to his headquarters at the Planter's House. During the day a number of prominent citizens called and assured him of their support. Late Sunday evening, about eleven o'clock, a crowd assembled in front of the Planter's House while a band played the "Star Spangled Banner," "Rally Round the Flag Boys," and a medley of patriotic tunes. Then the crowd began to call for Schofield. He soon appeared on the balcony, and was greeted with cheer after cheer. He spoke briefly: "Fellow Citizens: I am peculiarly gratified by this cordial reception on my return to Missouri, because it assures me that in the arduous and extremely delicate duties imposed upon me by the government I shall have the cordial support of every unqualifiedly loyal citizen." He said that he realized the "exceedingly delicate and intricate duties" imposed upon him, and that without the support of the loyal citizens he could "scarcely hope to succeed, while with their earnest co-operation we can accomplish everything." He would, he continued, attempt to "carry out to the letter" the instruction of the government, as well as the wishes of the "truly loyal citizens of Missouri." It would be his "earnest endeavor" to bring about a

4. *Ibid.*, p. 293.

state of "peace, happiness, and prosperity" as speedily as possible.
These remarks were frequently interrupted with outbursts of applause and finally responded to by three rounds of cheers for the
general.[5]

As flattering as his reception was, Schofield's appointment to
command in Missouri was not without opposition. The St. Louis
*Daily Missouri Democrat* carried an editorial on May 17, headed
"The Shuttlecock in Motion Again," voicing the editor's displeasure
with the change of commanders. Another change of command in
"this ill-starred department, contrary to the wishes of the loyal
people" was "a very unpleasant one." "Can the authorities in Washington," the writer continued, "be more interested in protecting
traitors than loyal men?" Editorials in the same vein continued for
the next several days. But if Schofield had some influential enemies
in Missouri, he also had firm backing in Washington, which would
soon be even stronger.

Now that he was in command of the Department of the Missouri, which encompassed Missouri, Kansas, part of Arkansas, and
the Indian Territory, Schofield determined that he would shortly
have Little Rock in Federal hands. He began collecting troops in
the eastern part of the state preparatory to an offensive against
the capital. But on June 2 urgent requests for reinforcements came
from Grant through Halleck. Schofield had 43,000 men in his department, and he immediately sent almost half of them to Grant[6]—
an act which gave great satisfaction to both the President and the
general-in-chief.[7] Then he mustered Governor Gamble's militia
to police Missouri. He continued to hold Helena, Arkansas, and he
had a force at Fort Gibson, Indian Territory, within easy striking
distance of the Arkansas line.[8] Schofield was still eyeing Little Rock.
If he could hold Missouri with half the number of men Curtis
had used and capture the capital of Arkansas at the same time,
perhaps his tribulations in Missouri would not be for naught after
all. But as things turned out, the invasion of Arkansas had to wait.
There were too many troublesome matters in Missouri.

Slavery, the most thorny of all questions in Missouri in 1863,
was demanding Schofield's attention. From December 29, 1862,

5. *Missouri Republican* (St. Louis), May 25, 1863.
6. Schofield, *Forty-Six Years*, p. 90. This is from a memorandum furnished
the President on October 1, 1863.
7. *O.R.*, Ser. 1, XXXIII, 355.
8. Monaghan, *Civil War*, p. 277.

until March 23, 1863, the state legislature had been in session at Jefferson City, attempting to deal with the emancipation issue. The question was not so much whether the slaves should be freed, for many realized that slavery was on its way out, but rather if emancipation should be gradual or immediate. Governor Gamble had spoken to the legislature in joint session and called for a plan of gradual emancipation. Emancipation was a subject of interest and concern to almost all of Missouri's people, and there was much discussion of it in the early months of the year. The newspapers were filled with editorials regarding the matter. Public meetings were held in many areas of the state. But the legislature took no action in the form of legislation, eventually becoming more involved with the election of United States senators. Furthermore, the national Congress was then considering compensation for Missouri and the legislature wanted first to see what would be done in Washington.

In September, 1862, Lincoln had pledged himself to appeal to Congress to offer the border states a plan for emancipation with compensation. In his annual message to Congress in December, Lincoln proposed such a plan for Missouri and urged its adoption. The House then passed a bill to award $10 million to Missouri slave-owners and sent it to the Senate. The Senate offered $20 million if Missouri provided for emancipation before July, 1865, and only $10 million if she postponed it to July 4, 1876. A committee of the two houses then conferred and could not agree on how much money was needed for Missouri. The Missouri Senate tried to help by appointing a committee to study the state's needs. To the surprise of no one, this committee could not reach an agreement either. By the end of March, 1863, both the national Congress and Missouri's legislature had adjourned without taking action on the emancipation issue.[9]

This did not quiet the people of Missouri, especially the immediate emancipationists, or "charcoals," as the St. Louis *Missouri Republican* had dubbed them. These people were clamoring for a new state convention to take definite action on the slavery question. Fearful that the radicals, if left alone, would eventually be successful in their plans, Governor Gamble and his supporters decided to convene the state convention (which had been summoned

9. Bill R. Lee, "Missouri's Fight Over Emancipation," *Missouri Historical Review* (April, 1951), pp. 256–70.

four times already since early 1861) while the conservatives still held sway in a majority of Missouri's counties. Some form of gradual emancipation, they felt, would certainly be preferable to immediate freedom. In April, 1863, the governor issued a proclamation calling together the state convention, which was to convene on June 15, to "consult and act upon the subject of the emancipation of slaves and such other matters as may be connected with the peace and prosperity of the state."[10]

Thus, when Schofield assumed command of the department in late May, the state convention was drawing nigh. Because of his relationship with the governor, as well as his position in the military and his relation with the national government, it was natural that he should take a keen interest in the proceedings of the convention. He favored a somewhat more "radical" policy toward emancipation than did the governor. This is clearly shown by his letter of June 1, 1863, addressed to Mr. John E. Williams, president of the Metropolitan Bank, New York, which was printed in the New York *Tribune* and again in the St. Louis *Missouri Republican* just four days before the state convention met. In that letter Schofield said he regarded universal emancipation as "one of the means absolutely necessary to a complete restoration of the Union," and stated that he had great hope that the state convention would "adopt some measure for the speedy emancipation of slaves."[11] This letter is especially interesting in view of the fact that he was later accused of being a "clay bank," that is, soft toward slavery.

Schofield personally urged the governor to adopt a policy on the Negro question which was more in harmony with the views of the national administration and of the northern people. Gamble did make a speech at the state convention in which he advocated emancipation in a much shorter period than the convention could finally be prevailed upon to adopt. Schofield said that he also used his influence with members of the convention to the same end.[12] On the other hand, Schofield wired the President, seeking to gain some concession which might make a compromise between the warring factions more possible. On June 20, he asked Lincoln whether he could, directly or indirectly, pledge the President's

10. *Ibid.*, p. 270. Earl J. Nelson, "Missouri Slavery, 1861–1865," *Missouri Historical Review* (July, 1934), p. 261.
11. *Missouri Republican* (St. Louis), June 11, 1863.
12. Schofield, *Forty-Six Years*, p. 71.

support to the protection of slavery in Missouri during any temporary period preceding emancipation that might be decided upon by the convention.[13]

The President responded that his "impulse" was to say that such protection would be given, but since he could not know exactly what shape an emancipation act would take, he did "not wish to pledge the general government to the affirmative support of even temporary slavery. . . ." Since he had urged the slave states to adopt emancipation, it would be his object not to thwart what any of them might "in good faith do to that end." Schofield was authorized to act "in the spirit of this letter, in conjunction with what may appear to be the military necessities of your department." The President concluded, "Although this letter will become public at some time, it is not intended to be made so now."[14]

An ordinance was passed by the convention which provided, in effect, that slavery should cease July 4, 1870. Slaves over forty years old were to remain with their masters for life; those twelve and under would serve until they were twenty-three; and those of all other ages would remain in servitude until July 4, 1870.[15] The convention adjourned on July 1.

By this time Schofield was involved with another problem— seemingly minor at first, yet threatening to destroy his influence in Missouri as well as his favor with the President. On June 27, while Schofield was at Jefferson City involved with the state convention, the St. Louis *Daily Missouri Democrat* published the letter of May 27, in which Lincoln had explained why he had removed Curtis and instructed Schofield to maintain a neutral position between the two factions of Unionists in Missouri. Upon returning to St. Louis, Schofield, naturally regarding the letter as confidential, wondered how William McKee, editor of the paper, had gotten it. Certainly Lincoln had no desire for it to be published. Had it somehow been obtained from his own headquarters? Or had a copy sent by Lincoln to Curtis been slipped to a *Democrat* reporter? Whatever the case, McKee seemed determined to exploit his advantage. On July 7, the paper carried a page-one editorial entitled, "The President's Warning." "The present," the article ran, was "a very good time to remind the commanding general of the depart-

13. *O.R.*, Ser.1, XXII, part 2, 330.
14. *Ibid.*, pp. 331–32.
15. Lee, "Missouri's Fight," p. 271.

ment of the friendly admonition given him by the President. . . . " The editor was "much afraid General Schofield had not given due heed to the warning" for the "very contingency against which it advised [was bidding] fair to occur." Schofield was on too friendly terms with Governor Gamble to suit the *Democrat,* and above all, he had been endorsed by that "organ of all the Copperheads of Missouri," the St. Louis *Missouri Republican.* This alone proved he must be a traitor in the Union camp. "Of what act of hostility to the Union cause had General Schofield been guilty," McKee queried, "that he shall receive such an endorsement?"

Schofield sent a note to the *Democrat* calling upon one of the proprietors to come to see him. The man responded promptly but knew nothing of the publication of the letter, other than that Mc-Kee was responsible. Schofield asked the proprietor to tell McKee to come and see him. When the editor failed to appear, Schofield sent a written note by one of his staff officers who was a friend of McKee's. When several days had passed with no response from McKee, Schofield on July 12 sent the provost-marshal to bring him in. McKee then told Schofield that a copy of the letter had not come from his headquarters, but refused to say where it had come from. He requested ten days' time—to consider answering further, so he claimed—whereupon he was paroled.[16] The *Democrat* was soon denouncing the arrest as "foolish and unwarrantable,"[17] while the *Republican,* in its discussion of "The 'Pestilent' Letter" evidently sympathized with Schofield's desire to learn if there was an untrustworthy officer on his staff.

A message was on the wires at once to Lincoln from a congressional friend of McKee's. The Honorable H. T. Blow stated that the editor's arrest was "unkind, unjust, against the spirit of your instructions, and an insult to the supporters of the Union and the government." The President replied that he did not think the publication of a letter "without the leave of the writer or the receiver" could be justified, but neither did he think the case was of "sufficient consequence to justify an arrest," especially since, through a parole, the arrest was merely nominal. To Schofield, Lincoln wrote on July 13 what must have been a disturbing message: "I regret to learn of the arrest of the 'Democrat' editor. I fear this loses you the middle position I desired you to occupy.

16. *Missouri Republican* (St. Louis), July 13 and 15, 1863.
17. *Daily Missouri Democrat* (St. Louis), July 13, 1863.

I have not learned which of the two letters I wrote you it was that the 'Democrat' published but I care very little for the publication of any letter I have written. Please spare me the trouble this is likely to bring." Lincoln hoped that "this small matter," as he described it, could be dropped on both sides without further difficulty.[18]

Schofield defended himself. He was satisfied, he wrote, that the facts in the case had been misrepresented to the President precisely for the purpose of making it appear that he had departed from the "middle position" which Lincoln wanted him to maintain. McKee's politics "had nothing whatever to do with his arrest," except that his position as editor of a leading Union journal had caused Schofield to be "much more indulgent" than he would have been toward an ordinary offender. It seemed "probable," Schofield continued, that McKee obtained the letter through some friend of General Curtis, to whom, he presumed, the President had sent a copy, and not through some person on his own staff as it first appeared. If this was true, Schofield expressed his willingness to stop proceedings in the matter and to "pardon the offender without knowing who he may be."[19] Evidently Lincoln never told Schofield whether he had sent a copy of the letter to Curtis or not. Schofield did drop the charges. While his feelings in this matter are understandable, he did subject himself to unnecessary trouble.

Meanwhile the war was picking up tempo in the South. On July 7, Schofield received the welcome news that Vicksburg had fallen. Once more the way seemed open for active operations in Arkansas. On July 8, Schofield wrote to Grant, "I congratulate you most heartily upon your glorious triumph. . . . " It was very important to his own department, Schofield continued, that he be able to occupy the line of the Arkansas River as soon as possible. He hoped that Grant could now send back a substantial portion of the troops Schofield had sent him.[20] Grant's reply was sympathetic, but not very encouraging. He said he would send the soldiers as soon as he possibly could. But he did not know when Sherman's siege of Jackson would end, and he had sent two brigades up the Yazoo River and one to Natchez, leaving only three at Vicksburg.[21]

18. *O.R.*, Ser. 1, XXII, part 2, 366.
19. *Ibid.*, p. 374.
20. *Ibid.*, part 1, 19.
21. *Ibid.*, p. 20.

On July 13, Schofield received an alarming report from General John W. Davidson that Sterling Price, with 15,000 men, was marching toward southeastern Missouri to attack Bloomfield. The report was in error, but Schofield notified Grant of this supposed move, urging him to send a force to eastern Arkansas at once, so that they might trap and crush Price between them. He also notified Halleck, who ordered General Benjamin M. Prentiss to move west from Helena. Learning of Halleck's orders to Prentiss, Schofield ordered Davidson, with 6,000 cavalry, to advance from Bloomfield into Arkansas via Chalk Bluff to make contact with Prentiss. Davidson began his advance on July 17, and shortly after Grant sent a division of infantry to Helena, all the troops that he had who were "not worn out with fatigue."[22]

It is not clear just when Schofield and Davidson discovered that they had been deceived by a captured lieutenant from a Confederate regiment. Schofield had received Davidson's report, primarily based on the prisoner's information, on July 13, the same day he had received Lincoln's message expressing his fear that the affair with McKee had lost Schofield the "middle position." Perhaps this disturbance and the consequent necessity of writing Lincoln a long explanation of his side of the matter caused Schofield to evaluate Davidson's report about Price less carefully than he otherwise would.

But the end result, happily, was what Schofield had wanted all along. An operation meant to destroy Price in a pincer movement would ultimately unite Davidson and General Frederick Steele at Clarendon on the White River for an advance against Little Rock.[23] Schofield had suggested to Grant on July 8 that Steele, because of his acquaintance with the Arkansas territory, should be sent to command the invasion force. On August 3, General Stephen A. Hurlbut, acting under Grant's orders, relieved Prentiss, placing Steele in command.[24]

For a time there was confusion as to who had the overall direction of the Arkansas expedition, Schofield or Hurlbut. On July 27, the general-in-chief wrote Schofield that the Arkansas force would "act under your general orders," and sent a similar message to Grant the same day.[25] Three days later Halleck apparently

22. *Ibid.*, part 2, 367, 374, 376, 385.          23. *Ibid.*, pp. 429–31.
24. *Ibid.*
25. *Ibid.*, part 1, 22.

reversed himself, telegraphing Schofield that the troops he sent would unite with those from Hurlbut's corps and be temporarily under Hurlbut's command.[26] Schofield wrote Davidson accordingly, directing him to take orders from Steele, who would act under the orders of Hurlbut.[27] He likewise informed Hurlbut that he had directed Davidson to take orders from Steele. But Hurlbut was nevertheless confused. He wrote Grant about "a matter as to which I am not sure what to do." Steele reported to him. He had Grant's orders to organize the Arkansas expedition and the infantry was also from his corps. But, he reminded Grant, "you have also sent me a dispatch from General Halleck that troops serving in this expedition shall be under command of Major General Schofield." Hurlbut wondered whether he was responsible for the expedition and if so, how far?[28] Grant replied that since the troops under Steele were operating in Schofield's department they would be subject to his orders according to Halleck's dispatch, but Hurlbut, being closer to Steele than Schofield, should give him any aid he could in men and supplies.[29]

The question was of minor significance in the final analysis. Steele was proceeding with his own plans of operation, much as Schofield had anticipated that he would. In his letter to Hurlbut on August 6, Schofield had written that he "had not thought it necessary to enter much into detail concerning the plan of operations." From his previous campaign in Arkansas, General Steele was "thoroughly acquainted with the country" and with Schofield's views as well as those of the general-in-chief regarding "the . . . operations in Arkansas."[30]

On August 10 General Steele began his advance, proceeding up the White River beyond Clarendon, to Devall's Bluff, where he established a base of operations, preparatory to a farther advance. On September 1 he was ready to move again. The enemy, under Sterling Price, was entrenched three miles northeast of Little Rock on the north bank of the Arkansas River. After a lengthy reconnaisance to the north, Steele was convinced it was impracticable to turn the Confederate position from that direction. It would

26. *Ibid.*, part 2, 409.
27. *Ibid.*, part 1, 24.
28. *Ibid.*, part 2, 464
29. *Ibid.*, p. 465.
30. *Ibid.*, part 1, 22.

overextend his supply line.[31] Instead he would throw Davidson's cavalry to the south of the Arkansas, easily fordable following a severe drought in August, and have his troops advance up that side as the infantry moved against the Rebel works on the north bank.

Davidson's task was made easier by the lack of an experienced Confederate cavalry general to oppose him. General L. Marsh Walker had just been killed in a duel by General Marmaduke, who was subsequently arrested. Davidson defeated the Rebel cavalry, under the temporary command of a colonel, and then drove toward the city.[32] Price discovered his position was being turned and fell back rapidly, abandoning the capital of Arkansas to the Union army. Davidson's troopers rode into Little Rock about dark on the evening of September 10. At long last Arkansas' capital was in Federal hands, and the entire campaign had cost only 137 casualties.[33]

31. *Ibid.* p. 476.
32. Thomas A. Belser, Jr., "Military Operations in Missouri and Arkansas, 1861–1865," (Ph.D. dissertation, Vanderbilt University), pp. 582–83.
33. *O.R.*, Ser. 1, XXII, part 1, 482.

# V. "The Most Revolting Hostilities"

THE LITTLE ROCK triumph might have been more satisfying to Schofield had it come at some other time. In late August and September, 1863, the border between Missouri and Kansas was in such turmoil that Schofield scarcely had time to celebrate the capture of the Arkansas capital. The immediate source of his difficulties was an unsavory character from Ohio, William Clarke Quantrill, twenty-six-year-old gambler, horse thief, pillager, murderer, and butcher, who first makes his appearance in the *Official Records* as "the notorious Quantrill."[1]

Schofield by now was no novice in dealing with marauders. From the opening of hostilities in 1861, Missouri, Kansas, and northern Arkansas had been the scenes of a bitter and relentless guerrilla warfare. On his previous assignments in Missouri, Schofield had often been forced to deal with guerrillas. The border of Kansas and Missouri especially had been, as Schofield candidly expressed it, "the scene of the most revolting hostilities during the past two years."[2] The summer of 1863 was certainly no exception to the rule. Soon after he took over command of the Department of the Missouri in May, the renewal of guerrilla activity caused Schofield to create two new districts to combat Quantrill and others of his

1. Kenneth P. Williams, *Lincoln Finds a General*, 5 vols. (New York, 1959), V, 123.
2. *O.R.*, Ser. 1, XXII, part 1, 15.

stamp. On June 9, by General Order Number Forty-eight, he set up the District of the Border and that of the Frontier. The District of the Border, where the guerrilla war was centered, was the northern portion of Kansas and the two western tiers of Missouri counties north of the thirty-eighth parallel and south of the Missouri River. The District of the Frontier was the rest of Kansas, the Indian Territory, and the two western tiers of Missouri and Arkansas counties south of the thirty-eighth parallel. General James G. Blunt, with headquarters at Fort Scott, commanded the latter, while Brigadier General Thomas Ewing, Jr., brother-in-law of William T. Sherman, was given command of the former—the most troublesome of all the districts—establishing his headquarters at Kansas City.[3]

Ewing believed that the Missouri militia had been too soft in dealing with the pro-southern population of the area which was supporting the guerrillas. The only possible way to destroy the guerrillas was to strike at this root of their power. He began by arresting and confining at Kansas City a considerable number of the wives, mothers, and sisters of some of the most notorious members of Quantrill's band.[4] But by the end of July, Ewing had decided that more drastic action was required. On August 3, he wrote Schofield that since two-thirds of the families in western Missouri were kin to bushwhackers and were "actively and heartily engaged in feeding, clothing, and sustaining them," several hundred families of the "worst guerrillas" should be transported to Arkansas. Thus the guerrillas would be deprived of their aid, and, just as important, the guerrillas whose families had been removed would probably follow them out of the state.[5] On August 14, Schofield agreed to Ewing's plans, but cautioned him that because of the "expense and trouble" which the banishment of the guerrilla families would entail, as well as "the suffering it may cause the children and other comparatively innocent persons," the number removed should be "as small as possible" and confined to those of "the worst character."[6]

3. *Ibid.*, part 2, 315.
4. Albert Castel, "Order No. 11 and the Civil War on the Border," *Missouri Historical Review* (October, 1959), p. 359. Richard S. Brownlee, *Gray Ghosts of the Confederacy: Guerrilla Warfare in the West, 1861–1865* (Baton Rouge, 1958), pp. 115-16.
5. *O.R.*, Ser. 1, XXII, part 2, 428, 429.
6. *Ibid.*, pp. 450, 451.

On the same day that Schofield approved Ewing's plans, a large three-storied brick building in Kansas City, which was being used as a prison for the guerrilla's women, collapsed during a wind storm. Among the women in the building were three sisters of "Bloody Bill" Anderson and a young cousin of Coleman Younger, both men being members of Quantrill's band. One of the Anderson girls, Younger's cousin, and several others were killed in the tragedy. A rumor circulated that Ewing had directed his soldiers to remove the girders under the structure. The guerrillas swore revenge.[7] Then, only four days later, General Order Number Ten, authorizing the removal of guerrilla families, was sent out from Ewing's headquarters. One writer has remarked, "Coupled with the death of their women in Kansas City, Order Number Ten seemed to scream for retaliatory measures."[8] Possible excuses can be found, but the fact remains that Quantrill and his blood-thirsty lieutenants had for some time planned a raid on Lawrence, Kansas.[9]

On the morning of August 19, Quantrill, with three hundred followers, rode west from his hideout in Jackson County, toward the Kansas border and Lawrence. At sunrise on August 21, the guerrilla chief, wearing a black slouch hat with a gold cord, and four revolvers in his belt, halted his men and rode along the column. "Kill every man big enough to carry a gun," he said. "Burn every house." Listening were such well-known killers as Frank James, the Youngers, George Todd, and, of course, "Bloody Bill" Anderson.[10] The sleeping town of almost two thousand inhabitants had no warning of the impending doom. By the time that the guerrillas departed about 9 A.M., approximately 180 men and boys had been killed, and the town was a smoking shambles. Various small Union forces were soon in pursuit of the raiders. Among these was one from Leavenworth headed by Ewing. Another was headed by Senator James H. Lane of Kansas who was meant to be a prime target for Quantrill's band but had escaped from his home, clad only in his nightshirt, by fleeing across a field

7. Brownlee, *Gray Ghosts*, p. 119.
8. *Ibid.*, p. 121.
9. William E. Connelley, *Quantrill and the Border Wars* (New York, 1956), pp. 297, 308 ff. Brownlee, *Gray Ghosts*, p. 121.
10. Monaghan, *Civil War*, p. 281. Brownlee, *Gray Ghosts*, p. 123. Connelley, *Quantrill*, p. 335, gives a different account, saying that many of the guerrillas hesitated, and Quantrill rode along the ranks saying: "You can do as you please. I am going into Lawrence." He spurred forward and the guerrillas followed, to a man.

behind his house to the cover of a ravine. Some of the guerrillas were overtaken and received no better than they had given. Ewing placed the number killed at not fewer than a hundred, and he telegraphed Schofield, "No prisoners have been taken, and none will be."[11]

As word of the Lawrence massacre spread, a wave of revulsion swept rapidly over the North, and the people of Kansas clamored for vengeance. Governor Thomas Carney of Kansas wrote to Schofield: "Lawrence is in ashes. Millions of property have been destroyed, and, worse yet, nearly 200 lives of our best citizens have been sacrificed. No fiends in human shape could have acted with more savage barbarity than did Quantrill and his band. . . . I must hold Missouri responsible for this fearful, fiendish raid. . . . There can be no peace in Missouri, there will be utter desolation in Kansas unless both [guerrillas and southern sympathizers], are made to feel promptly the vigor of military law."[12] Senator Lane was almost as vigorous in his pursuit of Schofield as he had been of Quantrill. Schofield had always been too moderate to suit Lane, and his relationship with Governor Gamble was still more reason why Lane opposed him, since he and the governor were political enemies. Now, he thought, was his opportunity to have Schofield removed. On August 25, he joined Congressman A. C. Wilder in telegraphing Lincoln, "The imbecility and incapacity of Schofield is [sic] most deplorable. Our people unanimously demand the removal of Schofield, whose policy has opened Kansas to invasion and butchery." Probably, he continued, there would be a collision between outraged Kansans and the military.[13] Not surprisingly, the St. Louis *Daily Missouri Democrat* jumped on the anti-Schofield band wagon with an "I told you so" article on August 24. "Who Is Responsible?" the *Democrat* cried. "Who caused the removal of the former Department Commander, whose administration had been a marked success. . . . Who imposed upon the Department an officer whose first administration . . . was a failure . . .?"

On the same day that Wilder and Lane sent their telegram to Lincoln, General Ewing issued an order which to some extent moderated the passions of Kansas but caused much hardship and suffering in Missouri. This was his famous General Order Number

11. Connelley, *Quantrill*, p. 353. *O.R.*, Ser. 1, XXII, part 2, 479–80.
12. *O.R.*, Ser. 1, XXII, part 1, 576.
13. *Ibid.*, part 2, 475.

Eleven. It required all the inhabitants of the western Missouri counties of Jackson, Cass, and Bates not living within one mile of specified military posts to vacate their homes by September 9. Those who by that date established their loyalty to the United States government with the commanding officer of the military station nearest their place of residence would be permitted to remove to any military station in the District of the Border or to any part of Kansas except the counties on the eastern border of that state. Persons failing to establish their loyalty were to move out of the district completely or be subject to military punishment.[14] The order was generally regarded as an act of retaliation for the destruction of Lawrence. Actually such a measure had previously been considered by both Ewing and Schofield. In fact, Schofield, on the very same day that Ewing published the order, sent him the draft of an almost identical order. "I am pretty much convinced," Schofield wrote Ewing in the letter accompanying the draft, "that the mode of carrying on the war on the border during the past two years has produced such a state of feeling that nothing short of total devastation of the districts which are made the haunts of guerrillas will be sufficient to put a stop to the evil."[15] The major difference between Schofield's draft and Ewing's order was that Schofield's was more harsh.

In spite of Order Number Eleven, many persons in Kansas were determined to personally see that the western Missouri counties "paid" for the outrage on Lawrence. On August 26 a mass meeting was held in Leavenworth at which it was resolved that all interested parties should meet at Paola on September 8 for the purpose of "recovering stolen property," that is, invading Missouri to wreak devastation there. General Lane stormed about the state, damning Schofield, whom he sneeringly referred to as "Skowfield"[16] and whose moderate policy he blamed for all the misery of Kansas. And on August 27, a short telegram arrived from the President. Lincoln enclosed a copy of the dispatch he had received from Wilder and Lane, but omitted their names. "The severe blow they have received," the President said, "naturally enough makes them intemperate even without there being any just cause for blame. Please do your utmost to give them future security and to punish

14. *Ibid.*, p. 473.
15. *Ibid.*, p. 471.
16. Monaghan, *Civil War*, p. 289.

their invaders."[17] The next day Schofield wrote a long letter to Lincoln in which he said that he had "strong reasons" for believing that the authors of the telegram to the President were among those who were endeavoring to organize a force for the purpose of general retaliation upon Missouri. "Those who so deplore my 'imbecility and incapacity,'" he continued, "are the very men who are endeavoring to bring about a collision between the people of Kansas and the troops under General Ewing's command." Schofield had "not the 'capacity' to see the wisdom or justice of permitting an irresponsible mob to enter Missouri for the purpose of retaliation, even for so grievous a wrong as that which Lawrence suffered." He closed with an apology for the length of the letter which in justice to himself or to truth, he said, could hardly be made shorter.[18]

During the first week of September, Schofield visited Kansas in an attempt to restore order. While in Leavenworth he had an interview with Lane, who explained "his view of the necessity, as he believed, of making a huge portion of western Missouri a desert waste." He urged that he be allowed to lead all the "citizens" who might volunteer for such an enterprise, the whole to be under the direction of the district commander. When Schofield refused, Lane suggested that Schofield himself should lead them and gave his personal pledge that they would "abstain entirely from all unlawful acts."[19] If Schofield did not agree, the senator said he would appeal to the President. Schofield was convinced that Lane's main object in proposing that he should lead the band into Missouri was to have him held responsible for the murder and robbery which in all likelihood would result. Schofield flatly refused, publishing General Order Number Ninety-two on September 4, prohibiting armed men not in the military service from passing from one state to the other.[20] If Lane intended to enter Missouri, the senator would have to cross swords with Schofield. Radicals in both Missouri and Kansas clamored all the more for Schofield's removal. At Paola on September 8 Lane blasted Schofield in another crude and intemperate attack. "We've got the brains on Schofield, big!" he told a loudly applauding audience. "I don't

17. *O.R.*, Ser. 1, XXII, part 2, 479.
18. *Ibid.*, pp. 483, 484.
19. *Ibid.*, part 1, 573.
20. *Ibid.*, p. 575.

pretend to hold Old Abe responsible for the acts of Schofield; I hold that officer himself responsible, and I don't think another man so inefficient and wanting in brains as Schofield could be found to issue such an order as his celebrated No. 92 document. When he was appointed I went to Washington to have him removed. Gamble kept him in." The crowd responded with shouts of "Let's go to Missouri. Down with Schofield and Ewing. "We'll hang Gamble."[21] But the Paola meeting, where a great throng was supposed to organize the "invasion" of Missouri, was taking place in the rain, with only a few hundred present. All they did was listen to Lane and pass resolutions.[22]

Not the least of Schofield's objects in visiting Kansas was "to see for myself," he said, the condition of the border counties in both Kansas and Missouri and determine what modification, if any, ought to be made in the policy which Ewing had adopted with General Order Number Eleven. After spending several days in the area, talking with people "of all shades of politics" who were affected by it, Schofield was "fully satisfied" that the measure was "wise and necessary." It was "harsh," but he added, it was also "humane."[23] Having returned to St. Louis, he telegraphed Halleck on September 11 that he had approved Ewing's order after two modifications. Destruction of crops would not be carried out, and loyal people would be allowed to return as soon as they could do so safely.[24] First-hand knowledge had caused him to be more lenient than his proposal of August 24 had indicated.

Although Schofield undoubtedly believed that the order was necessary, the banishment of old men, women, and children probably occasioned more suffering than he had envisioned. Nor did it have the desired effect, for guerrillas continued to roam the area, looting the deserted homes and smokehouses, and rounding up the stray hogs, cattle, and chickens which owners had been forced to leave behind. Its long-range effectiveness was never thoroughly tested, since it was modified in late November and disapproved in January, 1864, when Schofield was no longer in command.[25] On the other hand, it is not difficult to understand why Schofield resorted to such a measure in a situation which had be-

21. *Daily Missouri Democrat* (St. Louis), September 14, 1863.
22. Williams, *Lincoln*, V, 127.
23. *O.R.*, Ser. 1, XXII, part 1, 574, 575.
24. *Ibid.*, part 2, 523.
25. Castel, "Order No. 11," pp. 366, 367.

come intolerable. And, if the policy had been continued without modification, perhaps it would have ultimately been effective.

The proposed invasion of Missouri had come to naught, but Schofield's tribulations were far from over. On September 15 the general-in-chief telegraphed, requesting that "all troops that can possibly be spared" be sent to the Tennessee River "to assist General Rosecrans."[26] It would "hardly be possible," Schofield replied, for him to send any troops. He was being compelled to call out Missouri militia to relieve troops he had sent to Steele in Arkansas, and "the radical papers" were opposing it, doing "all in their power to create dissatisfaction in the militia."[27]

On this same day, Lincoln issued a proclamation which Schofield must have welcomed. He suspended the writ of *habeas corpus*. His proclamation was largely aimed at those who resisted the draft and made it impossible for anyone in the military or the naval service to obtain a writ that would free him from custody. Nor could a person secure a writ if he had been arrested for resisting the draft, "or for any offense against the military or naval service."[28] On September 17 Schofield issued an order in which he held that the President's suspension of the writ of *habeas corpus* applied to all militia units that he had called or would call into service.[29]

Schofield had good reason for this order. A few days before when he had called out two St. Louis regiments of the Provisional Enrolled Militia to send to New Madrid to replace the 25th Missouri, which was under orders to reinforce Steele, radical politicians and papers had suggested resistance. Some of the men had mutinied, taken over the boat on which they were being transported, run it ashore, and gone home. Schofield had them rounded up, held the leaders in the military prison to await a court-martial, and put the others "at hard labor" on some blockhouses being built at Rolla.[30] The President's proclamation proved a timely aid, and requests by the militia for writs on the ground that they had been illegally "restrained of liberty" were denied.

In his order of September 17, Schofield, in addition to stating that Lincoln's proclamation would apply to the militia, also said that martial law would be enforced against all persons who should

26. *O. R.*, Ser. 1, XXII, part 2, 533.
27. *Ibid.*
28. Williams, *Lincoln*, V, 128.
29. *O.R.*, Ser. 1, XXII, part 2, 546.
30. *Ibid.*, pp. 542, 543. Schofield, *Forty-Six Years*, pp. 84, 86.

in any matter encourage mutiny, insubordination, or disorderly conduct, or try to create disaffection among troops. He concluded with a statement about a very touchy subject: "any newspaper which shall contain publications in violation of this order will be suppressed."[31] If this was disturbing, shortly after it Schofield issued an order which should have been reassuring to reasonable men. An election was soon to be held in Missouri, and Schofield sought to protect the polls and all lawful assemblages of persons seeking to vote. Any officer, soldier, or civilian, he said, who sought to intimidate a qualified voter from the exercise of his right was to be punished by a court-martial or by a military commission.[32] On September 26 Halleck wrote Schofield sending the President's written approval of his order of September 17, but advising "the exercise of great caution and discretion in the execution of this order, especially toward the newspaper press."[33]

As September was drawing to a close, Schofield was continuing to experience trouble, not only from guerrillas, but from the outrages perpetrated by certain of his own troops. A party of the Sixth Missouri Cavalry murdered a Union man in his own house near Sikeston, twenty miles east of Bloomfield, robbed another's store, and otherwise terrorized the country. General Clinton B. Fisk, who reported the outrages, said no officer was with them and concluded that "many citizens are killed and robbed by them."[34] Fisk had more pleasing news to report a few days later. Troops under his command had killed more than one hundred guerrillas and captured more than fifty, among them "some of the most desperate characters in the state," along with "the notorious Jeff Thompson and his staff."[35]

But more trouble was on the way. On September 22, Jo Shelby, with 600 troopers, started on a 1,500-mile raid into Missouri—the longest cavalry raid of the war. However, Schofield was not notified that Shelby was north of the Arkansas River until October 1. By then he was probably more concerned with the delegation of radicals from Kansas and Missouri who had gone to see the President to try and have him removed from command of the Department of the Missouri. Headed by Jim Lane, a 70-man

31. *O.R.*, Ser. 1, XXII, part 2, 547.
32. Williams, *Lincoln*, V, 131, 132.
33. *O.R.*, Ser. 1, XXII, part 2, 574.
34. *Ibid.*, p. 542.
35. *Ibid.*, p. 566.

delegation had arrived in Washington on September 27 and spent two days in preparing an address to present to Lincoln. On September 30, they stated their case at the White House. Claiming to represent the will of the Republican party in Kansas and Missouri, the group maintained that peace between the states could be restored by the removal of Schofield. In addition to demanding that he be replaced, the delegation wanted the system of enrolled militia broken up and persons restrained from voting who were not legally entitled to do so.[36] Lincoln then asked for specific errors committed by Schofield. The answers given, according to John Hay, Lincoln's personal secretary, were trivial.[37] Yet the delegates were united in wanting Schofield dismissed. Lincoln was not ready to have his department commander "railroaded" for no good reason and suggested that the committee give him time to consider their complaints. Lane and his delegates *demanded* an answer *at once*. Lincoln said he would answer them *at once*, not orally, but in writing![38]

On the same day Schofield received a dispatch from the President, transmitting a report (which proved false) from Leavenworth, that Colonel James H. Moss was driving Union families out of Platte and Clay counties.[39] Schofield ordered Ewing and Oden Guitar to investigate. Guitar reported that "the whole thing" was "an infamous falsehood, gotten up to aid the radical delegation in Washington in their revolutionary scheme."[40] In passing the result of his investigation to Lincoln, Schofield wrote on October 2, "A few men who claim to be loyal, but who have been engaged in murder, robbery, and arson, have been driven out." The leader of the group, a man Lincoln once pardoned at Gamble's request, but who was then engaged in an effort to overthrow the state government, had manufactured the report, which was, Schofield concluded, "a base attempt of my enemies to influence your action."[41]

On October 3, the St. Louis *Daily Missouri Democrat* carried an account of the address presented to the President by the radical delegation. Having read it, Schofield immediately telegraphed

36. *Ibid.*, p. 604.
37. Nicolay and Hay, *Lincoln*, VIII, 216–19.
38. Monaghan, *Civil War*, p. 292.
39. Schofield, *Forty-Six Years*, p. 93.
40. *O.R.*, Ser. 1, XXII, part 2, 587.
41. *Ibid.*, p. 591.

Lincoln, branding "so much of it as relates to me" as "not only untrue in spirit, but most of it is literally false. If an answer or explanation is on my account desirable, I shall be glad to make it."[42] The next day Schofield received a one-sentence telegram from the President which must have relieved much of his apprehension: "I think you will not have just cause to complain of my action."[43]

On October 5 Lincoln gave his reply to the delegation. Reminding them that "we are in Civil War," he described the various shades of opinion which had developed around the main question of slavery and its relation to the Union, how actual war had impassioned people in the views they held, and finally, how old grudges and the opportunity for plunder had led to murders and atrocities under whatever cloak best covered the occasion. "These causes," Lincoln observed, "amply account for what has occurred in Missouri, without ascribing it to the weakness or wickedness of any general. . . . Without disparaging any," the President affirmed, "with confidence that no commander of that department has, in proportion to his means, done better than General Schofield." Lincoln had directed him to act "solely for the public good" and neither anything the delegation had presented nor anything the President had otherwise learned had convinced him Schofield had been unfaithful to the charge. He was well satisfied that "the preventing of the threatened . . . raid into Missouri was the only safe way to avoid an indiscriminate massacre. . . . Instead of condemning," Lincoln said, he "therefore approved" what he understood Schofield did in that respect.

The charges that Schofield had purposely withheld protection from loyal people, and facilitated the objects of the disloyal, were "altogether beyond" his "power of belief." In regard to disbanding the militia, the President declared that "few things" had been "so grateful to my anxious feelings as when . . . the local force in Missouri aided General Schofield to so promptly send so large a general force to the relief of General Grant. . . ." Lincoln also stood behind Schofield in regard to the *habeas corpus* proclamation. "With my present views," the President informed the delegation, "I must decline to remove General Schofield."[44]

Lincoln's long document, covering three full pages in the *Official*

42. *Ibid.*, p. 595.
43. *Ibid.*, p. 601.
44. *Ibid.*, pp. 604–7.

*Records,* must have been a satisfying one for Schofield to read. He
had taken a big risk in defying Lane, but the senator and his delegation went home defeated. As usual, however, there was little
time for rejoicing. Shelby and his raiders were still in Missouri.
Schofield attempted to determine from the confused and con-
flicting reports of his garrison commanders and sources all over
western Missouri just where Shelby was and what he was doing.
First he decided that the Confederates would strike for Shelby's
hometown of Waverly; then he assumed it was merely a border
raid and that Shelby would soon return to Arkansas. After Shelby
captured Warsaw, Schofield realized that he was making a serious
movement toward the Missouri River. Even then Schofield was
misled by the garrison commander at Springfield, who reported
that the Rebels were making for Jackson County. Union troops
from southern, western, and northern Missouri were directed to
concentrate in that area. As they moved to block the west, Shelby
was moving east toward Tipton, Boonville, and Jefferson City.[45]

The capture of Tipton revealed his location and direction of
march. General Egbert B. Brown with 2,000 men moved quickly
from Sedalia to Boonville to cut him off. Brown attacked on the
evening of October 11 and again at dawn the next day. Shelby
broke north toward Marshall where he made a stand on the morning
of October 13. When he was almost surrounded, Shelby formed his
command and charged at what he considered to be the weakest
point of the Union line. Breaking through the gap torn in the
Federal ranks he headed westward as far as Waverly and then
veered south toward the Confederate lines in Arkansas. He was
pursued by Union forces under Brown, Ewing, and John McNeil.[46]

By November he was back within the Rebel lines, claiming to
have killed or wounded about six hundred Union soldiers, burned
two forts, destroyed miles of rails and telegraph line, destroyed
ordnance and supplies estimated to the value of $1,050,000, gained
eight hundred recruits while losing less than two hundred men,
and prevented Schofield from sending reinforcements to Rosecrans
after his defeat at Chickamauga.[47] Schofield reported to Lincoln
that the raider had been expelled after losing half his men and

45. *Ibid.,* pp. 588–631.
46. Daniel O'Flaherty, *General Jo Shelby, Undefeated Rebel* (Chapel Hill,
1954), pp. 200–204. *O.R.,* Ser. 1, XXII, part 1, 626–28, 639–41, 674–76.
47. *O.R.,* Ser. 1, XXII, part 1, 678.

gaining no recruits except the robbers under Quantrill. "This is gratifying," he said as he ended his dispatch, "as showing that the rebel power in Missouri is completely broken."[48] Shelby's report, while somewhat exaggerated, was more nearly accurate; but at least the Rebel raider was no longer plaguing Schofield's department.[49]

In fact, the department was more peaceful than it had been in several months. The radical delegation had been rebuffed by Lincoln. Quantrill presented no immediate problem. Guerrilla war had comparatively subsided. James G. Blunt, however, continued to be a thorn in Schofield's side. It is difficult to know whether Schofield held any personal feeling against Blunt or not. There is no doubt that Schofield's first impression of Blunt was a favorable one.[50] Possibly as his opinion of Blunt as a military commander changed and Blunt evidenced extreme bitterness toward Schofield, he may have developed a personal dislike for a man who would speak officially of him as an "incompetent" and a "coward."[51] But there is nothing in the tone of his official correspondence (or any other source the writer examined) which would indicate this.

It was not long after Schofield appointed Blunt to command the District of the Frontier that he began to receive reports of various irregularities in Blunt's recent administration of the Department of Kansas, then reduced to a district under Schofield's Department of the Missouri.[52] On July 15 Schofield telegraphed the War Department, stating: "I have received, from . . . sources, official and unofficial, reports of fraud, corruption, and maladministration in the Department and District of Kansas, while under the command of Major General Blunt, which seem to demand official investigation."[53] Schofield recommended that a court of inquiry be appointed by the President, with full power to inquire into the whole matter. Shortly after this Blunt wrote an intemperate and resentful "private" letter to Secretary Stanton. He com-

48. *Ibid.*, part 2, 677.
49. Monaghan, *Civil War*, p. 296.
50. JMS to Henry W. Halleck, November 18, 1862, Schofield MSS. *O.R.*, Ser. 1, XIII, 21.
51. *O.R.*, Ser. 1, XXII, part 2, 736.
52. Thomas Ewing to JMS, July 9, 1863, Schofield MSS. *O.R.*, Ser. 1, XXII, part 2, 326, 327, 393.
53. *O.R.*, Ser. 1, XX, part 2, 319.

plained that Schofield did not point out the "irregularities" of which he was guilty. Reviewing his own exploits for the benefit of the secretary—he had advanced against an enemy "greatly superior" in numbers, fought four successful battles in sixty days, "destroying" a "formidable" Rebel army—he said he supposed these were the "irregularities" of which he was guilty. Schofield was not the only object of Blunt's ire. "Baser traitors" did "not exist in Jeff Davis' dominion" than the Fort Leavenworth quartermaster and commissary; "two greater thieves" did not live than the governor of Kansas and the superintendent of Indian affairs.[54] A few days later he sent a similar letter to Lincoln. The President replied: "I regret to find you denouncing so many persons as liars, scoundrels, fools, thieves, and persecutors of yourself."[55]

An investigation was conducted, and with its results in hand, Schofield wrote Halleck on October 1: "I am compelled to relieve Major General Blunt from his command." When Lincoln was informed, since the radical delegation was then in Washington demanding Schofield's removal and Blunt was a friend of Lane, the President wired back: "If possible you better allow me to get through with a certain matter here before adding to the difficulties of it. Meantime," the President added, "supply me the particulars of Major General Blunt's case."[56] Schofield responded that he would send the papers in Blunt's case and defer action until he knew the President's "pleasure regarding it." He desired, Schofield continued, "if possible, to diminish and not to increase your difficulty."[57] Two weeks later Schofield reminded the President: "The papers in General Blunt's case were forwarded to the adjutant-general on the third instant. May I ask to know your pleasure concerning the proposed change?"[58] Apparently Schofield received no specific answer to this query, but on October 19, he received a letter of instruction from the President, dated October 1, in which Lincoln left Schofield with broad discretionary powers, concluding, "In giving the above directions, it is not intended to restrain you in other expedient and necessary matters not falling within this range."[59] In his October 1 dispatch to Halleck concerning the removal of Blunt, Schofield had requested a competent officer to be sent to take his place. When Halleck sent Brigadier General

54. *Ibid.*, 735–37.        55. Williams, *Lincoln*, V, 106.
56. *O.R.*, Ser. 1, XXII, part 2, 588.        57. *Ibid.*, p. 589.
58. *Ibid.*, p. 663.        59. *Ibid.*, p. 586.

John B. Sanborn, Schofield on October 19 issued an order directing Sanborn to relieve John McNeil from the command of the District of Southwestern Missouri, and McNeil to relieve Blunt as commander of the District of the Frontier.[60]

Blunt was not ready to be relieved of his command. In spite of the order, he went ahead with his immediate plans. Reports involving him with illegal activities continued to come in, but it was difficult to find enough evidence to warrant action on these charges. Finally, on December 9, Blunt wrote Secretary Stanton from Fort Smith explaining his "present position." Since General Order Number 118 had directed that he be relieved of command at Fort Smith, he had moved to that place to find that General McNeil had already assumed command seven days previous. Blunt admitted that while he had "acquiesced in this action," he had "never formally relinquished the command." I deem it my duty," he continued "to say that I shall not report to General Schofield by letter from Leavenworth City as directed in his order." In fact, he would not "hold any further intercourse or communication with him, except to prefer charges against him for incompetency and cowardice. . . ." Blunt could not "acknowledge General Schofield as my superior officer until he is a major general." If, however, the President had assigned a colonel to command the department who was "a true soldier and a gentleman," he "should not have demurred. . . ."[61]

Two days later Blunt walked into McNeil's headquarters and in the presence of several officers and men bragged of his letter to Stanton and read a copy of it, especially for the benefit of Champion Vaughan who was investigating the situation for Schofield. Vaughan was outraged, writing Schofield that the time for "temporizing with the defiers of regulations, law, and common decency" had passed.[62] Schofield did not seem too disturbed. In spite of all Blunt's intemperate protests, there was really nothing which he could do. Blunt eventually took up his new assignment of recruiting Negro regiments on the border.[63]

No doubt Schofield was weary of the continual abuse which had been heaped upon his head by the radicals in both Missouri

60. *Ibid.*, p. 666.
61. *Ibid.*, pp. 735–37. Blunt, "Civil War Experiences," pp. 246–47.
62. *O.R.*, Ser. 1, XXII, part 2, 742, 743.
63. Monaghan, *Civil War.*, p. 295.

and Kansas. He later wrote that it was "with sincere pleasure" that he received a summons in December from the President to come to Washington.[64] He talked with Lincoln several times during the visit. Knowing a presidential nomination was drawing nigh, Lincoln was especially anxious to unravel the political situation in the West. In Kansas, Senator Lane, while friendly to the President, was still bitterly opposed to Schofield. On the other hand, Governor Carney opposed Lincoln but was friendly to Schofield. There seemed to be no way to resolve the difficulty while Schofield remained in command of the department. Schofield told Lincoln frankly that he did not believe that he could ever reconcile the differences. In fact, he did not think any general, as department commander, could satisfy the Union people of both Missouri and Kansas. Schofield was ready to leave and Lincoln wanted to divide the old Department of the Missouri into three parts and try to assign to each a commander suited to its peculiarities. The President hoped to influence the Senate to confirm Schofield's long-sought nomination as a major-general, after which he promised to appoint him to a more important command. Thus matters stood in January, 1864, when Grant, then commanding the military division of the Mississippi and soon to be elevated to the command of "all the armies," telegraphed that it was necessary to relieve General John G. Foster from the command of the Department and Army of the Ohio because of ill health. When asked whom he wanted for the command, Grant replied, "Either [General James B.] McPherson or Schofield." Halleck showed the dispatch to Schofield, to whom "nothing in the world," he said, "could be better." When the proposition was presented to Lincoln, the President replied, "Why Schofield, that cuts the knot, don't it?"[65]

On January 22, 1864, Schofield turned over his department duties in Missouri to General Rosecrans and started for Knoxville, Tennessee, "without regret and with bouyant hopes of more satisfactory service in a purely military field."[66] On February 9 he relieved General Foster as commander of the Department of the Ohio. At that time Confederate General James Longstreet was still in East Tennessee apparently threatening Knoxville. Schofield prepared his force to assume the offensive against the Rebels. But on March 15 Grant ordered him to send the entire Ninth Corps

64. Schofield, *Forty-Six Years*, p. 106.        65. *Ibid.*, p. 110.
66. *Ibid.*, p. 112.

to the Army of the Potomac. With such a reduction in his command Schofield had to be content to observe Longstreet leisurely withdraw from Tennessee to join Lee in Virginia. Nevertheless the long-sought military opportunity was at hand.

In late March, Sherman, then commanding all the armies between the Alleghenies and the Mississippi, came to Knoxville and disclosed the general plans for his coming summer campaign.[67] While Grant went for Lee, Sherman would go for Joseph E. Johnston, commanding the Confederate Army at Dalton, thirty miles south of Chattanooga. Sherman's force would consist of approximately 100,000 men, made up of three armies, and Schofield was to command one of the three. This was the chance he had wanted— to hold a responsible command in a major military campaign directed by a general of established ability.

A few days after conversing with Sherman, Schofield received a letter dated April 7 from Senator John B. Henderson of Missouri, a friend who had worked for his appointment as a major general. The letter informed him that the Senate had failed to confirm his nomination and urged him to "whip somebody anyhow" in order to compel the Senate to confirm him. On April 15 Schofield replied: "No doubt" he might "easily get up a little 'claptrap' on which to manufacture newspaper notoriety." But he had "the approval and support of the President, and the secretary of war, General Halleck, General Grant and General Sherman." He would "not give a copper for the weight of anybody's or everybody's opinion in addition to, or in opposition to theirs," and would never "resort to 'humbug'" for the purpose of securing his own advancement. If he could not gain promotion by legitimate means, he did not want it at all. Finally, he concluded, he found "this letter is both too long and too ill-natured," as he felt too much as if he "would like to 'whip somebody anyhow,'" so he would stop where he was.[68]

Schofield had done, under difficult circumstances, a reasonably good job as commander of the Department of the Missouri—especially in view of the complexities of the situation. Now, directing the Army of the Ohio in Sherman's campaign to end the war in the West, his military abilities as a field commander in heavy battle promised to be well tested in the months ahead.

67. Sherman, *Memoirs*, II, 7, 8.
68. Schofield, *Forty-Six Years*, p. 119.

# VI. Marching with Sherman

MAY FLOWERS were blooming and the warm sun bathed the north Georgia landscape as Sherman's 100,000 pushed South in 1864. George H. Thomas' Army of the Cumberland, 60,000 strong, was the center of Sherman's line, pushing the enemy straight on. James B. McPherson's Army of the Tennessee, with about 25,000, and Schofield's Army of the Ohio, about 14,000, were on either side of Thomas, driving for the Confederate flanks and forcing the enemy to fall back. To hold the line against this Federal onslaught, Confederate General Joseph E. Johnston could muster no more than 60,000—or approximately the same as Sherman's center under Thomas.

The Confederates initially held a very strong position northwest of Dalton. At the deep and narrow "Buzzard Roost" gorge which ran through a mountain range known as "Rocky Face," they had prepared extensive fortifications. The place was originally selected by General Braxton Bragg after he was driven from Chattanooga. Johnston had since been strengthening the position for nearly six months. Sherman climbed to a summit, looked down into the gorge, and saw it was practically unassailable from the front. He decided to "turn the end."[1]

The Army of the Tennessee, on the Union right, drew the first flanking assignment: to strike through Snake Creek Gap for Johnston's railroad, about twenty miles in his rear at Resaca.

1. Jacob D. Cox, *Atlanta* (New York, 1882), p. 29. Sherman, *Memoirs*, II, 32.

Sherman ordered Schofield to push his force forward on the left and join with Thomas in pressing the enemy strongly all along the line, thus holding him in position. He hoped that when Mc-Pherson fell upon the railroad, Schofield and Thomas could rush in at any sign of retreat and catch the Confederates in confusion.[2]

Schofield's Army of the Ohio, the same which Ambrose E. Burnside commanded in the defense of Knoxville in November, 1863, was little more than an army corps in actual size. It was composed of three divisions, the first commanded by Brigadier General Alvin P. Hovey, the second by Brigadier General Henry M. Judah, and the third by Brigadier General Jacob D. Cox. On Sunday, May 8, Schofield moved his right, Judah's division, to the northern point of Rocky Face Ridge. There they connected with Thomas' left. On his own left Schofield swung Cox's division about a mile eastward toward Varnell's Station to better protect his flank. Hovey's division in the center remained in reserve.[3]

The next day Schofield and Thomas pressed steadily forward, skirmishing briskly with the enemy and driving him back. As he passed close to one of his regiments, Schofield overheard the words of a veteran who remarked, "I like the way the old man chaws his tobacco."[4] Schofield's army was advancing across a valley east of "Rocky Face," and directly toward the main Confederate works. It was late afternoon when the Rebels were finally driven inside their main fortifications. The Confederates then opened up a heavy rattle of musketry, supported by artillery, which did not cease until after dark.[5]

Just about that time Sherman received word from McPherson. He was within five miles of Resaca! Sherman burst out exuberantly that he "had Joe Johnston dead!" and renewed his orders to Schofield and Thomas to be poised for immediate pursuit.[6] But McPherson, upon drawing closer to the enemy, decided Resaca was too strongly fortified. He fell back to the mouth of Snake Creek Gap and dug in. Sherman received the disappointing news later in the night and realized his hope to crush Johnston at the beginning had failed. The weather must have seemed appropriate to the

2. Sherman, *Memoirs*, II, 32.    3. *O.R.*, Ser. 1, XXXVIII, part 2, 510.
4. Schofield, *Forty-Six Years*, p. 120.
5. *O.R.*, Ser. 1, XXXVIII, part 2, 510, 675.
6. Lloyd Lewis, *Sherman, Fighting Prophet* (New York, 1932), p. 357. Sherman, *Memoirs*, II, 33.

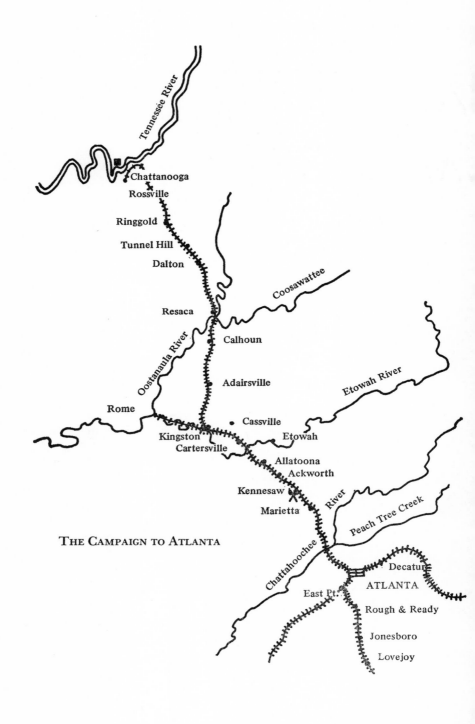

Tennessee River

Chattanooga
Rossville
Ringgold
Tunnel Hill
Dalton

Coosawattee

Resaca
Calhoun

Oostanaula River

Adairsville

Etowah River

Rome
Cassville
Kingston
Cartersville
Etowah
Allatoona
Ackworth
Kennesaw
Marietta

Chattahoochee River

Peach Tree Creek

THE CAMPAIGN TO ATLANTA

Decatur
ATLANTA
East Pt.
Rough & Ready
Jonesboro
Lovejoy

occasion: a storm blew in at night and continued the next day.[7]

His chance for a surprise gone, Sherman decided to send the whole army through the gap which McPherson held and move on Resaca.[8] About eight o'clock on the morning of May 10, Schofield began withdrawing his troops from their position in the line of battle. The enemy's infantry made no serious attempt to pursue, but his cavalry kept up a running fight, continually annoying the rear skirmish line. In spite of the harrassment, the army was withdrawn smoothly and swung around to the right where it took a position commanding the gap north of Rocky Face.[9] On May 12, Schofield marched south following the Army of the Cumberland to Villanow. The next morning he continued through Snake Creek Gap and went into position on the Union left in front of Resaca. Once more, Thomas was in the center and McPherson on the right. But, having realized what Sherman was doing, Johnston's Rebels were already at hand with a line of entrenchments covering the town and protecting their railroad.

On May 14, Sherman closed in. Schofield advanced toward the enemy's position at the head of Camp Creek—Cox's division on the left and Judah's on the right. Progress was slow. The ground was rough and broken, covered with dense woods and thick underbrush.[10] Near noon the Confederate skirmish line was contacted. Schofield ordered his men to attack. Cox's division scrambled forward at a double-quick, driving the enemy's skirmishers back before them. Artillery fire roared from the Rebel's works on the margin of a wood in front. The musketry lent its voice to the din of battle. The troops, charging with bayonets fixed, finally engaged in a fierce struggle for possession of the first Confederate line of entrenchments. The enemy gave way and fell back upon stronger fortifications. Again the division pushed forward to within about two hundred yards of the second line, and one regiment closed the gap to only fifty yards. But the Confederates were raking them with grape and canister as well as musketry, and this line could not be carried.[11]

7. L. G. Bennett and W. M. Haigh, *History of the 36th Regiment of Illinois Volunteers* (Aurora, Illinois, 1876), p. 579.

8. Earl S. Miers, *The General Who Marched to Hell: William Tecumseh Sherman and His March to Fame and Infamy* (New York, 1951), p. 80.

9. *O.R.*, Ser. 1, XXXVIII, part 2, 675.

10. Cox, *Atlanta*, p. 43. B. F. Thompson, *History of the 112th Regiment of Illinois Volunteer Infantry* (Toulon, Illinois, 1885), p. 203.

11. *O.R.*, Ser. 1, XXXVIII, part 2, 511, 676, 677. Thompson, *112th Illinois*, p. 203.

Schofield climbed up on a bald hill just in the rear of Cox's line and discovered that some parts of the enemy's main line of defense could be seen. Thinking Sherman would be interested, he sent a courier dashing to find the general. Soon Sherman appeared, along with Thomas, Joseph Hooker, and several staff officers. The whole party scrambled up the hill to survey the enemy's works. So large a group attracted attention, and a Confederate battery on the next ridge sent a shell crashing through and exploding in the branches of a dead tree close beside the Union officers. All of them scattered looking for cover except two. Schofield watched as Sherman and Hooker drew themselves to full height and with apparent indifference to danger, strode around in complete silence, each waiting for the other to seek cover first. Finally, "as if by some mysterious impulse," they simultaneously marched to the rear. Evidently, Schofield concluded, personal relations between the two were not completely satisfactory.[12]

Farther to the right, Judah's division also became heavily engaged. The division commander ordered a charge across an open field cut by a deep creek which proved to be nearly impassable for infantry. As the men struggled forward, they were subjected to a continuous artillery and musketry fire from an entrenched position covered by woods. The division was driven back with the greatest loss of life of any which engaged in the fighting before Resaca. Rumors were soon circulating that Judah was drunk when he ordered the charge. It did seem that the position had not been properly reconnoitered or such an attack would never have been attempted.

The next morning Lieutenant Colonel Isaac R. Sherwood, commanding the 111th Ohio regiment in Judah's division, went to Schofield's headquarters and complained of the gross negligence of his division commander. The reports Schofield heard must have convinced him that Judah was not qualified for his position. He relieved him from command on May 18 and Brigadier General Milo S. Hascall was assigned in his place.[13]

Sherman's army pressed forward at all points on May 15, but made no attempt to assault the fortified works around Resaca. Schofield swung his army farther to the east until he was on the

12. Schofield, *Forty-Six Years*, pp. 140, 141.
13. Isaac R. Sherwood, *Memories of the War* (Toledo, Ohio, 1933), pp. 105, 106. *O.R.*, Ser. 1, XXXVIII, part 2, 511.

Dalton and Resaca road, holding the extreme left of Sherman's line. The day's greatest success came at the other end of the Union line. There McPherson gained a ridge overlooking the town, from which his artillery could reach the railroad bridge across the Oostenaula River. Night was approaching and the Rebels continued trying to drive him back from the strategic position even after dark, but could not. The next morning Johnston had gone south, destroying the bridges.[14]

Sherman took up the pursuit, with Schofield's force moving east for a short distance and fording the Connasauga River at Fite's Ferry. The march was continued up the north bank of the Coosawattee River to Field's Mill, where Schofield camped for the night. The Coosawattee was too deep to ford, and on May 17, a trestle-foot bridge was constructed for the use of the soldiers. The trains and artillery were again ferried by flat boat, but not until several hours were lost waiting for the ordnance train of Hooker's corps to be floated across. Hooker was supposed to be crossing at Resaca with the rest of the Army of the Cumberland, and Schofield was quick to inform "Fighting Joe" of the trouble he was causing.[15] But Schofield's protest was to no avail. It was nearing 10 P.M. before the last of his command finally got across the river.

Since the Army of the Cumberland had been advancing directly from Resaca once they repaired the burned bridges, Schofield determined to push south anyway. He finally halted the column, sometime between two and three o'clock on the morning of May 18, at Big Spring on the road to Adairsville.[16] There was still little rest to be had. Reveille sounded about 5 A.M. and the march was again taken up, the troops swinging along for about eight miles in a line almost due south. Late in the evening Schofield received a dispatch from Sherman revealing his anxiety to bring on a battle: "If we can bring Johnston to battle this side of Etowah," he said, "we must do it, even at the hazard of beginning battle with but a part of our forces."[17] With every day's advance Sherman's lines of communication were being stretched out a little more.

Johnston had formed his new line between Kingston on the west and Cassville on the east. All appearances indicated that he

14. Sherman, *Memoirs*, II, 35, 36. *O.R.*, Ser. 1, XXXVIII, part 2, 511.
15. JMS to Joseph Hooker, May 17, 1864, Schofield MSS.
16. *O.R.*, Ser. 1, XXXVIII, part 2, 679. Thompson, *112th Illinois*, p. 205.
17. Cox, *Atlanta*, p. 56.

was prepared and willing to fight. Indeed he was. The road south from Resaca forked at Adairsville, and Johnston had hoped Sherman would divide his army, moving part of his force on the fork toward Kingston and part on the fork toward Cassville. Johnston had just added another division to Leonidas Polk's Corps, and his numerical strength was then at its greatest. He planned to fall with full force upon the flank of one of Sherman's advancing columns. Sherman, however, did not approach in massed columns as Johnston expected. Instead he had his ends spread wide, McPherson some six to eight miles west of Thomas' center, and Schofield, moving with Hooker's corps, about four to six miles to the east of Thomas. The spread was so wide that Johnston discovered his own flanks were in danger. About nightfall on May 19, Schofield's cannon suddenly began to enfilade the Confederate right wing. And when his corps commander, Hood, did not attack at the time ordered, Johnston abandoned his general orders for an attack and began retiring once more. Schofield was soon pushing the enemy's rear guard, but Johnston crossed the Etowah River at Cartersville and burned the railroad bridge, retreating without any serious difficulty.[18]

For the next two days Sherman gathered supplies at Kingston while Johnston's Rebels took up another strong position along the railroad at Allatoona Gap and pushed one corps westward toward Dallas. On May 23, Sherman moved again. He had seen Allatoona Pass in 1843 when serving in Georgia as a lieutenant and had no intention of following Johnston into such a trap. Leaving his railroad, he decided to swing the whole army to the west of Johnston, toward Dallas, and send the Army of the Tennessee striking again for Johnston's left flank.

Schofield was to take twenty days' rations, cross the Etowah at the site of burned out Milam's Bridge (Etowah Cliffs), and advance so as to come up once more on the left of the main army. Two pontoon bridges were laid for this purpose, but when Schofield reached the river Hooker had commandeered them and was again crossing first. The afternoon was lost in waiting for the XX Corps to pass.[19] At daybreak on the twenty-fourth, a day which

18. Lewis, *Sherman*, p. 361. Basil Henry Liddell-Hart, *Sherman, Soldier, Realist, American* (New York, 1929), pp. 254, 255. Cox, *Atlanta*, pp. 55–57.

19. Cox, *Atlanta*, p. 66. *O.R.*, Ser. 1, XXXVIII, part 2, 680. JMS to W. T. Sherman, May 22, 1864, Schofield MSS. Although Schofield complained about Hooker pre-empting his roads, he attributed this to Hooker's desire to advance as fast as possible, and to the size of the Army of the Cumberland, which made

proved extremely hot,[20] Schofield pushed across the Etowah, continued across Richland Creek, and proceeded to the forks of the roads leading to Acworth and Burnt Hickory. There he struck camp for the night, having taken position on the left rear of the Army of the Cumberland. This position was maintained until late afternoon of the following day when Schofield received news that Hooker's advance guard had found the enemy.[21] Hooker's leading division had crossed a bridge at Pumpkin Vine Creek and pursued some enemy cavalry down the road heading due east for Marietta. About four miles from the bridge, they struck a heavy infantry force at New Hope Methodist Church, and a sharp battle was raging. Sherman wanted support for Hooker as soon as possible.[22]

Schofield sent Hascall's and Cox's divisions down the road to Burnt Hickory and from there headed directly south on the road to Dallas. He could hear the din of musketry ahead, but, as he was then getting in the rear of Hooker's wagons, progress was slow. A storm came up and it began raining. The men splashed along through the mire, but at midnight they were still west of Pumpkin Vine Creek. Schofield halted the column, ordered bivouack for the night, and then rode forward through the drenching rain to learn the situation and receive further orders from Sherman. The night was pitch dark, and as he tried to pick his way around some wagons his horse fell with him into a gully. He was rather painfully injured and forced to relinquish his command to Cox during the next two days' operations.[23]

When Schofield took over again on May 28, there had been little change in position. The Army of the Ohio had edged up on Hooker's left, and the entire Union line lay confronting the Confederate line along Pumpkin Vine Creek. Fierce skirmishing continued all along the front for several days and nights. A soldier in Schofield's army later said he "could almost swear" that the "roar of artillery and the rattle of musketry never ceased, day or night."[24] Sherman tried to withdraw the Army of the Tennessee from his

it nearly impossible for all the corps to move by the roads assigned and still meet a schedule. Schofield, *Forty-Six Years*, p. 139.

20. Thompson, *112th Illinois*, p. 207.
21. Cox, *Atlanta*, p. 74.
22. Sherman, *Memoirs*, II, 43, 44.
23. *O.R.*, Ser. 1, XXXVIII, part 2, 512. Cox, *Atlanta*, p. 75.
24. John A. Joyce, *A Checkered Life* (Chicago, 1883), p. 111.

right and swing it in to relieve Hooker's right at New Hope, but
the Confederates attacked so fiercely that McPherson was not able
to move. It was not until June 2 that the Army of the Tennessee
finally extricated itself and relieved both Hooker's and Schofield's
troops. Schofield then pivoted around to the extreme left of the
Union line, struggling over rough hill country, densely timbered
with scrubby pines and black jack. Gulches, formerly worked for
gold, added to the dismal scene.[25] He finally went into position
facing east on the road between Dallas and Burnt Hickory near
the head of Allatoona Creek.

Sherman again resumed his flanking movement, this time on
the Confederate right, and Schofield's army was in the key position.
With General Daniel Butterfield's division of the XX Corps supporting his left rear, Schofield advanced Hascall on the left, Cox
in the center, and Hovey on the right. The line plowed through
the dense woods and thickets until it suddenly struck the Rebel
skirmish line, and the bullets began to hum. About this time the
rain started again—another spring thunderstorm. Schofield's men
kept pushing forward. Confederate artillery was trained upon the
blue line, and it became difficult to distinguish the roar of artillery
from the peal of thunder. The enemy was driven back for a mile
or more, across Allatoona Creek and into his entrenched line.
Schofield then deployed his troops as far to the left as possible,
and skirmishers reported they had reached the extremity of the
Confederate line but could not overlap it. Schofield decided he could
turn the flank with Butterfield's division. A staff officer was sent
galloping to inform the division commander of the situation. Then,
on second thought, Schofield decided to go himself. He explained
the enemy's vulnerable position and asked Butterfield to send in
a brigade to outflank the Confederates. But that officer had been
instructed only to "support" Schofield, which he interpreted to
mean staying in supporting distance, and he would do no more.
It was then too late in the day for Schofield to move troops from
his right and the chance was lost.[26]

His men spent a very uncomfortable night. The ground was
too wet and muddy to lie or sit upon and the rain had wet them
to the skin. Many occupied themselves putting up temporary

25. N. A. Pinney, *History of the 104th Ohio Volunteer Infantry from 1862 to
1865* (Akron, Ohio, 1886), p. 41. Joyce, *Checkered Life*, p. 110.
26. *O.R.*, Ser. 1, XXXVIII, part 2, 512, 681. Schofield, *Forty-Six Years*, p. 130.

breastworks and kept moving to avoid being chilled.[27] At dawn
on June 3, Schofield sent Hovey's division stepping around behind
Cox and Hascall, with orders to drive for the rear of the Confederate right. Hovey gained the Dallas and Acworth road near
Allatoona Church, having completely turned the enemy's position.
The Confederates in front of Schofield then abandoned their line
and fell back once more.[28] Meanwhile, still farther to the left,
Hooker's Corps likewise secured a lodgment on the Dallas and
Acworth road. Johnston soon appreciated the danger of his position and that night (June 4) retired to a new line of entrenchments on a ten-mile arc along the hills covering Marietta—his
right on Brush Mountain, his center on Pine Mountain, his left
on Lost Mountain.

From the fourth to the ninth of June Schofield lay in position
near Allatoona Creek on the Dallas and Acworth road. Sherman
shifted Thomas' army around on Schofield's left, and McPherson's
force followed, coming up still farther to the east on the railroad
in front of Acworth. The positions of June 2 were thus reversed,
Schofield becoming the right of Sherman's army, as he had previously been its left. Sherman was also busy bringing supplies forward to Allatoona Station and insuring his communications with
Chattanooga.[29] Rain came down almost daily, and Schofield may
have felt fortunate that the Army of the Cumberland and the Army
of the Tennessee had to do most of the plowing through the mud
while his troops simply waited.

About the time the armies were in their new positions, Frank
Blair, Jr., arrived with two divisions of the XVII Corps and joined
McPherson's Army.[30] Schofield decided to ride over to his camp
and renew old acquaintances. When he arrived, McPherson was
also there with several other officers. To the pleasant surprise of
everyone, Blair had brought along several hogsheads of ice and a
number of baskets of champagne. "Of course," wrote Schofield, "we
did not disdain such an unusual treat in the enemy's country."[31]
Following the afternoon's festivities, McPherson suggested that
Schofield should visit his camp and the two started off at a gallop.
After enjoying a good camp supper, Schofield paid for the day's

27. Thompson, *112th Illinois*, p. 215.
28. *O.R.*, Ser. 1, XXXVIII, part 2, 512.
29. Sherman, *Memoirs*, II, 50.
30. *Ibid.*, pp. 24, 51.
31. Schofield, *Forty-Six Years*, pp. 138, 139.

pleasantries by a hard night ride of about fifteen miles to get back to his headquarters camp. He rode in sometime in the early morning hours trying not to look at his watch.[32]

Serious business was taken up again on June 10. The whole army moved forward, feeling for the enemy. Schofield followed the general course of Allatoona Creek, traveling southeastward. His "army" was now consolidated into two divisions as Hovey had become discontented and asked to be relieved.[33] Hascall's division advanced on the left near the Burnt Hickory and Sandtown road. Cox moved on Hascall's right to Kemp's Mill, where he once more contacted the Confederate skirmish line and dug in for the night. On the Union left, McPherson's army had advanced about six miles to "Big Shanty," another station on the railroad, while Thomas was bringing up the center of Sherman's line.

Heavy rains continued for the next few days. Schofield slowly edged forward through the water-soaked fields. A brisk skirmish was kept up daily with the Rebels. On Tuesday, June 14, there was a partial cessation of the rain, and Sherman directed the armies to hasten forward as close to the enemy's works as possible.[34] Schofield advanced Hascall's right and Cox's center and succeeded in turning the enemy's left. There was a sharp but brief resistance, and the men in gray fell back to another line. This "cat and mouse" game continued for the next several days—in spite of the rain which sometimes came in torrents. The Confederates were gradually forced back over a series of ridges connecting Lost Mountain with Kennesaw Mountain, then across Mud Creek, and next, behind Noyes Creek. On June 20, Cox's division forced a crossing of the latter and fortified a bridgehead on its east bank.[35] The main enemy force had been backed up to the fortifications on Kennesaw Mountain.

On the twenty-second Sherman rode the whole line and ordered Thomas to advance Hooker's corps. He sent a letter to Schofield to keep his army in close support of Hooker as a strong right flank.[36] Schofield sent his right, under Cox, down the Sandtown road to the intersection of the Powder Springs and Marietta roads, where they began to entrench. Hascall's division on the left

32. *Ibid.*
33. *O.R.*, Ser. 1, XXXVIII, part 2, 512.
34. Cox, *Atlanta*, p. 97.
35. *O.R.*, Ser. 1, XXXVIII, part 2, 513.
36. Sherman, *Memoirs*, II, 57.

moved toward Marietta and connected with the right of Hooker's corps at Kolb's farm. Schofield, displeased with the position, then reconnoitered with Hooker, hoping to advance to more favorable ground. But the Rebels had decided that the Union advance was already too far. The Confederate infantry, in heavy force, was suddenly discovered moving out toward the Federal line. The attack fell first upon Schofield's advance guard, the 14th Kentucky, which was covering his reconnaissance. Ordering that regiment to hold the enemy in check, Schofield commanded the rest of Hascall's division to speed up the entrenching operations. He sent word to Cox to leave one brigade in position and bring up three brigades on his right as soon as possible. The 14th Kentucky gave a good account of itself, holding on for nearly an hour and one half, retiring to the main line only when ordered to do so.[37]

It was then late in the afternoon, and the fighting became general all along Hooker's right and Schofield's left. Union infantry and artillery poured a withering fire into the gray ranks as the blue line held firmly.[38] But Hooker was worried. About 5:30 he sent a brief message to Sherman: "We have repulsed two heavy attacks and feel confident, our only apprehension being from our extreme right flank. Three entire corps are in front of us."[39] Sherman was angry. Why did not Hooker report to Thomas' headquarters? Besides, there were only three corps in Johnston's army. They all could not be in front of Hooker. And why was he concerned about his right flank? Sherman knew Schofield was there, just as he had been ordered. The insinuation that Schofield was not doing his work was unjust.[40]

Early the next morning, Schofield was with Hooker on the Powder Springs road, near the position where their commands joined, when Sherman rode up. It was raining again, and the three stepped inside a little church standing by the road. Sherman handed Schofield Hooker's message of the previous evening. Sherman later wrote that when Schofield read it he was "very angry," and that "pretty sharp words" passed between Schofield and Hooker.[41] Schofield later said that he "did not remember" being

37. *O.R.*, Ser. 1, XXXVIII, part 2, 513.
38. *Ibid.*, p. 683.
39. *Ibid.*, part 4, 558.
40. Sherman, *Memoirs*, II, 57, 58.
41. *Ibid.*, p. 59.

"very angry," though he thought Sherman was.[42] Whether he was angry or not, Schofield told Sherman that the enemy attack struck his troops before Hooker's and offered to show him the dead men of his advance division lying farther out than any of Hooker's. Sherman accompanied Schofield as they rode over the ground and viewed the dead. Sherman then rode off with Hooker, reproving him "more gently," according to Sherman, "than the occasion demanded. . . ."[43]

During the next two days Schofield extended his right as far as seemed prudent in an effort to make the enemy thin out his lines correspondingly. Sherman had decided to stop turning the ends. The weather was clearing up, and for the first time in the campaign he decided upon a head-on assault. In a dispatch to Washington on June 25, he summarized his plan briefly: "I shall . . . make him [Johnston] stretch his line until he weakens it and then break through."[44] Meanwhile, the roar of artillery was being kept up "like a continual long roll," all along the line, day and night. A soldier in Schofield's army thought the Confederate stronghold on Kennesaw Mountain presented "a magnificent spectacle" at night. "Sheets of white flame" poured forth from the Confederate guns on the mountain. Shells, "like so many sky rockets," rose from the Federal batteries and arched toward the enemy position. Over all were "the weird, unearthly reflections on the clouds."[45]

Sherman called a conference of his army commanders and later claimed that they all agreed there was "no alternative but to attack 'fortified lines,' a thing carefully avoided up to that time."[46] There is reason to believe that Schofield did not favor such an assault. As he later wrote, there were certainly other alternatives to an assault, one of which was successfully used a few days later. There is no doubt that Thomas was opposed to the attack.[47] And Schofield said that he believed McPherson also questioned the

42. Schofield, *Forty-Six Years*, p. 134.

43. Sherman, *Memoirs*, II, 57, 58. Schofield, *Forty-Six Years*, pp. 132, 133. Schofield wrote that Hooker did not refer to his (Schofield's) immediate right in his dispatch to Sherman, but to the extreme right of the army. Hooker believed Johnston had drawn his main force from around Kennesaw and was about to strike the right flank of Sherman's line.

44. Liddell-Hart, *Sherman*, p. 265.

45. Pinney, *104th Ohio*, p. 45.

46. Sherman, *Memoirs*, II, 60.

47. Schofield, *Forty-Six Years*, pp. 142, 143. Richard O'Conner, *Thomas: Rock of Chickamauga* (New York, 1948), pp. 272–74.

wisdom of the assault at Kennesaw. Although the army commanders, and others, may have doubted the advisability of such an undertaking, their opposition was deferential. The responsibility, of course, was Sherman's, and he was becoming impatient.

Monday morning, June 27, was the day picked for the grand effort. McPherson's Army of the Tennessee would feint with its extreme left, while attacking in earnest at the west base of Kennesaw. Thomas' Army of the Cumberland would select a point in the center for its assault, and Schofield's Army of the Ohio would serve as a decoy, pushing forward near the Marietta and Powder Springs road, threatening the extreme left flank of the enemy.[48] Schofield was instructed to begin his demonstration on June 26, with the hope of inducing the Rebels to send reinforcements to their left, thus weakening the points where the real attack would be made by McPherson and Thomas. Schofield sent Colonel James W. Reilly's brigade of Cox's division forward on the Sandtown Road toward Olley's Creek. The troops were soon engaged in a brisk skirmish, but managed to occupy some hills close to the stream. The enemy's dismounted cavalry, supported with artillery, held a strong position just across the creek. Schofield brought up Colonel Robert K. Byrd's brigade, about a mile to the left, where a bridge was built across the swamplike water. Crossing the stream, these troops, covered by artillery, soon occupied a hill northeast of that held by the Confederates in front of Reilly's brigade and began to entrench on all sides. Thus Schofield had managed to push out a separate redoubt. He connected the advanced brigade with his line on both the right and left by a chain of pickets and covered the interval between with his artillery. Sherman was pleased, and the Confederates were uneasy. Still, Johnston did not feel that he could detach from other portions of his line to drive Schofield back.[49] The Confederate position remained strong at the center.

Early on the morning of June 27 Sherman's artillery opened all along the line, preparatory to the assault. Schofield continued his advance on the right. Colonel David Cameron's brigade was thrown across Olley's Creek, in rear of Byrd's, and, advancing down the south bank, struck the enemy in flank. Reilly's brigade moved farther down the stream, forced a crossing under protection of

48. Cox, *Atlanta*, pp. 118, 119.
49. *Ibid.*, pp. 119, 120. *O.R.*, Ser. 1, XXXVIII, part 2, 514.

artillery fire, and pressed to the attack in front. After a brisk fight, the Confederates gave way. Schofield had Cox's entire division east of the creek and occupying the position the enemy had just forsaken. He was also advancing Hascall's division toward Marietta on his extreme right flank.[50]

The hands on the clock neared eight o'clock. The pounding of Kennesaw ceased. McPherson's and Thomas' armies surged forward and upward toward the entrenchments on the mountain side. The din of musketry and roar of artillery was terrific as they marched toward death. An idea of what the Union line faced is given by the remark of a Confederate private. For two hours, he said, "every man in our regiment killed from onescore to fourscore, yea, fivescore men," for "all that was necessary was to load and shoot."[51] Schofield's men could hear the noise of battle off to their left and rear. While the slaughter progressed, Schofield continued his more cautious advance. Taking advantage of the enemy's preoccupation, Cox's division pushed forward once more, advancing some two miles until a crossroad was reached. One of these roads rounded the ridge of hills which separated Olley's Creek and Nickajack Creek and led into the principal road from Marietta to Sandtown. The nature of the hills bordering Nickajack Creek prevented the Confederate line from being extended farther south. And the position was an excellent one from which to strike Johnston's railroad near Smyrna, five miles south of Marietta. The importance of the position was immediately obvious. If Sherman were forced to resume his flanking operations, Schofield was occupying strategic ground. Schofield ordered Cox to entrench on an advanced hill overlooking the Nickajack and hold on firmly. This was the only success gained anywhere that day. Thomas and McPherson both suffered heavy losses.[52] In four days Sherman was turning the Confederate left again, advancing down the Sandtown Road, heading for the Chattahoochee River and Atlanta.[53]

During the afternoon of July 3 the Army of the Tennessee filed past Schofield and took the advance. While this was going on, Schofield and McPherson sat on their horses, observed the move-

50. *O.R.*, Ser. 1, XXXVIII, part 2, 514, 683.
51. Sam R. Watkins, *"Co. Aytch," Maury Grays, 1st Tennessee Regiment* (Jackson, Tennessee, 1952), p. 218.
52. JMS to W. T. Sherman, June 27, 1864; JMS to J. D. Cox, June 27, 1864, Schofield MSS. Cox, *Atlanta*, pp. 123, 124.
53. *O.R.*, Ser. 1, XXXVIII, part 2, 514, 515, 683. Sherman, *Memoirs,* II, 62.

ment, and reminisced about the days of their youth. McPherson confided that he had become engaged to be married. He was wondering when there would be an opportunity to return to Ohio for the occasion. Schofield replied that as soon as Atlanta was captured there would be ample time.[54] Neither could know that McPherson had only three weeks to live.

Meanwhile, Joe Johnston was watching as Schofield and Mc-Pherson's strong right flank was drawing closer to Atlanta than the Confederates. Johnston had evacuated the formidable lines at Kennesaw during the night of July 2, entrenching in a position already prepared behind Nickajack Creek. Within forty-eight hours he was falling back again, racing to take up a new position in the works just north of the Chattahoochee—before Sherman's right wing slammed in first.[55] The Chattahoochee, the last great natural barrier to Sherman's advance on Atlanta, was at Johnston's back, but to hold his line Johnston had prepared what Sherman thought was "one of the strongest pieces of field fortification I ever saw."[56] There were six miles of earthworks, with ditches and abatis, and over two hundred pieces of artillery. For miles to the right and left of this six miles were long lines of cavalry and pickets with occasional forts and artillery, usually placed at the fords and ferries. There was one good bridge—behind Johnston's main line—and the waters were turbid and swollen.[57] This massive bridgehead was the unwelcome sight confronting the Union army as it came up on July 5. Sherman decided he would have to "study the case a little."[58]

Schofield was occupying the center as his Army of the Ohio approached the river. McPherson went into position on his right front, facing the enemy line in a southeasterly direction down to Turner's Ferry. Thomas came up on the left and pressed right up against the center of Johnston's bridgehead. Schofield was stationed at Smyrna Camp Ground, near the railroad, in position as a movable column to be used in any direction.[59] Soon Sherman was scattering troops up and down the river, hunting for fords by

54. Schofield, *Forty-Six Years*, pp. 136, 137.
55. Cox, *Atlanta*, pp. 132, 133.
56. Sherman, *Memoirs*, II, 66.
57. George Redway, "A Bloodless Victory," *National Tribune*, September 18, 1902.
58. Cox, *Atlanta*, p. 134.
59. *Ibid.*

which to turn the flank again. Colonel Israel Garrard's cavalry found a ford twenty miles up the river to the northeast, at Roswell. but Sherman wanted something closer. On the other flank, he had Stoneman's cavalry, aided by McPherson, carrying on a demonstration, hoping to hoodwink Johnston. It was Schofield, however, whom Sherman was looking to for this assignment.[60]

On July 7 Schofield made a reconnaissance of the Chattahoochee for several miles north of Pace's Ferry. Moving northeastward up a deep ravine, separated from the river by a parallel ridge some two hundred to three hundred feet high, he examined the course of a stream known as Soap's Creek. After flowing generally south for some miles, it cut through the ravine for a considerable distance and emptied into the Chattahoochee after making a short curve. There was a spot below the mouth of the creek, known as Phillip's Ferry, which appeared to be held by only a light force. It would be difficult to cross in the face of strong resistance, but it was very favorable for a surprise. He just might get across the river before the Rebels knew what had happened. This looked like the crossing for which he had been searching. Sherman thought so too. Schofield wanted to reconnoiter more fully the next day, but Sherman had learned that the main body of the enemy's cavalry was several miles downstream on the Confederate left. The time to act was at hand. Schofield was instructed to cross as soon as possible and entrench on the east bank.[61]

At daylight on the eighth Schofield marched, Cox's division in the lead—ready to cross by surprise if possible, by force if necessary. From Cameron's brigade he chose some fifty "tall and strong" men.[62] These constituted his advance, which Schofield planned to put across the Chattahoochee at an old fish dam, about half a mile above the mouth of Soap's Creek. The water would be up to their mouths at times and the footing on the piled up stones would be slippery. If they made it across, the rest of the brigade would follow immediately. At the same time, a pontoon bridge, set up in the creek far enough from its mouth to be concealed from the enemy, would emerge into the main stream, loaded with the 12th Kentucky infantry from Byrd's brigade. The pontoons should be

60. Sherman, *Memoirs*, II, 69.
61. *O.R.*, Ser. 1, XXXVIII, part 2, 515. Sherman, *Memoirs*, II, 69. Redway, "Bloodless Victory."
62. Special Field Orders, No. 46, July 7, 1864, Schofield MSS.

in place across the Chattahoochee in a matter of minutes. The rest of Byrd's brigade would advance simultaneously to the river's edge, on the run, covering the pontoons with their fire if necessary, and crossing as soon as the bridge was in position. Artillery would be stationed just behind the crest of the ridge at the river, ready to be wheeled into position at the instant the crossing commenced. The area was heavily wooded, right down to the water's edge, and it should be easy to remain out of sight until the appointed time. The bank on the other side of the river appeared to be about eight feet high. Beyond lay open, level bottom, less than a hundred yards wide, and beyond that, a rather steep hill, rising perhaps two hundred feet, and covered with timber. At the top lay what appeared to some of the men to be a line of earthworks.[63]

Half past three in the afternoon was the time set for the crossing. Schofield, atop the ridge, could see nothing on the opposite side but a cavalry outpost with a single piece of artillery. He gave the signal to advance.[64] About fifty men emerged from the woods and started scrambling along the broken rocks in the swift current at the fish dam, holding their guns and ammunition over their heads. Some never expected to get across alive. A few slipped and went under, but were helped up and pushed on.[65] Twenty pontoon boats shot out from the mouth of Soap's Creek, loaded with the Army of the Kentucky, their oarsmen pulling for the other side as fast as possible. In a moment the fifty at the fish dam were clambering safely up on the Rebel side, and others were ready to follow. Deploying in a skirmish line the advance made for the timbered area. Not a shot had been fired. Suddenly the Confederate cannon opened with a "boom." They had seen the pontoons coming across the river! But it was too late. Musketry fire opened on them from all along the river bank. The Union artillery was pushed quickly into position and opened fire. And the group already across the river was blazing away at them from the flank. Not another cannon shot was fired by the Confederates. After a short musketry exchange the astonished Rebels abandoned the field, leaving their one piece of artillery. It was a bloodless victory. Schofield had not lost a single man. By night he had laid

---

63. Redway, "Bloodless Victory." *O.R.*, Ser. 1, XXXVIII, part 2, 515. Cox, *Atlanta*, pp. 138, 139.
64. Cox, *Atlanta*, p. 139.
65. Redway, "Bloodless Victory."

a bridge, and Cox's entire division was across and securely entrenched. In the night of July 9, Johnston, seeing his line of retreat again endangered, withdrew his main force, abandoning the Chattahoochee, and taking up a new line along Peachtree Creek.[66]

Schofield's men, together with the rest of Sherman's army, were soon splashing in the Chattahoochee, basking in the sun, and playing cards on the river bank.[67] Nearly a week was consumed in building bridges, bringing up supplies, and strengthening the garrisons in the rear. On July 17 Sherman was ready to move again. He approached the enemy in a giant wheeling movement, slanting to the east. Schofield was the spoke in the middle. Thomas was the hub to his right, and McPherson was the rim, marching some fifty miles and swinging from Thomas' right until he came around in rear and on the left of Schofield. McPherson was breaking up the railroad into Atlanta as he progressed.

As the movement continued on the eighteenth, Sherman got hold of an Atlanta newspaper and learned that Johnston was no longer in command of Confederate forces. John Bell Hood, his left arm dangling useless at his side since Gettysburg, his right leg amputated at Chickamauga, was now directing Rebel fortunes.[68] Sherman knew Schofield and McPherson had been Hood's classmates at West Point. And Thomas had been one of his instructors there. He inquired what the man was like. Schofield replied that Hood was bold, rash, and "courageous in the extreme." This was the general opinion of McPherson and Thomas also. Evidently, the Union officers reasoned, the President of the Confederacy was tired of his army retreating. Hood could be expected to fight. Word was sent to all division commanders to be prepared for battle "in any shape."[69] The Union army would not have long to wait.

Meanwhile, Schofield, with Hascall's division in the advance, was striking south and west toward the outskirts of Atlanta at Decatur. Some two miles out of the town, he encountered a heavy force of Confederate cavalry. But the enemy could do no more than hinder his progress. By mid-afternoon July 19, Schofield's lead division was tramping into Decatur, breaking the telegraph line and tearing up a mile of the railroad. The depot, with a large

66. *O.R.*, Ser. 1, XXXVIII, part 2, 515, 516. Redway, "Bloodless Victory." Lewis, *Sherman*, p. 381.
67. Lewis, *Sherman*, p. 381.
68. Dyer, *The Gallant Hood*, p. 320.
69. Sherman, *Memoirs*, II, 72.

amount of army stores and wagons was already burning furiously, fired by the retreating Rebels. When about a mile and a half east of the town, Schofield had sent Cox's division filing off to the right, taking the Atlanta road to Pea Vine Creek. This stream, running nearly due north, was a branch of the south fork of Peachtree Creek, which flowed into the Chattahoochee. It was only about four miles from Atlanta. Cox entrenched on its north bank on the Peyton plantation. During the evening the right of McPherson's Army of the Tennessee swung into Decatur and relieved Hascall's division. The latter then assumed position in reserve to Cox.[70]

The next day Schofield inched in still closer, Cox's division advancing a mile or more against very stubborn resistance. At the same time, McPherson was bringing up a strong left flank. Then Hood thought he saw his chance—a gap was visible between Schofield and Thomas. The Confederates came pouring in about noon, when the Union troops were resting and eating. The brunt of the attack struck Hooker's corps which was driven back; but "Old Slow Trot" Thomas soon plugged the gap. Thomas got some field batteries in a good position and directed a furious fire of canister on a mass of the enemy. Soon communication between the Army of the Ohio and the Army of the Cumberland was established once more. The advance was continued, and Hood's men fell back into their entrenched position.[71]

The next day Schofield strengthened his works and cut roads, opening communication with the Army of the Tennessee on his left. His batteries engaged in a lively duel with the Confederate artillery and the skirmish pits kept up a deadly fire all day. After Hood's sally on July 20, Sherman was expecting Atlanta to be evacuated. But Hood, seeing that McPherson's flank was "hanging in air," was bringing four divisions around to his right and preparing to roll up Sherman's left. About one o'clock on the morning of July 22, Schofield's pickets discovered that the enemy had abandoned the strong line of parapets, "Peach Tree line," in his front. There was no enemy in front of Thomas either. At dawn, Schofield and Thomas pushed rapidly toward Atlanta. The Rebels had fallen back within their works immediately around the city.

70. *O.R.*, Ser. 1, XXXVIII, part 2, 516, 571, 572, 686, 687. Cox, *Atlanta*, pp. 153, 154.
71. Lewis, *Sherman*, p. 383. *O.R.*, Ser. 1, XXXVIII, part 2, 516.

Schofield advanced to within about twelve hundred yards of the
Confederate works and began to fortify a line in front of the
Howard House on the Atlanta road. Sherman was with Schofield,
and from the open ground in front of the Howard house the
two could plainly see the whole Rebel line. The line was strongly
manned, with guns in position at intervals. Sherman still thought
Hood was preparing to evacuate the city.[72]

It was about ten o'clock, and Schofield was dressing forward
his lines when McPherson rode up with his staff. Sherman and
McPherson walked back toward the Howard house where Sherman
drew a map of the operations he proposed to make when the
Army of the Tennessee had finished destroying the railroad at
Decatur. Schofield's men were skirmishing fiercely with the Rebels,
and his batteries roared as they hurled round-shot toward Atlanta.
Similar but fainter sounds could be heard all along Thomas' line
to the right and McPherson's to the left. Suddenly, about noon,
a louder and brisker note came in the firing. It was off to the
left—McPherson's men. And then artillery was heard back toward
Decatur, some five miles in the rear. What did it mean? Mc-
Pherson, exchanging hurried words with Sherman, swung into his
saddle and galloped off toward the sound of firing in his front
which was still gaining in volume. But Sherman was most disturbed by the roar of artillery back toward Decatur, where his
trains were parked. There was no cavalry to guard the army's left
rear. The night before, Sherman had sent away all of Garrard's
cavalry division with orders to destroy two bridges and tear up
railroad track some thirty miles to the east. Sherman ordered
Schofield to send a brigade of infantry back to Decatur at once.
Schofield called upon Cox who immediately dispatched Reilly's
brigade to the rear.[73]

McPherson had been gone only a few minutes when one of his
staff officers dashed up to the porch of the Howard house where
Sherman was pacing. Alighting from a horse covered with sweat,
the man reported that McPherson, riding into a wooded area,
had been either killed or taken prisoner. Shots had been heard, and
his horse came back riderless and bloody. Sherman instructed the
officer to go and find General John A. Logan, to tell him to take

72. *O.R.*, Ser. 1, XXXVIII, part 1, 72; part 2, 516, 572, 687. Sherman, *Memoirs,*
II, 75.
73. Sherman, *Memoirs,* II, 76. Lewis, *Sherman,* p. 384.

command of the Army of the Tennessee and drive the enemy back. To make doubly sure that the message would get through, Sherman dispatched one of his own officers to Logan with the same orders. He sent couriers racing to find Thomas, telling him to push toward Atlanta, since Hood had apparently withdrawn much of his force from his left in order to strike the left and rear of the Union line.[74]

As soon as it was evident that the Army of the Tennessee was heavily engaged, Schofield, leaving his picket line in position, with a reserve behind the parapets, had begun drawing the larger part of his troops out of the line and massing them in his left rear. Here they would be in position to reinforce the Army of the Tennessee if necessary. Within an hour after McPherson rode away from the Howard house, an ambulance arrived, bearing his lifeless body. Sherman directed that it be carried inside the house where a door was torn from its hinges and the limp body laid upon it.[75] While the remains of his friend lay in the house, Schofield remembered that Sherman, deeply affected, remarked that the whole of the Confederacy could not atone for the sacrifice of one such life.[76] Many shots were then striking the Howard house, and fearing it would catch fire, Sherman ordered that McPherson's body be taken to Marietta.

Meanwhile, the Army of the Tennessee was fighting for its life, with Confederates driving at them from three sides and sometimes from four. Schofield proposed that his and Thomas' reserves should go to their assistance, preferably by making a counterattack on the left flank of the Rebels, attempting to cut them off from Atlanta and the rest of the Confederate army. But Sherman preferred to "let the Army of the Tennessee fight its own battle."[77]

Late in the afternoon the Confederates sallied forth from

74. Sherman, *Memoirs*, II, 77.
75. *Ibid.*, pp. 77, 78.
76. Schofield, *Forty-Six Years*, pp. 145, 146.
77. *Ibid.*, p. 148. In his memoirs Sherman implied that Schofield and Thomas could have gotten into Atlanta if they had tried hard enough. (II, 80) But Schofield points out in his memoirs that he was occupied in forming an infantry reserve to meet the enemy if Logan's troops did not drive them back, and that this was done with Sherman's knowledge and approval. He further states that there was never any question of his attempting to "make a lodgment in Atlanta" that day; that the ground in his front made the enemy's position practically unassailable anyway" (p. 147).

Atlanta (a move which Sherman believed Hood intended to be simultaneous with the morning attack on the left). The onslaught was directed mainly against Leggett's Hill and along the Decatur railroad. At the latter point, General Charles R. Woods' division, which was the extreme right of Logan's command, found itself driven back and cut off from the rest of the Army of the Tennessee. Sherman sent Woods back with orders to attack and then ordered Schofield to bring all his cannon to a hill overlooking the position. Although in both his official report and his memoirs Sherman gave credit for the movement to Schofield, Schofield said it was Sherman who placed the batteries in position and directed their fire.[78] The shells were soon whistling over the heads of Woods' men and enfilading the parapets from which the Union troops had been driven. With this assistance the division regained the entrenchments which it had lost. The Army of the Tennessee was rallying all along the line and at last driving the enemy back toward Atlanta. Since Logan's infantry proved sufficient, most of Schofield's forces, except the artillery, were not engaged, beyond heavy skirmishing, in "the Battle of Atlanta."[79]

The next day Schofield brought all his troops back into line, occupying substantially the same position in front of the Howard house as before the battle. Every fifteen minutes each of his batteries fired a shot into the city. Firing from the artillery and the skirmish pits was continued at intervals during the following days. On the night of July 26, the Army of the Tennessee, General Oliver O. Howard now commanding, was withdrawn from Schofield's left and swung to the right and rear, around the northern outskirts of Atlanta. Sherman was moving to cut off all entry to the city except from the south, hoping finally to draw the Rebels out of Atlanta by threatening the only remaining railroad—the line from Macon.[80] Schofield placed his main body of troops in entrenchments on the southeastern flank, stretched out an advanced picket line to his left, and made frequent demonstrations upon the Confederate right, thus masking the disappearance of Howard's men. At nightfall on July 27, Howard's troops were facing Atlanta from the west. The next morning the last of his three corps (Logan's) was coming into position when Hood, once more think-

78. Sherman, *Memoirs*, II, 81. Schofield, *Forty-Six Years*, p. 147.
79. *O.R.*, Ser. 1, XXXVIII, part 2, 572. Schofield, *Forty-Six Years*, p. 147.
80. *O.R.*, Ser. 1, XXXVIII, part 5, 291.

ing he would catch Sherman's flank "in air," sent Stephen D. Lee's corps to the attack near Ezra Church. Logan's men had covered themselves with a rough breastwork of logs and repulsed the Confederates with great loss.[81] After this Hood did not venture forth again.

Simultaneously with Howard's movement to the west, Sherman attempted to break the Macon railroad with his cavalry. General Edward M. McCook's troopers were to drive from the west and George Stoneman's from the east. They were to join about thirty miles below Atlanta at Lovejoy's Station on the night of July 28, proceed south, and destroy the railroad. After this work was accomplished, Sherman said, Stoneman could continue south and attempt to release Union prisoners at Macon and Andersonville. But Stoneman disregarded his instructions to join up with McCook, riding instead due south to Macon. He destroyed a large amount of property and did some damage to the railroad below the town. He was also captured, with about six hundred of his command. McCook made a lodgment on the railroad, but without help from Stoneman he was forced to turn back and narrowly escaped being captured.[82]

The cavalry had failed. The railroad would have to be broken by the infantry. Sherman called on Schofield for the task. After dark on August 1, Garrard's cavalry, dismounted, slipped into Schofield's trenches while the Army of the Ohio swept in a semicircle around the northern edge of Atlanta, passing in rear of Thomas Howard and coming up on the right flank of the Union army.[83] Late the next afternoon, Schofield was positioned along the north branch of Utoy Creek, about two miles from his objective—the railroad at East Point.[84] To give more punch to the blow Sherman instructed General John M. Palmer to join Schofield with the XIV Corps and placed this corps under Schofield's control so there would be a unified action.

Dawn on August 5 was the time Sherman set for the attack, but there was anything except unity of action. About mid-afternoon of August 4 Schofield received word from Palmer, who claimed seniority over him, that he would "co-operate" with Schofield, but

81. Liddell-Hart, *Sherman*, p. 290.
82. *Ibid.*, pp. 288, 289. Lewis, *Sherman*, pp. 402, 403.
83. Liddell-Hart, *Sherman*, p. 291.
84. *O.R.*, Ser. 1, XXXVIII, part 2, 517, 688.

would "not obey either General Sherman's orders or yours, as they violate my self-respect."[85] Sherman, having investigated Palmer's claim to seniority which was based on a technicality, informed Palmer that night that he had decided in favor of Schofield. He told Palmer, quite pointedly: "The Sandtown road and the railroad, if possible, must be gained tomorrow, if it costs half your command. I regard the loss of time this afternoon as equal to the loss of 2,000 men."[86]

About midnight Palmer replied, still refusing to obey orders, and asked to be relieved of his command.[87] If there were underlying irritating factors in Palmer's stand, they are not known.[88] Schofield later wrote that he had but a very slight personal acquaintance with Palmer, and if there was any cause of ill-feeling between the two, he had never suspected it.[89]

General Richard W. Johnson, the senior division commander of the XIV Corps, replaced Palmer, but, perhaps sympathizing with Palmer, proved to be far from ready to support the movement heartily. He, in turn, was replaced by General Jeff C. Davis, who held the command for the rest of the war. On August 5, Reilly's brigade, supported by the whole of Cox's division, tried to break through the Confederate line about a mile below Utoy Creek. Some of the men reached the enemy's parapets, but the attack failed, with the loss of about four hundred men who were caught in the entanglements and abatis.[90] The next day Hascall succeeding in turning the position, and Schofield advanced his whole line close up to the enemy below the creek. But he could not gain a foothold on the railroad. Sherman sent word to suspend aggressive operations and "dig in." As the order was given to begin fortifying, Schofield heard an old volunteer, as he laid aside his gun, "Well, if digging is the way to put down the rebellion, I guess we will have to do it."[91]

The August heat bore down and nothing further, except for the incessant skirmish firing, was done on the right flank for

85. *Ibid.*, part 5, 355.
86. *Ibid.*, p. 356.
87. *Ibid.*, pp. 356, 357.
88. George T. Palmer, *A Conscientious Turncoat: The Story of John M. Palmer, 1817–1900* (New Haven, 1941), p. 149.
89. Schofield, *Forty-Six Years*, p. 151.
90. *O.R.*, Ser. 1, XXXVIII, part 2, 689.
91. Schofield, *Forty-Six Years*, p. 155.

over two weeks. On the night of August 25 Sherman moved again, marching to occupy the Macon railroad once and for all. The armies of Howard and Thomas made a grand left wheel to the southeast, pivoting on Schofield.[92] By August 28 Howard and Thomas were astride the Montgomery railroad between Fairburn and Red Oak—busily ripping up the tracks on a Sunday afternoon. At noon on the twenty-eighth, Schofield evacuated his works and moved into position as the left wing of the general advance, moving on a seven- or eight-mile front and striking southeastward toward the Macon railroad.[93]

It was August 30 before Hood, who had thought Confederate cavalry raids on Federal communications were forcing the Union army to withdraw, realized Sherman was attacking, not retreating. Then he quickly sent William J. Hardee with two corps to Jonesboro, some twenty miles south of Atlanta, to protect the railroad.[94] On the thirty-first, Schofield drove for the railroad near Rough 'and Ready, gaining a firm hold about a mile and a half south of the station.[95] Thomas gained the rails at two points farther to the south, while Howard's army was confronting Hardee's Rebels still farther below at Jonesboro.

That night Schofield received instructions from Sherman to "break the road good as you move south."[96] Later in the night, after he had gone to sleep, another message came from Sherman. He requested Schofield to take orders during the next day's movement from General David S. Stanley, Schofield's senior in date as a major general, whose corps was entrenched on Schofield's right. Since their commands would form a common movement, Sherman was hoping to ensure cooperation by thus eliminating a possible source of friction.[97] Schofield replied that he differed with Sherman's opinion on the question of rank, holding that an army or department commander's position took precedence over any other officer of the same grade, even though senior in rank; nevertheless he would "act heartily in accordance with [Sherman's] decision and execute [his] orders."[98] Schofield's view was subsequently

92. *O.R.*, Ser. 1, XXXVIII, part 2, 518.
93. Liddell-Hart, *Sherman*, pp. 297, 298.
94. Lewis, *Sherman*, p. 406.
95. *O.R.*, Ser. 1, XXXVIII, part 2, 519.
96. *Ibid.*, part 5, 733.
97. *Ibid.*, p. 734.
98. *Ibid.*, p. 753.

upheld by the general-in-chief, Halleck commending Schofield for his conduct on the occasion as well as the tone of his protest.[99]

At daylight on September 1, Schofield moved Cox's division north to Rough and Ready and began "working on the railroad"— burning the ties and heating and twisting the rails—destroying about two miles of the Atlanta and Macon road.[100] Meanwhile, Sherman decided to close in on Hardee. He ordered Schofield and Thomas to advance south, converging at Jonesboro. Sherman intended for Stanley's corps, the left of Thomas' army, together with Schofield's Army of the Ohio, to come up on the northeast side of Jonesboro and roll up the Confederate right. Schofield later wrote that he did not receive the orders until after the fight at Jonesboro was ended. He said he heard the sound of battle to the south, rode rapidly to the head of Stanley's column which was not advancing, and learned that Stanley was searching for Thomas to get orders. Early in the morning, Schofield related, Stanley had said he was not entitled to the command and did not want it. Of course, Schofield could not relieve him of the responsibility. Schofield then took Hascall's infantry, which had taken the advance while Cox was destroying the railroad near Rough and Ready, and moved through the woods and fields to the left of Stanley's corps and toward the front. He was trying to find a way to reach the enemy's flank but was unable to do so.[101] This is in accord with Hascall's report, who said that in the movement he encountered an extensive swamp, which, owing to the lateness of the hour, prevented any farther movement.[102]

It was nearly dark before Stanley's troops began to deploy and attack—too late to be of any real value. During the night Hardee would slip out of the trap at Jonesboro, circle south, and entrench again at Lovejoy's Station, seven miles lower on the railroad. Sherman, though he did not say it in his report, held Stanley responsible for the failure to snare the Confederates.[103] Schofield would write that the erroneous interpretation of the law that threw the supreme responsibility at the crisis of battle upon "untried and . . . unwilling shoulders" was responsible for

99. H. W. Halleck to W. T. Sherman, October 4, 1864, Schofield MSS.
100. *O.R.*, Ser. 1, XXXVIII, part 2, 692.
101. Schofield, *Forty-Six Years*, p. 157.
102. *O.R.*, Ser. 1, XXXVIII, part 2, 574.
103. Sherman, *Memoirs*, II, 108.

the failure.[104] Stanley later wrote that he could "pick his [Schofield's] chapter on Jonesboro to pieces" but did "not think it worthwhile."[105] He did not explain what he meant.

On the night of September 1 Schofield read his orders for the next day's action. Sherman planned a double envelopment and triple attack on the Rebels at Jonesboro. Schofield was to press around to the east, attacking from the flank, while Thomas drove south down the railroad and Howard attacked from the west flank.[106] Daylight, however, would alter the situation greatly. Not only would Hardee be gone, but during the night, about 2 A.M., Schofield had heard explosions and firing in the direction of Atlanta. Similar noises were heard again near 4 A.M. He could see large fires back toward Atlanta. There were brilliant flashes followed at regular intervals by loud explosions, far too loud for any artillery. Then there would be very rapid explosions of shells. No battle he had ever seen would account for such phenomena. Hood was burning his magazines! He was abandoning Atlanta! Schofield sent a dispatch to Sherman: "All the circumstances indicate the burning of magazines at Atlanta."[107] He also sent an infantry reconnaissance to endeavor to learn more. About ten o'clock in the morning a Negro came in from Atlanta saying that the Confederates had retreated south during the night on the McDonough road, reportedly in confusion and disorder.[108] Hood was retreating, but not in confusion. The bulk of his force marched by a wide circuit to the southeast, passing through McDonough and then striking west to join Hardee at Lovejoy's Station, arriving during the night of the second and morning of the third.

There was never any real chance of intercepting the retreat unless the enemy columns had been located early in the morning of September 2. And at that time Sherman was still thinking he would entrap Hardee at Jonesboro. It was not until early morning, September 3, that Sherman received word from Henry W. Slocum, whose single corps had been left on the western outskirts of Atlanta, that the Confederates had indeed abandoned the city. Slocum had pressed into the city at daybreak of September

104. Schofield, *Forty-Six Years*, p. 158.
105. Stanley, *Memoirs*, p. 214.
106. *O.R.*, Ser. 1, XXXVIII, part 5, 754, 755.
107. *Ibid.*, p. 773.
108. *Ibid.*

2, finding the enemy trenches empty and catching a glimpse of a few of the Confederate rear guard as they moved south.[109]

September 2 was spent by Schofield in attempting to pursue Hardee's troops to Lovejoy's Station. It was a long and tedious march through the unfamiliar fields and woods, which, even when continued long after dark, only brought him partially into position on the left flank of the Union advance.[110] Little did it matter. Sherman had what he wanted. "Atlanta is ours and fairly won," he wrote Halleck.[111] He promptly discontinued offensive operations, gradually fell back, and occupied the city. There was great rejoicing in Washington. The campaign to re-elect Abraham Lincoln received a much-needed shot in the arm. On September 8 Schofield's army encamped on the eastern outskirts of Atlanta about Decatur, and the great campaign was ended. Sherman proposed to give his army a month's rest while he perfected his future plans. Schofield took advantage of the opportunity to attend to business in his Department of the Ohio. Within a few days he was on a train heading for Knoxville. A long hot summer had finally come to an end.

109. Lewis, *Sherman*, p. 408.
110. *O.R.*, Ser. 1, XXXVIII, part 2, 519.
111. *Ibid.*, part 5, 777.

# VII. West Point Classmates--Eleven Years Later

IT WAS EARLY November, 1864. Abraham Lincoln had just been re-elected President of the United States. Sherman was cutting a wide swath through Georgia as he slashed eastward and southward toward the sea. But Schofield was no longer with him. Returning from Knoxville and Louisville, he was reluctant to be a part of the great march. His command was shrunken from losses and expiration of terms of service. He wanted to take the Army of the Ohio back to Tennessee in order to replenish it with fresh regiments from the North.[1] Furthermore, the Confederates under Hood were presenting a new problem.

In late September Hood moved around Sherman's right, striking his railroad south of Chattanooga. Sherman followed, realizing "it was absolutely necessary to keep General Hood's infantry off our main route of communication and supply."[2] Then the puzzling Hood had moved westward to Gadsden, Alabama. Hood could "turn and twist like a fox," Sherman said, "and wear out my army in pursuit."[3] It began to look to some, especially General Thomas, tending to affairs of the Department of the Cumberland in Nashville, as if Hood were going to invade Tennessee. Sherman was not going to follow him to find out. He would let Thomas cope

1. *O.R.*, Ser. 1, XXXIX, part 3, 467, 468. Schofield, *Forty-Six Years*, p. 165.
2. Sherman, *Memoirs*, II, 146.
3. *Battles and Leaders*, IV, 441.

with Hood. Sherman took the majority of the troops which had
engaged in the Atlanta campaign and started for the sea.

Thomas had the task of organizing and molding an army in the
face of impending danger. His infantry would consist of General
David S. Stanley's Corps, about 12,000 men, and General Andrew
Jackson Smith's Corps, then in Missouri, about 10,000 strong. There
would be some 5,000 cavalry. And Thomas would have the garrisons and railroad guards which had been used during Sherman's
summer operations in Georgia. But many of these, their terms of
enlistment expiring, would soon be discharged.[4] Schofield said
that he thought Thomas' force was too small and requested to be
sent back to help him. However, it was not until he had marched
three days toward Atlanta, en route to Savannah, that Sherman
on October 30 ordered him to proceed to the nearest point on
the railroad and report by telegraph to General Thomas for
orders.[5]

Having contacted Thomas, Schofield prepared to move his corps
by rail to Tullahoma and then march to Pulaski, a small town
south of Nashville and near the Alabama line. But Thomas was
in a hurry, and after conferring with the superintendent of military roads he managed to arrange rail transportation all the way
to Pulaski, via Nashville. On November 3, Schofield started
Joseph A. Cooper's division from Dalton by train, leaving Cox's
division until further transportation could be arranged.[6] About
the same time "that devil [Nathan B.] Forrest," as Sherman described him, appeared at Johnsonville on the Tennessee River
west of Nashville. His cavalry soon destroyed a great quantity of
property and terrorized the Union colonel in command. Schofield,
with the advance of his troops, reported to Thomas on November 5
and was ordered at once to Johnsonville to dispose of the enemy
force. But Forrest had done his mischief, and no enemy was to be
found.[7] Leaving General Cooper and two brigades with orders to
fortify the post, Schofield returned to Nashville. The remainder
of his XXIII Corps arrived on the ninth, and two days later

4. Livermore, *Numbers and Losses*, p. 131. *O.R.*, Ser. 1, XLV, part 1, 54,
55. O'Connor, *Thomas*, p. 298.
5. Schofield, *Forty-Six Years*, pp. 164, 165.
6. *O.R.*, Ser. 1, XXXIX, part 3, 538. Jacob D. Cox, *The March to the Sea;
Franklin and Nashville* (New York, 1882), pp. 16, 17. Hereafter cited as
*Franklin and Nashville*.
7. *O.R.*, Ser. 1, XXXIX, part 3, 637, 653, 673–74.

Schofield left for Pulaski where he assumed command of the forces assembling there on the morning of November 14.[8]

Hood's invasion then appeared a virtual certainty. Unable to contend effectively with Sherman who greatly outnumbered him, Hood had decided to try to capture Nashville and there gain supplies and reinforcements. Plans after that were vague. Perhaps he would continue on into Kentucky to the Ohio River, or turn to meet Sherman if he should come back from Georgia, or maybe even move eastward through Cumberland Gap and join forces with Lee in Virginia by attacking Grant from the rear. Lee could then choose whether to "annihilate Sherman [Hood's words]" or march on Washington.[9] If nothing else, Hood's plans testify that "hope springs eternal within the human breast."

The general purport of Schofield's instructions from Thomas was that he should hinder Hood's advance as much as possible in order to gain time for the concentration of all available forces and especially for the arrival of Smith's command from Missouri.[10] He was not supposed to try to whip Hood himself. He had about 22,000 infantry consisting of Stanley's IV Corps and a portion of the XXIII Corps, and a small section of cavalry, probably 3,500, under General Edward Hatch.[11] Hood would be advancing with about 40,000.[12] These numbers, of course, did not remain constant during the ensuing campaign. Schofield's force was increased as he retired toward Nashville picking up garrison troops and more cavalry, especially after General James H. Wilson took command of the latter at Lynnville. The Confederate numbers decreased somewhat, particularly the cavalry which was spearheading Hood's invasion. By the time of the contest at Spring Hill and Franklin, the Confederates actually engaged were not a great many more than the Federals.

Schofield remembered Hood well from their days together at West Point. He said Hood was "a jolly good fellow" who had been a little discouraged by unexpected hard work. He had especially

8. *Ibid.*, XLV, part 1, 886.
9. John Bell Hood, *Advance and Retreat* (New Orleans, 1880), p. 266.
10. *O.R.*, Ser. 1, XLV, part 1, 340, 1085, 1108. J. D. Cox, *The Battle of Franklin, Tennessee, November 30, 1864* (New York, 1897), pp. 21 ff. Hereafter cited as *Franklin*.
11. Livermore, *Numbers and Losses*, p. 131. *O.R.*, Ser. 1, XLV, part 1, 52, 970. Cox, *Franklin and Nashville*, p. 18.
12. Thomas Robson Hay, *Hood's Tennessee Campaign* (New York, 1929), p. 78.

experienced difficulty with math. Hood had also been more interested in the girls than in his studies.[13] In a class of fifty-four, Schofield graduated seventh from the top, Hood tenth from the bottom.[14] But it was eleven years later and the contest was no longer academic.

Schofield had little more than arrived at Pulaski when Stanley greeted him with disturbing news, pointing out the isolated position the Federal troops were occupying. Upon hearing Stanley's objections to the position, Schofield, as yet unfamiliar with the terrain, halted Cox's division about four miles north of the town. There they were in position to cover a road from Lawrenceburg until Schofield had time to consider the situation.[15]

Indeed there was reason for concern. Pulaski was thirty miles south of Columbia and the crossings of the Duck River, from which ran the turnpike and the railroad to Nashville some forty-five miles north of Columbia. Sixteen miles to the west of Pulaski lay the town of Lawrenceburg with a direct road to Columbia by way of Mount Pleasant. This situation invited the superior Confederate force to race for the bridges at Columbia which were guarded by less than 800 men.[16] If Schofield's retreat were thus cut off, Hood might march directly into Nashville, the largest Union supply depot in the West. And to make matters worse Schofield's cavalry force was too small for the necessary scouting. General Edward Hatch's command would be facing the aggressive veteran Forrest, advancing with some 7,000 troopers. Accurate information regarding Hood's movements would be difficult to obtain.[17]

Soon aware of the danger of his exposed position, Schofield sent a dispatch to Thomas on Sunday afternoon, November 20, suggesting that he move his main force to Lynnville, halfway to Columbia. His message summarized the situation well. In fact it was almost prophetic: "If Hood advances, whether his design be to strike this place or Columbia, he must move via Lawrenceburg, on account of the difficulty of crossing Shoal Creek. Under cover of his cavalry he can probably reach Lawrenceburg without our

13. Schofield, *Forty-Six Years*, pp. 14, 29. Dyer, *The Gallant Hood*, p. 23.
14. *Official Register*, 1853, p. 7.
15. *O.R.*, Ser. 1, XLV, part 1, 885. Schofield, *Forty-Six Years,* p. 167.
16. *Battles and Leaders*, IV, 441, 442.
17 General Hatch thought Hood was advancing as early as Nov. 8. There were continual rumors of an advance. *O.R.*, Ser. 1, XXXIX, part 3, 708, 768.

knowledge and move his forces a day's march from that point toward Columbia before we could learn his designs, and thus reach that point ahead of us; or he might move upon this place, and, while demonstrating against it, throw his forces onto the pike north of us, and thus cut us off from Columbia and from our reinforcements. Lynnville would be free from these objections as a point of concentration for our forces. . . ."[18] Thomas replied that there was little hope of seeing Smith's troops before Friday and expressed hope that Pulaski might be held till then. But he agreed with Schofield that if Hood attempted to get in his rear, it would be necessary to retire to Columbia.[19] Although Schofield clearly believed it best to leave Pulaski, in deference to Thomas' wish to hold on if possible, he said he would "consider the matter more maturely before deciding." Anyway, he thought, Hood "cannot reach here before Tuesday at best." It had been raining for several days and the roads seemed almost impassable.[20]

At noon, November 21, he informed Thomas that he would move two divisions to Lynnville and leave Stanley at Pulaski with the other two. Then, if Hood advanced, Stanley could join him at Lynnville. Again he expressed his belief that Hood could not get this far "while the roads are so bad," and Smith might be able to join up before they got better. It would "be well to avoid the appearance of retreating when it is not necessary."[21]

Feeling assured that he had time to make his dispositions without haste, Schofield started Cox's division back to Lynnville on the morning of the twenty-second and planned to move Stanley back the next day, with Cox then continuing on to Columbia. On November 23 Stanley got underway around 2 P.M. and bivouacked at Lynnville late that night. Cox, meanwhile, had moved to within seven miles of Columbia when he called a halt for the night.[22] But on this day the movement of Hood's advance nearly kept pace with that of Schofield's.[23] Schofield, camping at Lynnville with Stanley, did not realize this until near midnight when he received a message from General Thomas H. Ruger in

18. *O.R.*, Ser. 1, XLV, part 1, 956.
19. *Ibid.*, p. 957.
20. *Ibid.*, pp. 957, 958.
21. *Ibid.*
22. *Ibid.*, pp. 974, 1020.
23. Hay, *Hood's Tennessee Campaign*, p. 81. Cox, *Franklin and Nashville*, p. 65.

Columbia revealing that Capron had been fighting the enemy all day and had been driven back to Mount Pleasant.[24] Now alive to the peril of the situation, Schofield, at 1 A.M., November 24, dispatched an urgent message to Cox, leading his advance: "All information indicates that Hood is nearer Columbia tonight than I am. . . . I desire you to march at once to or near Columbia and hold the enemy in check as far out as practicable long enough for Stanley to get in. . . . The question is to concentrate the entire force at Columbia in time."[25]

Without sufficient cavalry to inform him accurately of Hood's movements, Schofield had depended too much upon his conviction that the bad weather would retard Hood's movement. Hood was pressing him more closely than anticipated. However, Hood's infantry was not as close to Columbia as Schofield apparently thought. Schofield's dispatch was received by Cox about 4 A.M., and before daylight he was marching for Columbia.

About seven-thirty, when two miles from town, he arrived at a crossroad leading westward to the Mount Pleasant pike. Cox sent his trains on into Columbia and turned his command off to the left, striking for the pike, which he had learned was about a mile away.[26] Firing could be heard in the distance. Cox reached the pike at an intersection about three miles from Columbia. He was just in time to interpose his infantry, moving at the double-quick, between Forrest's cavalry and the brigade of Colonel Capron, which was being driven back rapidly. But Cox's infantry soon checked the Confederate cavalry, and a line was formed behind Bigby Creek. Schofield, at the head of Stanley's column, rode into Columbia about ten o'clock. As fast as the Union troops arrived at Columbia, Schofield set them to throwing up earth works to

24. O.R., Ser. 1, XLV, part 1, 1000.
25. Ibid., p. 1020. Years later Schofield said: "That action was magnified at the time, and afterward, into evidence of a race between our troops and the enemy for the possession of Columbia. In fact, Ruger's troops at Columbia were quite capable of holding that place against Forrest, and Hood's infantry was not within a day's march of either Cox or Stanley until after both had reached Columbia"—Forty-Six Years, p. 168. At 1 A.M. on Nov. 24, 1864, he said to Cox: "I have directed Gen. Ruger who is at Columbia, to communicate with you. His force there is very small"—O.R., Ser. 1, XLV, part 1, 1020. Schofield was right in saying that if Forrest had taken Columbia, there was no infantry support within less than a day's march. Forrest would have had a difficult time holding the town—probably an impossible one.
26. O.R., Ser. 1, XLV, part 1, 1020, 1021.

cover the approaches from the south, while the trains were sent across the river.[27]

After making an examination of the ground, Schofield was satisfied that Hood would try to turn his position, and he informed Thomas of his decision to prepare an interior and shorter line which could be held by about 7,000 men. When it became necessary he could retire to this line and send the greater part of his force north of the Duck River.[28]

On the morning of November 26, Schofield received Thomas' orders to hold the north bank of Duck River, keeping Hood south of the river until the Union forces could be concentrated to take the offensive, the orders indicating that Smith's force was arriving or about to arrive at Nashville. It had been raining all day, but Schofield now had a pontoon bridge across the river. That afternoon he ordered the bulk of his trains to the north bank and prepared to move infantry and artillery over after dark. However, the rain had rendered the approaches to the bridges practically impassable, so the crossing was postponed.

By that evening, leading infantry elements of Hood's army had deployed in front of Columbia, taking over from the cavalry. The next day the Army of Tennessee completed its deployment. That night at Confederate headquarters, three miles south of Columbia, Hood laid out a bold plan to execute a flank movement on the Union left. He would place the main body of his army at Spring Hill, twelve miles north of Columbia and directly across the one good road to Franklin and Nashville. He would then be in excellent position to attack Schofield's force as it moved northward.[29]

Schofield, expecting Hood to try a flank movement and believing he had held on as long as it was safe for him to do so, crossed Duck River the same night. He destroyed the railroad and pontoon bridges. The next day he was under heavy fire from Hood's troops. During the morning he sent dispatches to General Thomas discussing the situation and suggesting the concentration of his forces so that he could be ready for prompt movement. This had special reference to the withdrawal of Cooper's brigade from Centerville, where it had been placed by Thomas. Early in the

27. *Battles and Leaders*, IV, 443, 444. Cox, *Franklin and Nashville*, p. 65.
28. *O.R.*, Ser. 1, XLV, part 1, 1016, 1018, 1036.
29. *Ibid.*, p. 657. Hay, *Hood's Tennessee Campaign*, p. 82.

afternoon Schofield learned from General Wilson, now commanding the Union cavalry, that Forrest's cavalry had forced a crossing
of the river near the Lewisburg turnpike, about twelve miles to the
east, and had driven the Federal cavalry back past Rally Hill. Thus
the Confederate cavalry was on Schofield's left flank, but by nightfall it was still not certain whether Hood was using his infantry in
this movement. Schofield may well have considered Forrest's move
only a feint to draw him away from Columbia and thus leave open
the road from Columbia to Franklin for the advance of Hood's
army. It would have been foolish, on the basis of the information
he had, for Schofield to have pulled out of Columbia at that time.
He would have been giving the good road to the Confederates.

He relayed the information to Thomas and inquired where he
proposed to concentrate if it should prove true that Hood was
moving in force upon the Federal rear by the route his cavalry
had taken. He also asked for a pontoon bridge to be sent from
Nashville and placed across the Harpeth River at Franklin. No
answer reached Schofield until eight o'clock the next morning.[30]

The sun rose about seven o'clock on November 29. Shortly
before that hour Schofield received a dispatch from General Wilson,
dated 1 A.M., November 29.[31] Wilson said that information from
prisoners indicated that the whole of Forrest's cavalry was in his
front and that three pontoon bridges were being laid above Huey's
Mill for the passage of Hood's infantry. The bridges had been
expected to be ready by 11 P.M. of the preceding day. Wilson
believed that Hood was "aiming for Franklin," and advised that
Schofield ought "to get back to Spring Hill by ten A.M." with his
entire force.[32] Wilson then, instead of regrouping and riding for
Spring Hill to join Schofield and help secure his line of retreat,
continued to retire toward Franklin. Schofield would have no
cavalry assistance that day.

30. *O.R.*, Ser. 1, XLV, part 1, 341, 403, 1106–7, 1109–10.
31. Cox, *Franklin*, p. 26. Actually he received a duplicate of one written at
one o'clock, and sent from Hurt's Crossroads. The one o'clock original evidently miscarried. Schofield later wrote that he received the message "about
2 A.M."—Schofield, *Forty-Six Years*, p. 210. At 8:15 A.M. of the twenty-ninth he
informed Wilson: "I have received your dispatch of 1 A.M. and will act upon
it"—*O.R.*, Ser. 1, XLV, part 1, 1143. If Schofield had received this dispatch
"at about 2 A.M." he probably would not have waited until 8:15 A.M. to reply.
32. *O.R.*, Ser. 1, XLV, part 1, 1143, 1150, 1151. Schofield resented Wilson
telling him to "get back to Franklin without delay" as if he were giving the
orders. Notes on Cox's *Franklin and Nashville*, Schofield MSS.

Schofield was not at all sure that Hood was driving for Franklin or Spring Hill. But even though Wilson's information was based upon reports of prisoners, Wilson seemed so sure of its truth that Schofield determined to act upon it. He sent Stanley, with two divisions and the army's trains, marching for Spring Hill. He also instructed Ruger to pull in his detachments down the river and move "at once" to Spring Hill, leaving one regiment at the ruins of the railway crossing as an outpost till night. Cox's division was ordered to hold on at the river till night and then march for Spring Hill. This would prevent Hood from using the turnpike for moving his artillery. Schofield determined to find out for sure what Hood was doing. He directed Thomas J. Wood to send a brigade on a reconnaissance in force up the river and learn the truth in regard to the crossing of the enemy's infantry.[33]

He had little more than given the orders when he received General Thomas' dispatches of the evening before.[34] Thomas expressed the wish that Schofield should retain his position at Duck River till the arrival of Smith, if he were confident of his ability to do so. If it were true that Hood's infantry had crossed the river, he would have to make preparations to take up a new position at Franklin behind the Harpeth. Schofield wrote afterward that "the situation early in the morning [of the twenty-ninth] had been a very simple one," but that the receipt, about 8 A.M., of Thomas' dispatch of the previous evening had upset all his plans and that instead of getting back to Spring Hill and Franklin, he "determined to keep the main body of troops together and trust to Stanley's [one division] to hold Spring Hill until the army could reach that point."[35]

It is difficult to know whether Schofield was influenced more by the dispatches from Thomas or by his own idea of what Hood would do. Between seven-thirty and eight o'clock Hood opened a "lively" artillery fire from Columbia. Undoubtedly most of his artillery with some of his infantry was still in Schofield's front.[36] If Hood were crossing the river to the east with the greater part

---

33. *O.R.*, Ser. 1, XLV, part 1, 147, 148, 341, 1142, 1143.

34. Cox, *Franklin*, pp. 25, 27, 28. Schofield, *Forty-Six Years*, pp. 211, 212. Further evidence of this is attested by the orders to Ruger and Stanley, before and after 8, which are significantly changed, as well as his dispatch to Wilson of 8:15.

35. *O.R.*, Ser. 1, XLV, part 1, 1108. Schofield, *Forty-Six Years*, pp. 214, 215.

36. Cox, *Franklin*, p. 27.

of his infantry, he might strike down the right bank to attack
Schofield's left. He could probably do this by noon. This is apparently what Schofield assumed most likely. He countermanded
his first order to Stanley to take two divisions to Spring Hill, re-
taining Nathan Kimball's division, while Stanley continued on to
Spring Hill with George Wagner's division. Kimball was to place
his division east of the pike between Duck River and Rutherford's
Creek along with Wood's division to protect the flank. Post's
brigade of Wood's division was to continue its reconnaissance eastward to learn what Hood was doing. And Thomas Ruger's division
was directed to take position on the pike north of Rutherford's
Creek, about half way to Spring Hill. Thus Schofield deployed his
men to meet either possibility: a Rebel movement on Spring Hill
or a strike down the Duck River on his left flank. He then notified
Thomas that he would await the result of the infantry reconnaissance.[37]

The result came shortly after ten o'clock, for Schofield advised Stanley, then marching to Spring Hill, that "Thomas J.
Wood's reconnaissance shows a considerable force, at least, on this
side of the river," adding "I will try to hold the enemy until dark
and then draw back." Schofield later said: " I decided to hold on
to the crossing of Duck River until the night of the 29th, thus
gaining twenty four hours more for Thomas to concentrate his
troops. I did not apprehend any serious danger at Spring Hill, for
Hood's infantry could not reach that place over a wretched country
road much before night, and Stanley, with one division and our
cavalry [which was not there] could easily beat off Forrest."[38] This
story is confirmed by William M. Wherry in his account of the
campaign. Stanley, whose memoirs cannot be said to be favorably
disposed to Schofield, contradicts this, saying that "all said in
Schofield's book as to his foreseeing and providing to meet the
events as they unfolded, is the merest bosh." He "assumes a grand
superiority and wisdom, in each case at variance with the facts,
and appropriates circumstances entirely accidental and the run of
luck in our favor as a result of his wise foresight."[39]

37. William M. Wherry, "The Franklin Campaign," Schofield MSS. O.R.,
Ser. 1, XLV, part 1, 341, 342, 1141, 1142. Hay, *Hood's Tennessee Campaign*,
p. 99. Schofield, *Forty-Six Years*, p. 230. Cox, *Franklin*, p. 27.

38. O.R., Ser. 1, XLV, part 1, 1137, 1141.

39. Wherry, "Franklin Campaign." Wherry testifies the matter "was fully
considered and the decision deliberately made not to retreat at all that day—

Schofield was never inclined to shrink from taking credit for making the necessary dispositions to meet all contingencies. But it is not difficult to believe that Schofield would have considered the possibility that Hood might be trying to flank him at Spring Hill, and to have attempted a calculation as to whether or not the distance and condition of the roads would have allowed Hood to concentrate sufficient force there to make a lodgement on the line of retreat. Actually, it would be surprising if he had not done so. It took no great wisdom to recognize Spring Hill as Hood's possible objective.

November 29 proved to be a beautiful fall day. By 11:30 A.M., Stanley, riding with the head of Wagner's Second Division, was within two miles of Spring Hill when he was advised by a breathless courier that Forrest's cavalry was halfway between Rally Hill and Spring Hill—only about four miles out. The troops were at once double-quicked into the town, the leading brigade (Emerson E. Opdycke's) arriving about 12:30 P.M., just in time to help the garrison troops already at Spring Hill prevent Abraham Buford's division of Forrest's cavalry from occupying the town.[40] Stanley at once deployed his troops, Opdycke's and Joseph Q. Lane's brigades of Wagner's division forming a line from the railroad station, northwest of town, to a point some distance to the east of the village and providing a space in which to park the trains. Luther P. Bradley's brigade, after letting the artillery pass into town, was placed on a wooded hill about three-quarters of a mile east of the Columbia–Spring Hill Pike, commanding the approaches to the town from that direction. Most of the artillery was positioned on a rise south of town. Stanley's disposition of his forces apparently impressed Generals Hood, Benjamin F. Cheatham and Forrest with the idea that a large force was in front of them.[41]

---

Nov. 29th. The important point to hold was the crossing of Duck River at Columbia, so as to delay Hood's use of the turnpike, by which alone he could move any large amount of artillery and trains. It was . . . determined to hold that crossing until the night of the 29th after the cost was fully counted and the measures fairly estimated. . . . Hood failed at Spring Hill, solely because he could not bring up, before dark, troops enough to dislodge those General Schofield had placed there early in the day to hold him in check"—Stanley, *Memoirs*, p. 214.

40. *O.R.*, Ser. 1, XLV, part 1, 113, 229.

41. *Ibid.*, p. 113. *Battles and Leaders*, IV, 444, 445. Stanley, *Memoirs*, pp. 201, 202. Hay, *Hood's Tennessee Campaign*, p. 84. Stanley, in his *Memoirs*, p. 195, said of Nov. 29, 1864: "It was the biggest day's work I ever accomplished for the United States."

About 3 P.M. General Hood was at the crossing of Ruther-ford's Creek, two and a half miles from Spring Hill, with the head of Cheatham's corps (9,800 strong). Forrest's cavalry (about 5,000 effectives) had been in the Spring Hill area since noon. Alexander P. Stewart's corps (8,500) and Edward Johnson's division (2,500) were coming on behind Cheatham.[42] If Hood could drive Stanley's division (about 5,500 plus the garrison cavalry and infantry, alto-gether totaling perhaps 6,500 to 7,000) out of Spring Hill, the Federal army would probably lose its wagon train, and Schofield's main force might be cut off from Thomas' army at Nashville.

Traditionally this has been considered an outstanding Con-federate opportunity, which Hood somehow botched, to panic the Union army and deal it a mortal blow. What occurred in the Con-federate army at Spring Hill has been one of the great mysteries of the war. Explanations of Rebel failure have ranged from wild parties to the providence of God. The perplexity of the problem was recently demonstrated anew when an authority who once thought Hood should have crushed Schofield at Spring Hill re-versed himself, contending that the Federals simply "got there first with the most men," and Hood never had much chance to hurt Schofield's army.[43]

What happened at Spring Hill will probably never be satis-factorily explained. Some who might have shed light on the matter, such as Confederate General Pat Cleburne, were killed the next day at Franklin. Participants who lived to write accounts left records which are often confusing and contradictory about orders, locations, and times of day.[44] One of the most difficult matters to calculate is whether the Rebels, even if Hood and his subordinates had made no mistakes, had time enough on a short November day to march 20,000 men on country roads from Duck River to Spring Hill and deploy them for effective action against entrenched Union troops. It was 15 miles from the Davis ford over Duck River,

42. Hay, *Hood's Tennessee Campaign*, p. 85.

43. Stanley F. Horn, "The Spring Hill Legend," Civil War Times *Illustrated* (April, 1969), pp. 20–32.

44. J. P. Young, "Hood's Failure at Spring Hill," *Confederate Veteran*, XVI, 25–41. W. O. Dodd, "Reminiscences of Hood's Tennessee Campaign," and Benjamin F. Cheatham, "The Lost Opportunity at Spring Hill—General Cheat-ham's Reply to General Hood," *Southern Historical Society Papers*, IX, 518–41. Hood, *Advance and Retreat*. Campbell H. Brown, "To Rescue the Confederacy," Civil War Times *Illustrated* (December, 1964), pp. 13–15, 44–48.

where Hood crossed his infantry, to Spring Hill. And some of the soldiers had to march a mile or two before they even reached the ford.[45]

When one realizes that the *head* of Hood's infantry column was still two and a half miles from Spring Hill at three o'clock, that the Federals had 6,500 or 7,000 men entrenched at Spring Hill as early as two o'clock (supported with two batteries of artillery while the Rebel artillery was at Columbia), that the first Confederate infantry did not get in position to render assistance to Forrest's cavalry, which was low on ammunition, until about four o'clock, and that sunset is about 4:30 in late November with darkness coming by 5:15, he is forced to conclude that the Confederate chances to destroy the Union army have been magnified by some writers.[46]

On the other hand, one hesitates to say that the Rebel flanking movement could not have succeeded, that Hood had attempted the impossible. The contest for Spring Hill was so close that just a little change could have made a significant difference. A more capable Confederate commander, even a more healthy Hood (he lost a leg at Chickamauga and the use of an arm at Gettysburg), might have been able to eliminate some of the delay and confusion in organizing Rebel ranks for an assault in time to drive Stanley from Spring Hill before Schofield could reinforce him.[47]

Perhaps the greatest danger for the Union army at Spring Hill was at noon when, if Stanley had been just a little later, Forrest's troopers might have taken the town from the garrison defenders. But even if they had, it is questionable whether they could have held it in the face of an infantry assault by Stanley's division. Once it became clear that the Rebel efforts to drive Stanley's men out of Spring Hill were not going to succeed, the Confederate alternatives were limited. If the Rebels had succeeded in seizing the pike south of Spring Hill they would have been placing themselves between the two portions of the Union army, possibly in a more dangerous position than that of their enemy. And this would not have pre-

45. The writer has examined the route of march carefully and about fifteen miles is the shortest possible distance.

46. See the official reports of the Union and Confederate commanders, particularly Bate, Cheatham, Hood, Schofield, Stanley, Stewart, and Wagner, in the *O.R.*, as well as the sources cited in note 44.

47. It is not the purpose of this study to attempt to detail what went wrong in the Confederate army at Spring Hill. The reader is referred to Hay, *Hood's Tennessee Campaign*, and Horn, *Army of Tennessee*.

vented the Federals from leaving the pike and coming into Spring
Hill or continuing north on a parallel road farther to the west.
In fact it is possible that some of the Union army may have
marched into Spring Hill by such a route after turning off the pike
to the west about two miles south of the town.[48]

A better move for Hood would have been to make a lodgement
on the pike north of Spring Hill. This was what Schofield seemed
to fear most. Indeed, Forrest was on the pike north of town sometime earlier in the evening but left, probably because he did not
have enough ammunition. The Confederate ordnance wagons were
in the army's rear and, as already noted, Forrest's troopers were low
on ammunition earlier in the day. But an infantry lodgement on
the pike north of town, even if possible (which is doubtful in view
of the confusion in Confederate deployment caused by darkness
and other factors), would have done nothing to take away the
possibility of the Union army moving to the west and continuing
its retreat northward. And it would have taken a strong contingent
on the pike to prevent the Federals from breaking through. In any
event, Schofield did not have to continue his retreat. Stanley was

---

48. *O.R.*, Ser. 1, XLV, part 1, 742. Cheatham, "The Lost Opportunity," p.
527. It has always been assumed that the Federal army marched into Spring
Hill on the Columbia–Spring Hill pike. But it seems possible that this was
not the case. Evidence is furnished in the campaign report of Confederate
division commander, General William C. Bate. Bate, who had been instructed
by Hood to move west to the pike and then "sweep toward Columbia," approached the pike on the right of the Nat Cheairs house, which faces the
pike from the east. It was then getting dark, said Bate, and his leading
element—Caswell's battalion—fired on a Federal column approaching from
their left, a little south of the Cheairs house. Bate stated in his report that
"He [the enemy] veered to his left . . . and took a road leaving the pike. . . ."
Bate reported his contact with the Federal force to General Cheatham, his
corps commander, but Cheatham seems not to have been impressed. These
Federals who Bate says left the pike could have been from Ruger's division,
the leading element of Schofield's main body, advancing north from Columbia.
It seems only natural, considering how soldiers will follow one another in line
of march, that the entire Federal force could have filed off on the road to
the left and come into Spring Hill on a different road. This view is also
consistent with the personal reconnaissance which Confederate General
Edward Johnson said he made later in the evening, during which he saw
no Federals on the pike, and returned to his headquarters.
The road in question left the pike about two miles south of Spring Hill.
The Union army could have marched first west and then north again by a
country road which finally would have brought them onto a road leading
into Spring Hill from the west. By this road Schofield could have led the
army into Spring Hill, about two and a quarter miles distant.

in a good defensive position at Spring Hill. Schofield had all his trains and artillery and almost as many soldiers as Hood had. He might have placed the rest of his army in position and accepted battle at Spring Hill with a good chance of successfully meeting a Rebel attack.

It may well be argued that Schofield risked too much in staying so long at Columbia. The chances of placing his army in a dangerous position were too great when compared with what he hoped to gain: a little more time for Thomas to concentrate his forces at Nashville. And the writer strongly suspects that the affair at Spring Hill developed into a much tighter situation than Schofield expected (though, of course, Schofield never even intimated such a thing). Regardless of these factors, it seems clear that the Rebel's chances of cutting off Schofield at Spring Hill were not nearly as good as has generally been supposed in Confederate legend.

It was about 3 P.M. when Schofield became satisfied that he would not be attacked in force at Columbia, but that, instead, Hood was marching to seize his line of retreat at Spring Hill.[49] He then led Ruger's two brigades by a rapid march to Spring Hill, leaving staff officers to give orders to the other division commanders to follow shortly. Schofield's escort brushed away a Confederate picket from the road as he drew near Spring Hill, and he rode in about seven o'clock.[50]

Once in Spring Hill Schofield conferred with Stanley and learned that no help could be expected from Wilson's cavalry and that some of Forrest's troopers had been seen at Thompson's Station, about three miles to the north on the road to Franklin. Fearing that the enemy had occupied a favorable position across the turnpike, Schofield led Ruger's division to try to force a way through to Franklin.[51] To his surprise nothing was found at Thompson's but smoldering campfires, and the Union forces took possession of the crossroads without opposition. Schofield ordered his headquarters troop, under chief engineer Captain William J. Twining, to go at full gallop down the road toward Franklin and telegraph the situation to General Thomas. Twining was

---

49. *O.R.*, Ser. 1, XLV, part 1, 342. Cox, *Franklin*, p. 34.
50. *O.R.*, Ser. 1, XLV, part 1, 114, 342. Cox, *Franklin*, p. 34.
51. Wherry, "Franklin Campaign." *O.R.*, Ser. 1, XLV, part 1, 342. Cox, *Franklin*, p. 5.

also ordered to examine the means of crossing the river. Schofield then "sat motionless" on his horse and listened until the clatter of hoofs on the hard road died out in the distance. He turned and rode back to Spring Hill, satisfied that the road was clear. He arrived shortly after General Cox came in with his division, representing the rear of the army.[52]

It was then about midnight and the weather was frosty. Schofield ordered Cox to take the advance at once and march to Franklin, still twelve miles distant. Stanley was ordered to take charge of the trains and follow immediately. From about one o'clock until five o'clock of the morning of November 30, Stanley was occupied with getting about a thousand wagons, one at a time, across a single bridge at Spring Hill. About three o'clock a Confederate cavalry force attacked in "considerable force," but was beaten back after about a dozen wagons were lost. On the march the next morning Confederate cavalry again made a flank attack but was repelled.[53] Cox, who had taken an "easy gait" so as to avoid outmarching the trains (which would string out for about five to seven miles), approached the outskirts of Franklin around four-thirty in the morning.

In the meantime, Schofield, after issuing his final orders at Spring Hill, had ridden to the front and overtaken Cox. As they approached one of the outermost houses, Schofield ordered him to mass his division on both sides of the turnpike, leaving the way clear for the trains to come in. Weary men settled down to snatch a few minutes sleep or boil coffee while Schofield rode on into town to find Twining and learn the condition of the river crossings.[54] He hoped to find a pontoon bridge spanning the Harpeth which had been swollen by the recent rains. On November 28 and again at 1 P.M. on November 29, he requested a bridge.[55] With this he could get all his artillery and trains as well as his infantry across the river before Hood could arrive in sufficient force to attack. But there was no bridge.

52. Schofield, *Forty-Six Years*, pp. 173, 174. *Battles and Leaders*, IV, 447. Cox, *Franklin*, p. 34.
53. *O.R.*, Ser. 1, XLV, part 1, 114, 115. Stanley, *Memoirs*, p. 205.
54. Cox, *Franklin*, pp. 37, 38. W. W. Gist, "The Battle of Franklin," *Tennessee Historical Magazine*, VI (October, 1920), 220. Charles T. Clark, *125th Ohio Volunteer Infantry: Opdycke Tigers* (Columbus, Ohio, 1895), p. 332 *O.R.*, Ser. 1, XLV, part 1, 349.
55. *O.R.*, Ser. 1, XLV, part 1, 1107, 1108, 1138.

Schofield then rode quickly to the house of the F. B. Carter family, which Cox had commandeered as his headquarters. Rousing his division leader from a doze into which he had fallen, he spoke, according to Cox, with "a deep earnestness of feeling which he rarely showed."[56] The pontoons were not there, the county bridge was gone, and the ford hardly passable. But Schofield had made his decision. He would throw up a line of field works and fight, if he must, with a river at his back, thus hoping to save the wagon train. Cox was ordered to entrench upon the best line that could be located, placing the troops in position to hold Hood back until the trains could be crossed over the river. The artillery of the XXIII Corps was to be crossed by the ford as quickly as possible. When that of the IV Corps came in, Cox was to place it in position on the line. The first wagons which were already beginning to come in were ordered into the town and parked in the cross streets, leaving the main thoroughfare open.

Schofield then went to see what could be done to improve the means of crossing, upon which so much depended. The approaches to the ford received attention first. The banks on both sides had to be scraped since the grade was not practicable for heavy laden army wagons. There was a railroad bridge and a detail was ordered to ransack the town for planks to put this in condition for crossing. Then the approaches to it for wagons had to be constructed. The wagon bridge had been burned in a skirmish earlier in the season, but not wholly destroyed. The posts of the bridge were sawed off at the water's edge, and new cross beams and stringers attached and planked over. This was intended only for the passage of troops, but it was found that wagons could be crossed over it if care were taken. It was nearing noon, however, before any other crossing was practicable for wagons except the ford, which entailed a slow and laborious process. The pontoons for which Schofield had telegraphed two days before arrived from Nashville by train in the course of the morning—too late to be of help.[57]

As soon as the artillery reached the north bank Schofield ordered Giles J. Cockerill's battery of three-inch rifles placed in Fort Granger atop a high bluff overlooking the river. This was

56. Cox, *Franklin*, p. 39.
57. *Ibid.*, pp. 39, 49, 50. Clark, *125th Ohio*, p. 328. Bennett and Haigh, *36th Illinois*, pp. 647, 648.

approximately a mile from where the Union line was being formed and commanded the approach from the south and east. The rest of the cannon were parked nearby.[58] Schofield was finally in touch with his cavalry again. Wilson was some two and a half miles to the east on the road to Triune. One of Schofield's first acts at Franklin was to send directions to Wilson to cover his immediate flank and rear during the day. He revealed his lack of confidence in the cavalry: dispatching Thomas, he said: "I do not know where Forrest is. . . . Wilson is entirely unable to cope with him."[59]

Franklin lies in a bend of the Harpeth, with the opening to the south. From the river the land rises gently for a mile or more to the site of the Carter house, from which a plain slopes ever so slightly away, continuing a mile and a half to the Winstead Hills which form a southern enclosure. This area has been likened to the left hand, held palm up, and pointed south. The palm represents the village, the little finger and thumb the Harpeth River. The three fingers from the left to the right represent the Lewisburg, Columbia and Carter's Creek Pikes entering the town from the south. The Tennessee and Alabama railroad came up from the south, east of the Columbia Pike and crossed the Harpeth just east of the town and the turnpike bridge.[60]

At various times the town had been occupied and slight entrenchments thrown up on its southern outskirts. But these had become partially obliterated and were of little value. The thud of the pick and the clink of the shovel were heard once more. Men worked as rapidly as tired bodies would permit. Gradually an earthwork took shape with a slight ditch in front. John S. Casement's brigade, east of the Columbia pike, placed headlogs on their works and abatised their front with Osage orange branches. The losses among "Jack" Casement's troops would be relatively light. All along the line there were salient angles for crossfiring at intervals and embrasures for the artillery.[61]

Schofield's line extended in a rough semicircle, enclosing the

58. O.R., Ser. 1, XLV, part 1, 432.

59. Ibid., 1117, 1145, 1169.

60. Hay, Hood's Tennessee Campaign, pp. 118, 119. Hugh Walker, "Bloody Franklin," Civil War Times Illustrated (December, 1964), p. 18.

61. Pinney, 104th Ohio, p. 60. Levi T. Scofield, "The Retreat from Pulaski to Nashville," A Paper Read Before the Ohio Commandery of the Military Order of the Loyal Legion of the United States, December 1, 1886 (Cincinnati, 1886), p. 138. O.R., Ser. 1, XLV, part 1, 426.

town. Both the left, which began upon a knoll at the railroad yard close to the river, and the center were held by the XXIII Corps (Cox's and Ruger's divisions). These covered the Lewisburg and Columbia Pikes. Ruger's division extended on westward nearly to the Carter's Creek Pike. Here the line was broken, Kimball's division of the IV Corps occupying the right and extending north west toward the river. Wood's division of the IV Corps was placed at the fort on the north bank of the river to defend the trains and cover the flanks.[62]

By noon much of the apprehension of the Federal troops had been relieved. The placing of Kimball's division on the right would complete the line in front of the town. All the troops were in except Wagner's rear guards, still skirmishing in the distance beyond the Winstead Hills with the enemy's advance. The Columbia Road, which had been crowded all the morning with double lines of wagons coming in, was empty and relative quiet followed the rattling of wheels and the clatter of arms and tools. The troops at the breastworks were resting or getting their noonday meal. Many of them, too tired to get dinner, simply lunched on crackers and raw bacon and dozed. The day was bright and warm—a good example of Indian summer.[63]

Schofield was in town with Stanley at a house near the public square belonging to a Dr. Cliff. Cliff was a Union sympathizer and a friend of Stanley's from Ohio. Once Schofield had seen the necessary work well underway, he retired to this house and slept briefly. Then he ate dinner with Dr. and Mrs. Cliff.[64] Schofield, Cox, and Stanley did not expect an attack. In his campaign report Stanley wrote: "Nothing appeared so improbable as that they would assault."[65] And Cox later said, "None of us were quick to believe that a *coup de main* would be attempted."[66] The same opinion was held by many of the general officers.[67] Schofield held a formidable position. Hood had not been willing to attack fortified lines at Columbia. Now, with the trains in and the troops entrenched, an attack seemed most improbable. When Hood did move again,

62. Hay, *Hood's Tennessee Campaign*, p. 118.
63. Pinney, *104th Ohio*, pp. 59, 60. Cox, *Franklin*, pp. 62, 63.
64. Cox, *Franklin*, p. 68. John K. Shellenberger, *The Battle of Franklin* (Cleveland, 1916), p. 37.
65. *O.R.*, Ser. 1, XLV, part 1, 115.
66. Cox, *Franklin*, p. 68.
67. Gist, "Battle of Franklin," pp. 220–22. Thompson, *112th Illinois*, p. 267.

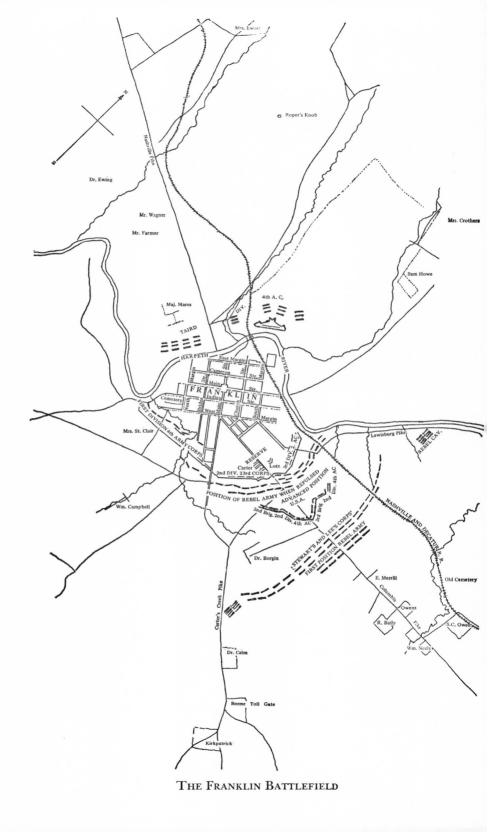

THE FRANKLIN BATTLEFIELD

Schofield expected him to try to turn his position by crossing the Harpeth to the east. All of the day's correspondence between Schofield and Thomas was based on this expectation.[68]

Wagner's division came in near noon and was directed to halt on the heights south of the town and observe the enemy, retiring if too severely pressed. The enemy came on with two heavy column's of infantry and Wagner fell back. Two of his brigades (Lane's and Joseph Conrad's) were halted about a quarter of a mile or less[69] in front of the main Union line and astride the turnpike from Columbia. The purpose was to compel Hood to disclose his intention. If an assault were attempted these brigades were to fall back within the main works.[70] If a flank movement developed they could swing eastward, the more quickly to check Hood until a new line of battle could be formed. Opdycke's brigade of Wagner's division came in and took position in back of the Carter house and west of the pike in a reserve status.[71]

Soon after Wagner's division was in, the head of Hood's army came over the Winstead Hills. Stewart's troops, leading the advance, began to file off the pike in line of battle to the east. A soldier in the 104th Ohio was observing from the Union line east of the pike. He watched for some time as the Rebel host continued to increase. Impressed with the splendor of the occasion, he later wrote that it was "one of the grandest pageants we had ever beheld."[72] The picture was soon to change, and Sam R. Watkins, a private in gray, would write: "Would to God that I had never witnessed such a scene."[73] Cheatham's corps was filing off to the west of the pike. Stephen D. Lee's corps, which was not all up, was being posted in reserve. Forrest's cavalry was stationed on both flanks. The artillery was not yet up, nor would it be.[74]

Schofield, meanwhile, anticipating the transfer of his troops across the river at dark, had moved his headquarters to the north side of the river to the house of a Mr. Alpheus Truett on the east side of the pike to Nashville. This was about a half mile from the

68. *O.R.*, Ser. 1, XLV, part 1, 1169, 1170, 1171. Cox, *Franklin*, p. 68.
69. *O.R.*, Ser. 1, XLV, part 1, 115, 231, 240, 270.
70. *Ibid.*, 342, 348, 349, 352, 1174. Stanley's instructions to Wagner were: "The General commanding directs that you hold the heights you now occupy until dark, unless too severely pressed. . . ."
71. *Ibid.*, p. 232.
72. Pinney, *104th Ohio*, p. 60.
73. Watkins, *"Co. Aytch,"* p. 218.
74. Hay, *Hood's Tennessee Campaign*, p. 119.

river and within easy riding distance of the vantage point at Fort Granger. About three o'clock he issued orders for the troops to be withdrawn at nightfall.[75] By then the Confederates had been in view for some time. They kept advancing slightly, stopping and correcting their lines at intervals. A soldier in the 26th Ohio watched from his advanced position on the west of the Columbia Pike: "One from a distance might easily imagine them out for drill or inspection or preparing for a grand review. It was an imposing sight."[76] Schofield did not visit the line to view the spectacle, evidently depending upon Cox to let him know if there were reason to expect an assault. Shortly before 4 P.M. the gray line, eighteen brigades strong, moved forward to the attack.

Schofield was riding with Stanley from the Truett house toward the river when Wherry met him with the news that the enemy was about to assault. Stanley galloped to the front to take command of his corps. Schofield turned to his left and rode into the fort. One account of the battle places Schofield still at Dr. Cliff's house when news came of the attack. Then, the writer says, "when Stanley started for the front, Schofield started for the rear. . . . After crossing the river Schofield rode to the fort . . . on the high bluff."[77] Evidently this account is wrong. Cox and Wherry both attest that Schofield's headquarters had been moved to the Truett house sometime around 2 o'clock.[78] And Stanley, in his memoirs, says, "I . . . was north of the Harpeth River, near Gen. Schofield's headquarters when [the battle began]."[79] This complements Wherry's account perfectly, and Stanley never showed any inclination to twist the truth to defend Schofield. Schofield said he was on the north bank of the river.[80]

Schofield was later criticized by some for remaining on the north bank at the Fort instead of assuming immediate command on the line. John K. Shellenberger speaks of him being "well beyond the range of every rebel bullet that was fired,"[81] and James B. Steedman spoke more bitterly: "We do not say that General Schofield is a rank coward, but we can, from personal knowledge, safely state

75. Cox, *Franklin*, pp. 68, 87.
76. Gist, "Battle of Franklin," p. 222.
77. Shellenberger, *Battle of Franklin*, pp. 39, 40.
78. Cox, *Franklin*, pp. 280, 281.
79. Stanley, *Memoirs*, p. 207.
80. Schofield, *Forty-Six Years*, p. 177.
81. Shellenberger, *Battle of Franklin*, p. 40.

that he possesses the 'rascally virtue called caution' in an eminent degree. . . . We never knew him to be reckless enough to expose his carcass to the fire of the rebels."[82]

Schofield's action is not difficult to understand. Dispatches from Wilson's cavalry gave him good reason to believe Hood was attempting to place a portion of his infantry across the Harpeth, two or three miles to the east.[83] This was what Schofield feared the most. Some kind of flanking attack was the reasonable move for Hood to make.[84] It was to meet just such a contingency that Schofield had placed Wood's division on the north bank, as well as positioning batteries in the fort. Shortly after three o'clock, he ordered a brigade to "move up the river" and help check the crossing of the enemy to the east.[85] If Hood were attempting to flank him, Fort Granger was the logical position for the Union commander, even if a simultaneous assault were being made on his front. Pre-

---

82. James B. Steedman, "Robbing the Dead," New York *Times*, June 22, 1881.

83. Shortly before 2 P.M., Wilson reported "rebel infantry approaching Hughes' Ford, three miles above Franklin, apparently with the intention of crossing." A little before 3 P.M. Wilson said: ["The movement] has not yet developed itself into anything more than the appearance of the enemy's infantry in the neighborhood of the river. Citizens say they can cross anywhere." In a 3 P.M. dispatch, Wilson reported: "enemy charged the picket at Hughes' Ford and he [bearer of the dispatch] thinks crossed." Upon receiving this message Schofield ordered a brigade of infantry to Hughes' Ford, "to check the crossing of the enemy at that point," and so sent word to Wilson–though Wilson later said he never got the dispatch—*O.R.*, Ser. 1, XLV, part 1, 1178. James H. Wilson, *Under the Old Flag*, 2 vols. (New York and London, 1912), II, 51. At the same time Schofield dispatched Thomas that Hood "now has a large force, probably two corps, in my front, and seems prepared [so recorded in Schofield's telegram-sent book, but in Thomas' telegrams-received book these words are "preparing" and "above"] to cross the river above and below. I think he can effect a crossing tomorrow . . . and probably tonight, if he attempts it. A worse position than this for an inferior force could hardly be found. . . . I have just learned that the enemy's cavalry is already crossing three miles below" [so recorded in Schofield's telegrams-sent book]—*O.R.*, Ser. 1, XLV, part 1, 1170. When reports came that the enemy was assaulting, the brigade which had been directed to Hughes' Ford was ordered to put itself on the left flank of the Fort instead—*ibid.*, p. 150.

84. Hood's own commanders were unfavorable to a head-on attack. Cheatham "did not like the looks of the fight," and Forrest strongly advised a flanking movement to the right across the river (just where Schofield expected it). With an infantry column to support, he said he could "flank the Federals out in 15 minutes." There is evidence that Cleburne did not favor the assault, though he did not live to take part in the later controversy. Much evidence from men in the Confederate ranks is of the same persuasion. Hay, *Hood's Tennessee Campaign*, pp. 120, 121. Gist, "Battle of Franklin," pp. 222, 223.

85. *O.R.*, Ser. 1, XLV, part 1, 1174.

sumably, Cox and Stanley could handle that. W. W. Gist, who is critical of both Schofield and Cox, admits, in another connection, that "the north bank of the river . . . would be the point of the greatest danger in case Forrest forced a crossing."[86] As Wherry said: "Fort Granger . . . was very close to the railroad bridge [which, planked over, afforded communication with the line] and was the prolongation of our left, only separated from the line of battle on that flank by the narrow stream. It overlooked the front nearly to the Columbia Pike at the Carter house, and was where communication with the reserves [Wood's division] and line of battle could best be had."[87]

The fort also afforded a view for some distance to the left and rear. It was only a little over a mile from Cox's headquarters on the line, not two miles as has been stated in some accounts. It was the place where he could best see the overall picture and determine what was happening; and, as Cox said, "where alone he could see the cavalry demonstrations on the left where Forrest and Wilson were . . . engaged."[88] Schofield has also been criticized for not riding to the front line earlier when the enemy began to deploy, in order to examine the situation in person. With field glasses, however, he could readily see what the Confederates were doing from the fort.

As Hood's lines advanced, a long line of rabbits scurried across the field. Several coveys of quail were flushed from their coverts.[89] Union batteries in Fort Granger began booming shells over the heads of the Federals and into the advancing lines. Union soldiers, watching behind cocked guns, waited in fear and suspense. The Confederate line gradually converged as the field narrowed in front of the Union works.

Wagner's two brigades, astride the Columbia Pike, became confused about how long to hold their ground and did not retire from their advanced position. They checked the Confederate avalanche momentarily, but then the Rebels came on harder than ever. They could see the foe on both flanks and they turned and ran. The Confederates raced them to the Federal line. For fear of hitting their own men, the Federal artillery on the pike

86. Gist, "Battle of Franklin," p. 220.
87. Cox, *Franklin*, p. 286, gives a copy of the letter which Wherry wrote to him.
88. Cox, *Franklin and Nashville*, p. 87.
89. Levi T. Scofield, "The Retreat from Pulaski," p. 133.

did not fire. Neither did a part of the brigades on each side of the pike. In the confusion some of the men in these brigades gave ground. The Confederates, encouraged by the unexpected Union blunder, poured in. A crucial moment was at hand when the battle had little more than started. But the break did not spread. Colonel Emerson Opdycke's brigade, resting some two hundred yards behind the main line, charged to plug the gap. The other troops rallied, and after a few minutes of hand-to-hand fighting the line was restored.[90]

The fighting at Franklin was as fierce, bloody, and horrible as any which took place in any battle of the Civil War. As the smoke of burned powder obscured the view and daylight faded into twilight and darkness, the Confederates charged again and again. The fighting continued until between nine and ten o'clock, with men firing at the flashes of guns. But the brunt of the action took place, and the contest was decided in little more than an hour, between about 4 and 5:30 P.M. Hood suffered 6,252 casualties. Schofield had 189 killed, and a total of 2,326 killed, wounded, and missing.[91] Hood lost 1,750 dead at Franklin, more than Grant at Shiloh, McClellan in the "Seven Days' Battle," Burnside at Fredericksburg, Rosecrans at Stone's River and Chickamauga, and Hooker at Chancellorsville.[92] Considering the relative smallness of the armies involved and the brief time they were engaged, the loss is all the more appalling.

While the infantry held the line, the cavalry checked Forrest's efforts to move on the east. Forrest's command had been divided, one division being on the Confederate left flank. Parts of two divisions did cross the Harpeth on the east but were hard pressed by Wilson's troopers, who outnumbered them. They retired about 5 P.M. Hood did not attempt to cross any infantry.[93]

When it became obvious that the enemy was repulsed, Schofield completed preparations to withdraw the army to Nashville.

90. *O.R.*, Ser. 1, XLV, part 1, 116, 270, 271, 256, 240, 349, 352–54. Much controversy has centered around the question of responsibility for the two brigades remaining in front once the Confederate line moved forward. Both Wagner and Cox, to judge from their official reports (and Cox contributed two reports, the second apparently to correct the errors of the first) deserve a part of the blame for the costly mistake.

91. Livermore, *Numbers and Losses*, pp. 131, 132. See also Schofield's campaign report.

92. Walker, "Bloody Franklin," p. 16.

93. Hay, *Hood's Tennessee Campaign*, p. 126.

Cox was sure that the line could be held and wanted to remain. But Thomas had directed that Schofield move back to Brentwood and Nashville. The enemy had been severely punished since Thomas sent the order, but Schofield felt that withdrawal was still the wisest move.[94] Once all the Union forces were concentrated at Nashville, the Confederate invasion would have no chance whatever of success. A description of Schofield as having "fled to the protection of the fortifications at Nashville"[95] after the Battle of Franklin is misleading. Not only is it inconsistent with earlier evidences of coolness under fire, such as at Wilson's Creek, but in addition the Union cavalry commander, Wilson, whose memoirs could hardly be described as sympathetic to Schofield, wrote that he supported the withdrawal and took note of the calmness which Schofield showed after the battle as he prepared to remove the troops to Nashville. Schofield was at the Truett house with Stanley when Wilson came in. Stanley's coat was bloody and his neck wrapped in bandages, as he had suffered a wound in the back of the neck. Schofield impressed Wilson as being calm, not "excited or disturbed to the slightest degree," but busy arranging the withdrawal. Schofield thanked Wilson for the cavalry's service in preventing Forrest from crossing the Harpeth: "It insures the safety of this army, for, notwithstanding our great victory . . . we should not have been able to withdraw from Franklin, or to maintain ourselves there, but for the defeat and repulse of Forrest's cavalry, which was evidently aiming to turn our left flank and throw itself upon our lines of retreat."[96]

Schofield sent Thomas news of the battle, instructed Wilson to hold his position until daylight, and then began withdrawing the infantry to Nashville.

94. *O.R.*, Ser. 1, XLV, part 1, 344, 1169–71. Cox, *Franklin*, p. 102.
95. Cox, *Franklin*, p. 287.
96. *Battles and Leaders*, IV, 467. Wilson, *Under the Flag*, II, 54.

# VIII. Schofield, Thomas, and the "Siege" of Nashville

THE CIVIL WAR bequeathed an almost inexhaustible legacy of questions concerning its leading contestants and engagements. These questions, not surprisingly, have run the gamut from the trivial—where did Stonewall Jackson get his lemons? What commentaries did he rely upon when he studied the Bible?—to mysteries and controversies which have a bearing upon the duration if not the outcome of the war—Was Grant truly a great general or merely a "butcher" who, given enough troops, finally bludgeoned the enemy into submission? Did the Lee of legend really exist or were the Union commanders in the eastern theater incompetents? One of the interesting questions of the war centers around the relationship between Schofield and Thomas on the eve of the Battle of Nashville, December 15–16, 1864. Did Schofield intrigue to replace Thomas as commander of the Union forces at Nashville? And one of the interesting controversies revolves about the significance of that battle. While one of America's foremost historians of the Civil War has disposed of the Battle of Nashville in less than two pages in one of his books, another well-known writer has contended that Nashville was the decisive battle of the war.[1] How significant actually was the engagement at Tennessee's capital city?

Near nine o'clock in the evening of November 30, General

1. Bruce Catton, *Never Call Retreat* (New York, 1965), pp. 411, 414. Stanley F. Horn, *The Decisive Battle of Nashville* (Baton Rouge, 1956), especially pp. v–xiii.

Thomas was at the Saint Cloud Hotel in Nashville when he received Schofield's victory telegram. Hood had struck and his assault had been thrown back with heavy losses. The news was a great relief. Through much of November, Thomas had seemed "reticent and gloomy" to those around him and habitually wore his hat pulled down over his eyes. Worrying over Schofield and the arrival of Smith, he had been especially troubled on this day. Now, wrote Colonel James F. Rusling, his assistant quartermaster, "his hat [was] up and [his] face all aglow."[2]

Schofield, with Thomas J. Wood, who had replaced the injured Stanley, rode in some time before midnight. Thomas greeted him, as Schofield remembered it, in his "usual cordial but undemonstrative way," and congratulating him, said he had "done well."[3] Schofield replied that he hoped "never again to be placed in such a position," and later wrote that he did not feel very grateful to Thomas.[4] While Schofield and Thomas were talking, Rusling came in with news that Smith was arriving. He had heard the steamboat whistles down on the Cumberland. Within minutes Andrew Jackson Smith walked in and Thomas "literally took him in his arms and hugged him. . . ."[5] Perhaps Schofield was impressed with the difference in the greeting Thomas gave the two. But soon they were all discussing the fight at Franklin. Early in the morning of December 1, Schofield, Thomas, Smith, and Wood had maps spread on the floor and were down on their knees examining the positions for the troops around Nashville.[6] The conference ended; Schofield, who had no sleep the night before and precious little for several days preceding, retired to his room and slept for nearly twenty-four hours.[7]

The one-legged Hood, having misled the Confederate government into believing that he had won a victory at Franklin while neglecting to inform them accurately of the extent of his losses, was once more strapped to his saddle and riding toward Nashville.[8] With one arm dangling useless at his side and 6,000 of his fighters

2. James F. Rusling, *Men and Things I Saw in Civil War Days* (New York, 1899), p. 86.

3. Schofield, *Forty-Six Years*, p. 226.

4. JMS to J. D. Cox, December 5, 1881, Schofield MSS. Schofield, *Forty-Six Years*, p. 226.

5. Rusling, *Men and Things*, pp. 87–88.

6. *Ibid.*

7. Schofield, *Forty-Six Years*, p. 226.

8. *O.R.*, Ser. 1, XLV, part 2, 643, 650.

dead and wounded on the plain north of the Winstead Hills in Franklin, he was a fitting symbol for the shattered army he led. Considering losses in earlier skirmishes, disease, and stragglers, he now had, at the most, 25,000 men.[9] He would be outnumbered more than two to one, but still he came to "invest" the city. And when the Battle of Nashville was fought he was still further weakened, having detached some of Forrest's cavalry and portions of two brigades of infantry to Murfreesboro, not to mention the hardships of the weather on his poorly equipped men.[10] It is very doubtful that Hood had 20,000 effectives in the line on December 15 when the battle began.

The Confederate commander's plan—a strategy conceived in defeat and desperation—was to entrench on the southern outskirts of the city, await the enemy's attack, and hope for reinforcements from Texas—so he later wrote.[11] On the morning of December 2, the line of battle began to form and the "siege" of Nashville began. Hood was far too weak to attack the city. Nashville was probably as strongly fortified as any city in America.[12] His hope for reinforcements was without foundation—possibly a later thought to try to justify his decision to push on to Nashville, for there is no evidence that he had any real reason to expect reinforcements.[13] Nor were there any acceptable alternatives. To swing around the Federals and head for the Ohio River was to invite an attack in flank and rear by superior Union forces. The Confederate invasion of Kentucky in 1862 was testimony that no significant number of Rebel recruits could be obtained in that state. To march for Virginia to join Lee was just as unrealistic. To retreat was to admit defeat. The Union commanders at Nashville were not incompetents who might be expected to play into Hood's hands with the type of reckless assault which enabled Lee to punish Burnside so severely at Fredericksburg—the only thing that might have given

9. Livermore, *Numbers and Losses*, p. 133. Hood himself claimed only 23,053 effective troops when he reached Nashville (*Advance and Retreat*, p. 299).

10. Horn, *Decisive Battle*, p. 69.

11. Hood, *Advance and Retreat*, pp. 299, 300.

12. Horn, *Decisive Battle*, p. 24.

13. Beauregard twice wrote Kirby Smith in the Trans-Mississippi Department, the only conceivable place he could think of where Hood might get reinforcements, but Kirby Smith never received the messages until the Battle of Nashville had been fought. When he finally replied on January 6, 1865, he explained in detail why he could send no troops to Hood. *O.R.*, Ser. 1, XLV, part 2, 639, 766.

Hood a chance at even a standoff. Thus having decided to come to Nashville, his greatest mistake for the unfortunates in his army, Hood did the only thing he could—wait until the Federals should drive him back in rout.

The Cumberland River loops around Nashville enclosing the city on the east, north, and west. The Union had built two lines of defense. The exterior line extended from the river on the east to the river on the west. The interior and shorter line ran from the Cumberland on the west in a southeasterly direction to the Franklin pike where it joined the exterior line.[14] With the arrival of Schofield and Smith, the Federal force at Nashville had been increased by over 30,000, bringing the total to about 53,000.[15] The exterior line, about twice as long as the Confederate, was held, from left to right, by the corps of Steedman, Schofield, Wood, Smith, and Wilson. The Rebel line lacked about four miles of reaching the river on the west and about a mile on the east. Even though it was shorter than the Union line it was too long for the number of troops that Hood had to defend it, and he still did not control all the roads into Nashville, the alleged reason for the line being as long as it was.[16]

There seemed to be only one problem for the Union—getting Wilson's cavalry better mounts and equipment. On December first, Thomas wired Halleck at Washington in something of an understatement: "If Hood attacks me here he will be more seriously damaged than he was yesterday; if he remains until Wilson gets equipped, I can whip him and will move against him at once."[17] This telegram soon inaugurated a series of proddings from Washington which did not cease until Thomas moved to the attack. Halleck turned Thomas' telegram over to Secretary Stanton who talked with the President that same day. Lincoln did not like the idea of Thomas laying in fortifications indefinitely until Wilson got equipped. It looked "like the McClellan and Rosecrans strategy of do nothing and let the enemy raid the country."[18] Stanton

14. Horn, *Decisive Battle*, pp. 24, 29.
15. Livermore, *Numbers and Losses*, p. 132.
16. To cover the long stretch between the western end of the infantry line and the Cumberland River Hood had only James R. Chalmer's division of Forrest's cavalry. Robert S. Henry, *First With the Most Forrest* (Indianapolis, 1944), p. 402.
17. *O.R.*, Ser. 1, XLV, part 2, 3.
18. *Ibid.*, pp. 15, 16.

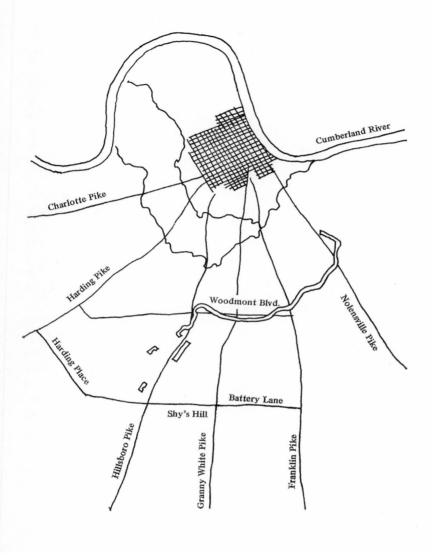

Cumberland River

Charlotte Pike

Harding Pike

Woodmont Blvd.

Nolensville Pike

Harding Place

Battery Lane

Shy's Hill

Hillsboro Pike

Granny White Pike

Franklin Pike

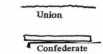

Union

Confederate

NASHVILLE: UNION AND CONFEDERATE LINES

wired Grant, giving him the President's reaction and telling him
to "consider the matter."[19]

Grant applied himself with characteristic bulldog tenacity,
sending Thomas two telegrams that same day advising an attack
"before Hood fortifies." He continued to write, directing Thomas
as to details and warning that Hood would wreck the railroads or
cross the river and move into Kentucky. On the sixth he wired,
"Attack Hood at once," and on the eighth the hero of Vicksburg
told Halleck that Thomas was too cautious to ever take the initiative, and if he "has not struck yet he ought to be ordered to hand
over his command to Schofield."[20] Grant's nervousness seems out
of character. But, like some others in Washington, he may not
have appreciated the hopelessness of Hood's situation, thus tending to exaggerate what Hood might be able to accomplish. On
the other hand, if he thought Hood's position hopeless, then he
could see no reason to hesitate in administering the *coup de grace*.
And he was being pressured from above.

Thomas was at last ready to attack, but at daylight on the
ninth freezing rain poured upon Nashville, continuing all day
and leaving the ground a sheet of ice. Sleet and snow fell on the
tenth. Men and horses could hardly walk and the attack was
delayed.

Schofield's role in these days became a matter of controversy
after the war. On the cold and icy evening of December 10,
Thomas invited his corps commanders to a meeting at the Saint
Cloud Hotel. Schofield, Wood, Smith, Steedman, and Wilson
listened as Thomas told them of Grant's orders to attack and then
expressed his belief that obedience was impracticable.[21] Wilson,
who later wrote an account of the conference, declared that as
he was the junior corps commander present in years as well as in
rank, he spoke first and expressed his full approval of Thomas'
decision to withhold battle. The other corps commanders were
equally outspoken, except Schofield, who "sat silent and by that
means alone, if at all, concurred in the judgment of those present. . . ."[22]

Schofield always told a different story, claiming that Thomas

19. *Ibid.*
20. *Ibid.*, pp. 17, 70, 96. Such an order was made out but cancelled.
21. Thomas B. Van Horn, *The Life of Major General George H. Thomas*
(New York, 1882), p. 320.
22. Wilson, *Under the Flag*, II, 100–102.

had been ordered to surrender his command (though he did not say to whom) unless he attacked Hood at once. One of the corps commanders asked Thomas to show them the order. Thomas declined, which Schofield said confirmed his belief that the successor could be none other than himself. Therefore, in order to save Thomas from the humiliation of being removed from command and without waiting for an opinion from the junior members of the council according to the usual custom, Schofield immediately replied that he would sustain Thomas in his determination not to fight until he was fully ready. Then all the other commanders expressed their concurrence.[23]

Still another account, that of Steedman, contradicts Schofield's and tends, with minor variations, to confirm that of Wilson. Steedman charged Schofield with "deliberate falsehood when he [said] that, as the ranking officer next to the commanding general, he waived his right to speak last and promptly sustained General Thomas." Schofield, said Steedman, spoke last and then only said he "would obey orders." Steedman went on to charge that Schofield, intriguing to replace his commander, had been telegraphing Grant that Thomas was too slow in his movements.[24] Schofield always denied the charges of "the viper," as he afterwards referred to Steedman. No dispatches to Grant were ever found.[25] And in 1881, when Steedman's accusations were published, Schofield wrote Grant, as "the only man able to effectively deny the charges," and asked him to pen a refutation. Grant wrote that he never received any messages from Schofield or anyone else disparaging Thomas. However, several of Thomas' biographers leave the impression that Schofield sent the messages and never mention Grant's testimony to the contrary.[26] A strong circumstantial case can be presented to substantiate their view.

Schofield himself said that he came in from Franklin believing that Thomas had been "unnecessarily slow" in concentrating his

23. Schofield, *Forty-Six Years*, p. 238. Cox, *Franklin and Nashville*, p. 105, said in a footnote, that he followed Schofield's account of the conference.

24. Steedman, "Robbing the Dead."

25. Sanford Cobb Kellogg, aide-de-camp to Thomas, thought that in 1879 the evidence had been removed from the War Department file. McKinney, *Education*, p. 403.

26. Schofield, *Forty-Six Years*, pp. 294, 295. Cleaves, *Rock of Chickamauga*, pp. 259, 260. McKinney, *Education*, p. 403. O'Connor, *Thomas*, pp. 360–63. Van Horn, *Life of Thomas*, p. 321, says that Thomas regarded Schofield as unfriendly to himself.

forces, had not fully informed him of his plans and above all, had not sent the pontoons which he requested to enable him to bridge the Harpeth until they were too late to be of use. Seventeen years later Schofield was evidently still keenly moved as he remembered. He wrote Cox: "General Thomas did not even attempt to help me, but cooly [*sic*] and curtly told me to use the bridge I had at Columbia."[27]

Schofield also wrote that he did not esteem Thomas' military abilities as highly as some others did.[28] No other evidence than his autobiography is required to believe this. If Steedman's account, which is bitter and indicates a considerable capacity for hatred, is accepted, Schofield had made remarks at Chattanooga showing he "envied and hated" Thomas because of the way the soldiers loved and honored him.[29] Thomas told Chaplain Thomas B. Van Horn, according to Van Horn, that he felt he would have an enemy in his command when first he heard that Schofield with his corps would join him from Georgia.[30] Shortly after the Battle of Nashville, Schofield did not hesitate to criticize Thomas' proposed spring campaign into the deep South in an unofficial letter to Grant on December 27, stating that it "would not be an economical or advantageous use of so many troops."[31] Schofield requested a transfer to Sherman's army. The next day he wrote a similar letter to Sherman.[32] And Thomas was not the only officer about whom Schofield complained to the general-in-chief. While in Missouri, of course, he had written Halleck complaining about General Curtis who was then his department commander.[33]

As further evidence against Schofield, it has been argued that when he was nearly dismissed from the U.S. Military Academy because of the blackboard obscenities affair, he felt that Thomas, is one of two out of a court of thirteen who did not vote for remission of the sentence, had been unjustly harsh to him. And it has been asserted that Schofield was in communication with Secretary Stanton who told him of the financial necessity of ending

27. JMS to J. D. Cox, December 5, 1881, Schofield MSS.
28. Schofield, *Forty-Six Years*, p. 242.
29. Steedman, "Robbing the Dead."
30. Van Horn, *Life of Thomas*, p. 321.
31. *O.R.*, Ser. 1, XLV, part 2, 377, 378.
32. JMS to W. T. Sherman, December 28, 1864, Schofield MSS.
33. JMS to H. W. Halleck, November 18, 1862, Schofield MSS. According to *O.R.*, Ser. 1, XIII, 793, this letter was "Not found." Also see *O.R.*, Ser. 1, XXII, part 2, 94, 95.

the war as quickly as possible since the floating of war bonds was becoming so difficult and the price of gold was dropping. Therefore, the armies must move![34]

What can be said in defense of Schofield? He wrote in his autobiography that he talked with Stanton in January, 1865, when passing through Washington, and only then learned of the financial necessity that the war be ended. If he had corresponded with Stanton on this subject previously, there is no record of it.[35] Schofield said he did not find out about Thomas' action when he was a cadet until 1868, when as Secretary of War, he had access to the records.[36] It is interesting to note that Colonel Henry Stone, on the staff of Thomas, if he knew of such intrigue, preferred to remain silent about it, saying: "Never had a commander a more loyal corps of subordinates. . . ."[37] Colonel Rusling, if he knew about the matter, likewise failed to mention it. And Wilson seemingly knew the story about Schofield's alleged dispatches only through Steedman's publication.[38]

But it is difficult to explain why Steedman would have invented his story of Schofield's intrigue. The writer has been able to discover no motive. And probably most significant, such intrigue would appear to be in character with what Schofield had done earlier in Missouri. At first glance it might seem difficult to explain the statement by Grant in defense of Schofield. In answer to Schofield's request Grant replied: "There never was any dispatch from you to me, or from you to any one in Washington, disparaging General Thomas' movements at Nashville. . . . I feel very sure that if any dispatches had been received from you I should now recollect it. . . ."[39]

Indeed it does seem that Grant would have "recollected" if Schofield sent him such dispatches! Would Grant have lied about it? It is interesting to remember that later during his Presidency when Grant discovered his private secretary among the culprits involved in the Whiskey Ring, he volunteered a written statement for the jury which helped his friend to escape. One might pursue

34. Ed Huddleston, "The Civil War in Middle Tennessee," The Nashville Banner, part IV, November 14, 1964.
35. Schofield, Forty-Six Years, p. 255.
36. Ibid., p. 241.
37. Battles and Leaders, IV, 457.
38. Wilson, Under the Flag, II, 100–102.
39. Schofield, Forty-Six Years, pp. 294, 295.

another line of thought, however. Is it likely that Grant would have lied when the truth (assuming that Schofield sent the dispatches) would have certainly helped to substantiate his own well-known criticisms of Thomas' slowness? If Schofield really sent the dispatches, then it might be reasoned that self-interest would have demanded the truth from Grant. On the other hand, when Grant wrote the statement to Schofield, Thomas had been dead eleven years. Grant might have felt that nothing was to be gained by further criticism of a man who had been so long in the grave. It may well have seemed to him that he should do what he could to squelch the story of Schofield's intrigue and thus help out a friend. Grant was usually loyal to his friends. It should also be noted that in searching the papers of Schofield the writer never found the letter from Grant or a copy of it, except in Schofield's auto-biography—published long after Grant was dead.

Whether Schofield sent such messages or not—and it seems likely that he did—and whether at the conference of commanders he spoke first, last, or at all, and regardless of whose account is accepted, the evidence is conclusive on one point: Schofield was never willing to acknowledge that there had been any necessity for Thomas' delay prior to the storm.

In addition to the testimony of Wilson and Steedman to this effect, there is an interesting statement in one of Schofield's letters to Cox. Addressing him from Rome, December 5, 1881, Schofield was obviously disturbed by the thought that his own words were being interpreted as condoning Thomas' delay at Nashville. He wrote: "I have been quoted as claiming priority in the support given by subordinates to General Thomas at Nashville in respect to his delay. I never meant to claim anything of the kind. On the contrary, I presume all the corps commanders deserve more credit than I do in that regard. What I do claim is very different, viz: that when the crisis came in which I alone could give him the effective support he needed to save him from impending humiliation, I promptly and emphatically gave him that support without waiting for the advice or opinion of anyone."[40]

Sherman and Grant both complained that Thomas was too slow. Some writers have discounted such criticism as simply professional

40. Schofield MSS. In his autobiography, Schofield wrote: "Indeed, Thomas could have given battle the second or third day after Franklin with more than a fair prospect for success" (236).

jealousy or a personal dislike for Thomas. But there was good reason to question Thomas' decision to wait about attacking. The usual reason given by his defenders for his delay is that he needed more time for Wilson to get the cavalry ready and that he wanted to be thoroughly prepared, planning the attack carefully and giving the Confederates no chance. The necessity of more time to prepare the cavalry has been exaggerated. What chance did the Confederates have and how long does it take to plan?

Forrest's troopers were less numerous and in poorer condition than when the campaign began, while the Union cavalry was more numerous and thus relatively stronger. The Rebels were greatly outnumbered and had just been severely hurt at Franklin. All the Union forces were united and their morale high. Were not the Rebels given much more time to recover from the shock of Franklin and prepare to receive an attack than the situation warranted? That the Confederates did not take full advantage of the opportunity to establish the best defensive line possible and could not obtain any reinforcements is, of course, beside the point in evaluating Thomas' decision to hold off the attack for more than a week. Thomas seemed, at least upon this occasion, to lack the killer instinct to press the foe relentlessly once he had an obvious advantage.

Intermittent sleet and freezing rain continued from December 11 until the fourteenth. The weather brought action along the picket lines to a near standstill, interfered with entrenching operations, and caused considerable suffering in the ranks.[41] The Confederates were not as well clothed and equipped as the Federal troops and suffered more. On the morning of the fourteenth, there was a welcome rise in the temperature. A warm sun began to melt the ice and frozen ground. Thomas planned to attack the next day and laconically wired Halleck: "The ice having melted away the enemy will be attacked tomorrow morning."[42] That evening he held a council of war with his corps commanders to discuss his plans of battle. These were basically the same as those for the previously postponed attack. As finally modified at Schofield's suggestion, they called for a feint on the Confederate right, while a grand wheeling movement by the entire Federal right wing overwhelmed the Confederate left. Wood's corps would form the hub

41. Gist, "Battle of Franklin," pp. 254, 257.
42. *O.R.*, Ser. 1, XLV, part 2, 180.

for this wheel, Smith's corps the spoke, and Wilson's cavalry the
rim. Schofield's troops would be in reserve near Smith's left to
become engaged as the course of events might dictate. There would
be a strong demonstration all along the line to hold the enemy
in position. Altogether Thomas would be hurling about 53,000
men at perhaps 20,000 Confederates, and Hood was without a
large portion of Forrest's cavalry.[43]

Schofield's role in the formulation of Thomas' plans of battle
also became a matter of controversy after the war. In 1870 the
Cincinnati *Gazette* and the Louisville *Courier-Journal* published
the orders of General Grant relative to the replacement of General
Thomas prior to the Battle of Nashville. There was an editorial
comment that such a move would have been disastrous. Soon
after this a letter appeared on the front page of the New York
*Tribune* of March 12, 1870, of anonymous authorship, severely
criticizing Thomas' conduct of the Nashville campaign. The writer
implied that General Schofield should have received credit which
went to Thomas.

It was stated, specifically, that it would "have been quite as
easy for Schofield to continue to command after the junction with
Thomas at Nashville, or to resume it after a few days, as it was
to exercise it at and before Nashville." The letter was critical of
Thomas' original plan of battle for the "mistake" of not using
10,000 men (Schofield's XXIII Corps) to advantage, placing them
in the left center where only a feint was to be made, rather than
in position to support Smith's corps which was making the real
attack on the right.[44] Furthermore, Thomas, the critic alleged,
was so fully convinced that the enemy had retreated at the close
of the first day of battle that he gave no orders to continue operations the next day, but ordered a pursuit. The *Tribune* letter
closed with reference to Thomas' generalship in a deeply "cutting"

43. *Ibid.*, part 1, 37. Livermore, *Numbers and Losses*, p. 133.
44. Schofield contended in his autobiography that he did not think Smith's
force was large enough for the real attack and suggested that his corps be
placed in position to support Smith. He claimed that Thomas readily acceded
and the plans were modified accordingly (*Forty-Six Years*, p. 243). Thus the
main attacking force was increased from about 10,000 to about 20,000. Thomas,
in his official report, made no allusion to Schofield's accepted change in plan,
unless the statement that the "original plan of battle, with but few alterations
was strictly adhered to," be so considered (*O.R.*, Ser. 1, XLV, part 1, 39).
Schofield did not appreciate Thomas' failure to give him credit for a suggestion
which he deemed of importance.

manner as "a common subject of pleasant conversation and jest among officers." And, "if his special friends had been so discreet as to 'let well enough alone,' 'Old Pap' Thomas might have died in the happy enjoyment of a reputation for generalship as well as for patriotism and heroic combat in battle." The letter was signed, "One who fought at Nashville."[45]

Thomas told members of his staff that he was certain the anonymous critic was Schofield. It seemed evident from the style of the author and the information at his disposal that he had been a highly placed officer at Nashville. And Schofield was the man most hurt by the opinions that he could not have successfully taken Thomas' place.

In actual fact it appears from a letter which Schofield wrote to Cox October 18, 1881, that William M. Wherry, adjutant-general to Schofield, wrote the letter from notes which Schofield had written, publishing it with Schofield's consent.[46] Thomas informed Colonel Alfred L. Hough that he was going to examine his papers on the Battle of Nashville and prepare an answer bringing to light all the circumstances surrounding it. That very day, March 28, 1870, he suffered a severe stroke of apoplexy and died about 7:30 in the evening. On the desk at which he had been working when stricken was a half finished account of his conduct of the battle.[47]

After the death of Thomas, Schofield refrained from any public criticism of his commander's conduct of the battle of Nashville until he published his autobiography in 1897. In it he dwelt at length on several points of criticism. It really made little difference whether Thomas or Schofield, or if neither Thomas nor Schofield, commanded at Nashville in mid-December, 1864. Under the circumstances of the heavy and irreplacable losses at Franklin, the lengthy and thinly manned Confederate line, and the inept condition of Hood, it is difficult to conceive of any way the Rebels could have stood against the blue juggernaut. The Union, with good execution, feinted an attack on the right and then hurled more troops against the Confederate left than Hood had in his whole army.

Shortly after four o'clock on the morning of December 15,

45. The letter is quoted in O'Connor, *Thomas*, p. 361.
46. Schofield MSS.
47. O'Connor, *Thomas*, pp. 363, 364.

Schofield's men began to move out of their works. Leaving only a picket line, which was later relieved by Steedman's troops, the main body of the corps shifted right to take battle position between the Hillsboro and Harding Pikes. A dense fog, which did not lift until mid-morning, hung over the valleys and concealed the movements. In places snow was still melting and the ground was softening.[48]

Steedman's feint on the east began near eight o'clock. About the same time the guns in the forts and the batteries along the line opened fire. Confederate artillery soon replied and the battle was on. Steedman moved against a battery planted in a rocky ravine, and although the position was not carried, the attack caused Hood to move troops from his center to strengthen his right.[49] Hood had been deceived briefly but he soon discovered Thomas' plans.

While this more or less sham battle proceeded on the Federal left, the main movement developed on the right. Wood, holding the center hub of the wheeling action, had the shortest distance to cover and was soon in position. Until shortly after noon most of his troops remained inactive, except for heavy skirmishing, and waited for the advance of Smith and Wilson to pull even. It was nearing ten o'clock when these two began their big sweep on the Federal right.[50] Their advance drove the thin line of Confederate skirmishers back rapidly. Schofield, following Smith's left, pushed Darius Couch's division forward, to be within supporting distance. He left Cox's division relatively stationary to the left of Couch.[51]

It was about noon when Wilson's and Smith's lines drew within striking distance of the Confederate works along the Hillsboro Pike. Meanwhile, Wood's left lay at the foot of the Confederate advance post on Montgomery hill. The position looked formidable but was actually only lightly held. Since it barred any farther advance, it had to be reduced. Artillery pounded the position, an assault was ordered, and the hill was taken with surprising

48. *O.R.*, Ser. 1, XLV, part 1, 405. Pinney, *104th Ohio*, p. 68.
49. Cleaves, *Rock of Chickamauga*, p. 262.
50. *O.R.*, Ser. 1, XLV, part 1, 437, 551. There was some confusion in co-ordinating their movements and thus the attack was later getting underway than intended. Wilson, in his memoirs, said McArthur's infantry, contrary to plan, crossed Wilson's front, instead of the cavalry's rear (Wilson, *Under the Flag*, II, 109-10).
51. *O.R.*, Ser. 1, XLV, part 1, 345.

ease. The blue line moved forward toward redoubts one and two, the main Rebel stronghold, and Wood's batteries began to shell number one.[52]

Farther to the right, the sound of battle was growing louder as the opposing lines drew closer together. Smith's right and Wilson's left converged on the redoubt fartherest to the south, the outermost outpost of the Confederate left. Here artillery dueled for about an hour, while dismounted cavalry and infantry edged closer. The position, held by only about a hundred defenders with four Napoleon guns, was soon overwhelmed. Immediately attention turned north to redoubt number four, which had suddenly opened fire on the victorious assaulters. It too must be reduced. The lines of Smith and Wood were closing in on the other redoubts. Hood's main line would soon be in dire peril.[53]

Schofield had been with Thomas. They were sitting on their horses in the rear of Wood's right and Smith's left. The position overlooked nearly the entire field. Occasionally a shell exploded near by, causing the horses to make a slight start. Thomas especially liked Schofield's field glasses and frequently reached for them as he surveyed the progress of battle.[54] Little was said. Thomas was hurling overwhelming numbers against the Confederate left. About one o'clock he decided to put in 10,000 more. Smith's advance had borne more to the left than Thomas intended. Schofield was ordered to swing his corps to the right, around the rear of Smith, and form on his right. Schofield quickly put his troops in motion and then rode forward through the slush and mud to find Smith. Smith was near the right of the line, and when Schofield told him of his movement, Smith extended his own line farther to the right.[55]

Schofield's troops, Couch's division in the lead, marched rapidly for about two miles, circling around Smith and crossing the Hillsboro Pike just north of redoubt number five, then in Federal hands. Cooper's brigade soon became heavily engaged. As it passed through an open field, it encountered artillery and musketry fire from a hill in front. Without waiting for orders, the troops double-

52. *Ibid.*, p. 129. *Battles and Leaders,* IV, 458, 459. Horn, *Decisive Battles,* pp. 88, 89.
53. *Battles and Leaders,* IV, 459. *O.R.,* Ser. 1, XLV, part 1, 438, 551.
54. Schofield, *Forty-Six Years,* p. 250.
55. *O.R.,* Ser. 1, XLV, part 1, 38, 345.

quicked it up the hill in the face of death while enemy fire from a stone wall on the left enfiladed their entire line. Nevertheless, the hill was carried. Three pieces of artillery and a number of prisoners were captured. At the same time one regiment changed direction to the left and overran the enemy position along the stone wall. The fighting was fierce. Cooper's brigade suffered more losses than all the rest of Schofield's corps during the two days of the battle.[56]

Immediately south of the hill carried by Cooper, the enemy occupied a still higher one which appeared to be a key position. If it were taken, Schofield could quickly possess the Granny White Pike and cut off one of the enemy's two lines of retreat. Schofield ordered Couch to carry this hill. But about the same time, the din of musketry increased on Schofield's right. The Confederates were counter-attacking and attempting to turn his flank. A sharp engagement then ensued in the valley which Cooper had just passed. Cox's division was coming up and two brigades were sent to support one of Couch's, already holding back the Rebels. Gradually the Confederates were driven back, but the engagement continued until darkness settled over the smoking hill.[57]

Schofield bivouacked for the night about halfway between the Hillsboro and Granny White Pikes. Couch's division dug in on the hill Cooper had taken, occupying a line running east and west; Cox's division was on a north and south line at a right angle from Couch's. Both faced the high hill south of Couch—Shy's Hill, as it would be known in twenty-four hours, named for Colonel W. M. Shy, 20th Tennessee Infantry Confederate, killed in the final effort to hold the position.

When the fighting ended on December 15, Wood and Smith had forced Hood out of his strongest redoubts and rolled up the left of his line. As a result Hood was pushed back well over a mile. He occupied a line only half as long as that of the previous day. But it was formidable. The right salient rested on an eminence known as Peach Orchard Hill, just east of the Franklin Pike, and the left on Shy's Hill, just west of the Granny White Pike. During the night hastily constructed breastworks were thrown up all along the line. Troops were moved from the right to strengthen

56. *Ibid.*, pp. 345, 369, 370, 371, 372.
57. *Ibid.*, pp. 345, 406.

the left which was expected to again receive the brunt of Thomas' juggernaut.[58] Hood was prepared to fight it out to the death.

Sometime after dark Schofield received his orders from Thomas. He found them puzzling. In substance, he was told to "pursue the retreating enemy early the next morning," taking the advance on the Granny White Pike, while the cavalry would start at the same time by a road to the right.[59] Schofield was convinced that Hood would not retreat. Mounting his horse, he rode into Nashville to find Thomas. Schofield later wrote that Thomas "seemed surprised at my suggestion that we would find Hood in line of battle . . . in the morning."[60] Schofield thought it likely that Hood might even launch a counter-attack on the Union right flank. Thomas then ordered that the cavalry remain in position until it became clear whether Hood would fight or retreat. He also sent some of Smith's troops (five regiments and a battery) to reinforce Schofield. These were used to plug a gap between Cox's and Couch's lines.[61] No new orders were issued anticipating the battle the next day. Evidently, the same general plan would be followed—holding down Hood's right and center and hammering his left. Schofield and Wilson's cavalry occupied the key positions.[62]

There is no order from Thomas such as Schofield described, to "pursue the enemy," recorded in the Official Records. Schofield knew this when he wrote *Forty-Six Years In The Army*. Since he has been accused of consciously attempting to make Thomas appear incapable of commanding, and since he said, more than once, that he never had a high regard for Thomas' ability, his account should not be accepted without substantial evidence.

If Schofield did not receive an order such as he described, his attempt to deceive was clever. In his official report, written only two weeks after the battle, which Thomas or some member of his staff would presumably read, Schofield began his summary of the second day of the battle with the statement, "In the night of the 15th I . . . received his [Thomas'] orders for the pursuit of the enemy on the following day." He continued: "Apprehensive that the enemy, instead of retreating during the night, would mass

58. Horn, *Decisive Battle*, pp. 108, 109. Dyer, *The Gallant Hood*, pp. 299, 300.
59. *O.R.*, Ser. 1, XLV, part 1, 345, 346. Schofield, *Forty-Six Years*, p. 244.
60. Schofield, *Forty-Six Years*, p. 245.
61. Cox, *Franklin and Nashville*, pp. 116, 117.
62. Schofield, *Forty-Six Years*, p. 245.

and attack our right in the morning, I requested that a division of infantry be sent to reinforce the right, which was ordered. . . ."[63] It is difficult to believe Schofield would assert this in his report if it were not true. Five regiments and a battery (about 1,500 men) were sent from Smith's corps to Schofield's line.[64] Knowing no such order as he described was to be found, why did Schofield, in his autobiography, specify that it was a written order?[65] If he were manufacturing the story, why not say it was oral?

It is not easy to determine what Thomas thought and did on the night of the fifteenth. In his report, he says: "The whole command bivouacked in line of battle during the night . . . whilst preparations were made to renew the battle at an early hour on the morrow."[66] He does not say what these preparations were. While the Official Records contain orders and instructions issued almost hourly, there is nothing in the record to show what general orders, if any, Thomas issued for the renewal of the battle the next day.[67]

Schofield's corps consumed much of the night entrenching. The enemy, just a few hundred yards in front, could be heard chopping wood, preparing to renew the struggle.[68] Friday, December 16, dawned chilly and slightly foggy. On the left and center Steedman and Wood moved forward early, driving the opposing skirmishers. By noon their lines joined in front of the enemy's right salient on Peach Orchard Hill. To Wood's right, Smith moved into line with Schofield, while Wilson's cavalry on Schofield's right made a wide detour, passed beyond the Confederate left, and drove to secure a lodgment on the Granny White Pike. Only the Franklin Pike would then be left as an avenue of retreat for Hood.[69]

Schofield, whose lines were already in contact with the enemy, spent the morning waiting impatiently.[70] The skirmishing in his front was lively, and his batteries opened a heavy fire on the Confederate line. Couch kept Schofield informed of the situation in his front. Early in the morning he sent word that the enemy was

63. *O.R.*, Ser. 1, XLV, part 1, 345, 346.
64. *Ibid.*, p. 434. Cox, *Franklin and Nashville*, p. 117.
65. Schofield, *Forty-Six Years*, p. 244.
66. *O.R.*, Ser. 1. XLV, part 1, 39.
67. Horn, *Decisive Battle*, p. 113.
68. *O.R.*, Ser. 1, XLV, part 1, 407.
69. *Battles and Leaders*, IV, 460, 461. Dyer, *The Gallant Hood*, p. 300.
70. Rusling, *Men and Things*, pp. 98, 99. Schofield, *Forty-Six Years*, p. 245.

fortifying the position.[71] A flanking column soon appeared on Schofield's extreme right and attempted to dislodge two brigades of Cox's division. Schofield ordered Cox to hold his position and prepare a brigade to move forward and second the movement of the cavalry when they should advance from the southwest. Several attempts were made to force Cox's brigades back, but all met with failure.[72]

By noon the Union and Confederate lines were not more than a few hundred yards apart at any point. Then the "blood-letting" began in earnest. On the Federal left a brigade of Wood's division made a fierce assault on Peach Orchard Hill, but was driven back. Then Steedman threw a Negro brigade at the salient. It was cut to pieces. When Hood saw the determined nature of the attack, he took a division from his left and sent it to succor the right. About the time that Hood was sending assistance to his right, Couch told Schofield that he believed he could carry the hill in his front, but would need assistance to hold it.[73] The artillery had leveled a part of the works and occasionally shells were passing over these ruins and falling at the backs of some of the enemy who were posted at an angle to protect their rear.[74] A little later Couch sent word that "the enemy is not in heavy force on Smith's front." Schofield was reluctant to attack,[75] believing it was not wise to assault except in connection with a general advance. Between one and two o'clock he sent Thomas word: "I have not attempted to advance my line today, and do not think I am strong enough to do so."[76] About the same time he sent Smith a request for a division of troops. Smith had no reserve and so informed Schofield.[77]

It was nearing mid-afternoon. The sky was dark and rain was beginning to fall. Schofield was standing on a small hill, a short distance behind his lines from which he observed the action. Wilson's dismounted cavalry was advancing from the south, apparently intending to carry a wooded hill beyond the enemy's flank and overlooking the Granny White Pike. About this time

71. *O.R.*, Ser. 1, XLV, part 2, 216.
72. *Ibid.*, part 1, 407.
73. *Ibid.*, part 2, 216. *Battles and Leaders*, IV, 413.
74. Henry Romeyn, "Hood's Campaign," *National Tribune*, June 27, 1889.
75. Cox, *Franklin and Nashville*, p. 119.
76. *O.R.*, Ser. 1, XLV, part 2, 215, 216.
77. *Ibid.*, part 1, 435.

Couch informed Schofield that one of Smith's divisions was preparing to assault the high hill in his front. The action then developed quickly. Schofield ordered Couch to support the assault. Wilson was riding to Schofield's position to find Thomas. He had intercepted a dispatch from Hood to James R. Chalmers: "For God's sake, drive the Yankee cavalry from our left and rear, or all is lost."[78] Thomas had been inspecting the Federal lines from right to left. He had just arrived at Schofield's position, and they had little more than exchanged salutations when Wilson rode up.[79]

The climax was near. Already one blue brigade was scrambling up Shy's Hill. General John McArthur of Smith's corps, impatient at the long waiting, was leading his men to the attack without orders. With bayonets fixed, they moved in two lines, not firing, cheering, or halting. Shell, canister, and musketry were thinning their ranks, but they kept climbing. Some who watched were given an eerie feeling by their silence. When they went over the top a great shout was heard from the troops watching on the left. Almost simultaneously two pieces of artillery, dragged up by dismounted cavalry, opened fire on the hill south of Shy's, and the horse soldiers were rushing the enemy from their rear. Two more brigades were following McArthur up the hill. At a sign from Schofield, Cox's division started on the run. Couch's line swept forward after McArthur.

In these few minutes, events transpired so rapidly that it is difficult to know the exact part played by each commander. Thomas gives credit and praise to all, finding fault with no one. His report is a matter of fact, but sheds little light as to the details of action. Schofield says that when Thomas arrived at his position, there was not time to give any orders. The troops were already in motion. Shouts to the left announced that McArthur had carried the enemy's works in his front. He does not mention Wilson being present.[80]

Colonel Rusling wrote that "no order reached Schofield from Thomas until Schofield had already advanced his men."[81] Colonel Henry Stone, a member of Thomas' staff, also gives an account similar to Schofield's. He states that "General Thomas . . . had

78. Wilson, *Under the Flag*, II, 115.
79. Schofield, *Forty-Six Years*, pp. 245, 246.
80. *Ibid.*
81. Rusling, *Men and Things*, p. 99.

no sooner reached Schofield's front than Gen. McArthur . . . set
to work." As the charge began, the cavalry advanced on the other
side. "Everywhere, by a common impulse, they charged the works
in front, and carried them in a twinkling."[82]

Cox says Wilson arrived at Schofield's position, where Thomas
was, just as McArthur led the charge up Shy's Hill. Then he states:
"At a sign from Schofield [his] division started also on the run. . . ."[83]

Wilson says that when he joined Schofield and Thomas some
of the shots from the cavalry's batteries, which were too high, were
passing over the enemy and falling in front of Schofield's corps.
"And yet he gave no orders to advance." Wilson says he pointed
in the direction of the cavalry moving against the left and rear
of the enemy, and impatiently urged Thomas to order the infantry
forward. Thomas scanned the field with what Wilson says he
thought was "unnecessary deliberation." Then Thomas directed
Schofield to attack. Wilson says nothing about McArthur's
charge, nor about Thomas' subsequent actions.[84] It should be
remembered that the feeling between the cavalry commander and
Schofield was not ideal. Schofield had been critical of Wilson's
cavalry before the Battle of Franklin—although he praised their part
at the Harpeth River and in the Battle of Nashville. It is obvious
that Wilson intended for all possible credit to go to the cavalry.
Certainly he gave the impression that if it had not been for him,
neither Schofield nor Thomas would have attacked.[85] Nevertheless,

82. *Battles and Leaders*, IV, 463, 464.
83. Cox, *Franklin and Nashville*, p. 122.
84. Wilson, *Under the Flag*, II, 115, 116.
85. *Ibid*. Cleaves accepts Wilson's record, and following the giving of orders
to Schofield, says Thomas rode over to Smith and pointed to the hills beyond:
"Order the charge." Aides were sent racing to Steedman and Wood, instructing
them to charge. The only source for Thomas' actions that Cleaves gives is
Wilson (*Rock of Chickamauga*, p. 266). McKinney followed in the same path
as Cleaves (*Education*, pp. 413, 414). Van Horn, who tended to glorify Thomas,
said Thomas rode to Schofield's position to hasten the attack. He directed
Schofield to advance, but he was reluctant, fearing to move because of the loss
of men it would entail. Thomas said: "The battle must be fought, if men
are killed." Then Thomas saw McArthur's men advancing and said: "Gen.
Smith is attacking without waiting for you; please advance your entire line"
(*Life of Thomas*, pp. 330–32).
  The Federal action on December 16 was rather haphazard. Whether it was
as uncoordinated as Schofield's memoirs suggest is a moot point. The informal
nature of the attack is evident from the following examples:
  A little after 10 A.M. Wilson dispatched Thomas, through Schofield, suggesting that his cavalry be transferred to the other flank of the army, since

when allowance has been made for Wilson's bias and all the available evidence considered, it seems that Schofield himself, so critical of Thomas for not attacking earlier, was not notably aggressive on the afternoon of December 16.

Some of the Confederates had been waving their colors in defiance and shouting to the enemy, "Come on, come on!"[86] Now the Federals were coming—by the thousands. Beset from the north, west, and south, the Confederates broke and ran down the hill toward their right and rear. As soon as the Federal line farther to the left saw and heard the action on the right, they too charged the works in their front. Everywhere, by a common impulse, the line seemed to be sweeping forward irresistably.[87] Hood wrote: "I beheld for the first and only time, a Confederate army abandon the field in confusion."[88]

The Franklin Pike afforded the only line of retreat, and Rebels by the hundreds were scrambling up hills and struggling through the valleys, making their way to it. Hood, with some of his officers, was on the pike in the drenching rain, trying to rally his men. There was no hope. A Confederate from Columbia said: "It was like trying to stop the current of Duck River with a fish

---

the country in his front was "too difficult for cavalry operations" (O.R., Ser. 1, XLV, part 2, 215, 216). He believed he could annoy the enemy more from that flank, "unless it is intended [underlining mine] that I shall push out as directed last night." Seemingly, Wilson was not quite sure what was expected of him.

Smith said he waited for Schofield's corps to take the initiative (O.R., Ser. 1, XLV, part 1, 435). Schofield later complained of receiving no orders from Thomas (Forty-Six Years, p. 245). His 1 P.M. dispatch saying that he had not attempted to advance his line that day may be consistently interpreted with such a statement (O.R., Ser. 1, XLV, part 2, 215, 216).

General McArthur acted largely on his own initiative in making the charge up Shy's Hill. He consulted Couch and found he had no orders to advance. McArthur then sent word to his superior, Smith, that unless he received orders to the contrary, he would assault the hill. Smith referred the question to Thomas, who had just arrived. Thomas wanted to wait until he heard from Schofield. In the meantime, McArthur simply ordered his men to "take that hill" (O.R., Ser. 1, XLV, part 1, 435; Horn, Decisive Battle, p. 140).

The culminating assault on Shy's Hill came as a surprise to the rest of the Union forces. In fact, the regiments of Smith's corps east of the Granny White Pike had just received orders to entrench for the night and were digging in when it was realized an attack was being made on their right (O.R., Ser. 1, XLV, part 1, 470).

86. Hood, Advance and Retreat, p. 302.

87. Battles and Leaders, IV, 464. O.R., Ser. 1, XLV, part 1, 40. Gist, "Battle of Franklin," p. 259.

88. Hood, Advance and Retreat, p. 303.

net."[89] Schofield pursued into the Brentwood Hills where darkness compelled his troops to stop.[90]

That night Schofield sent a dispatch to Thomas: "I . . . am satisfied Hood's army is more thoroughly beaten than any troops I have ever seen."[91] He also sent word that Forrest had been "killed certainly at Murfreesboro," as he had been advised by citizens. Forrest was still alive, but the former statement was true. Schofield talked with some of the Confederate officers who had been captured. He asked one of them when the Confederate troops had recognized the fact that they were beaten. The officer replied: "Not till you routed us just now." Schofield later wrote that he did not believe him then, for he thought they must have recognized their defeat at Franklin: or at least on the fifteenth at Nashville. "But now I think he probably told me the exact truth. I doubt if any soldiers in the world ever needed so much cumulative evidence to convince them that they were beaten."[92] On the night of December 16 they were convinced. And as they made their way toward Franklin in the dark night, at least one group had improvised a parody of the popular song "The Yellow Rose of Texas." The sodden, bloody troops were singing:

> So now we're going to leave you,
> Our hearts are full of woe;
> We're going back to Georgia
> To see our Uncle Joe.
>
> You may talk about your Beauregard
> And sing of General Lee,
> But the gallant Hood of Texas
> Played hell in Tennessee.[93]

The campaign in middle Tennessee was over. In a very real sense Sherman was right when he said "The Battle of Nashville was fought at Franklin," for after that contest there was no reasonable chance that Hood could have won at Nashville or could have

---

89. Watkins, "*Co. Aytch,*" p. 224.
90. *O.R.*, Ser. 1, XLV, part 1, 346.
91. Schofield, *Forty-Six Years*, p. 248.
92. *Ibid.*
93. Horn, *Decisive Battle*, p. 153. Bell I. Wiley, *The Life of Johnny Reb* (Indianapolis, 1951), p. 121, gives a slightly different version.

accomplished what he had set out to do—whatever it was. His army was half wrecked, there was no way of replenishing his losses, and he had lost the chance of preventing the unification of a far superior Federal force. To continue on to Nashville was a futile act of desperation.

# IX. The Thing Comes to an End

THE PURSUIT of Hood's broken army after the Battle of Nashville proved to be a terrible struggle for both armies. Possibly the worst enemy of Federal and Confederate was the weather, as rain, sleet, and snow, with below freezing temperatures, continually impeded progress and caused much suffering. The pursuit proper did not begin until the morning of December 17. The successful assault on Shy's Hill had been made so late on the sixteenth that darkness had soon nullified the efforts of the Union infantry to follow the fleeing Rebels. Wilson's cavalry had finally been checked in a spirited engagement on the Granny White Pike a few miles south of Shy's and just north of the lane leading east to the Franklin Pike at Brentwood. By morning of the seventeenth, Hood's force had crossed the Harpeth at Franklin and destroyed the bridges. General Thomas ordered a pontoon bridge to Franklin, but due to an unfortunate mistake, the pontoons were sent to Murfreesboro instead.

Schofield was a long way from Franklin anyway. By mid-afternoon of December 17 he had advanced down the Granny White Pike and on to the road which was the continuation of it only as far as the Little Harpeth River. From that point the road turned to the east, striking the Franklin Pike below Brentwood. Schofield could move no farther, for Smith's corps was massed in his front waiting for the pike to be cleared of the trains from Wood's corps. The road was in bad shape and Schofield reported it was "hardly

practicable for artillery."[1] It was December 19 before he managed
to get all of his command to Franklin. The next day he moved to
Spring Hill and on the twenty-second crossed Rutherford's Creek,
establishing his headquarters near Columbia. On a cold Christmas
Day he was still waiting for a second bridge to be completed over
the Duck River. At midnight he telegraphed Thomas that the
structure was nearly completed, the trains of Wood's and Smith's
corps might get over during the day, and as soon as he could
get the bridge he would move forward once more.[2] On the same day,
Hood's advance reached the Tennessee River at Bainbridge, Alabama, near Florence, where they began crossing on a pontoon
bridge. Forrest, who had joined up at Columbia, and the last
of the Confederate rear guard escaped across the Tennessee on
December 27.

The day before, Schofield received a dispatch from Thomas.
The general, "according to present indications," did not think
Schofield's troops would be needed at the Tennessee River. At
"last reports from Wilson and Wood," the enemy was "doing his
best to get out of the way." Thomas then presented the general
features of his plan for a spring campaign, operating from a base on
the Tennessee River. "What do you think of it?" he asked in
conclusion.[3] Schofield did not think much of it, and the same day
he wrote to General Grant at City Point, Virginia, requesting that
his corps be transferred to the East "where decisive work" was
to be done. "I am aware," he informed Grant, "that General
Thomas contemplates a 'spring campaign' into Alabama or
Mississippi. . . ." Such a campaign, in Schofield's opinion, "would
not be an economical or advantageous use of so many troops."
After all, there was little if any fight left in Hood's army, and
even "with time to organize and recruit, he probably could not
raise his force to more than half of the strength he had at
Franklin." Lee's army was "virtually all that is left of the rebellion."[4] "I go for concentrating against Lee," he told Sherman
in a very similar letter written on December 28.[5]

1. *O.R.*, Ser. 1, XLV, part 2, 234.
2. *Ibid.*, p. 349.
3. *Ibid.*, p. 362.
4. *Ibid.*, pp. 377, 378.
5. JMS to W. T. Sherman, December 28, 1864, Schofield MSS. Schofield wrote
in his autobiography: "Had Thomas' plan been carried out, he would have
been ready, with a fine army splendidly equipped, to start from the Tennessee

As the new year began, Thomas was proceeding with his plans for the spring campaign. On the first day of January, 1865, Schofield was ordered to move the XXIII Corps to Clifton, on the Tennessee River, and there embark for Eastport, Mississippi. Having arrived at Eastport, he was to "prepare for an early prosecution of the campaign."[6] The following day Schofield marched from Columbia and reached Clifton on January 8. While he was waiting to embark for Eastport, the orders which he had been hoping for came from Grant. He was to move at once with the XXIII Corps to Annapolis, Maryland.[7]

The transfer was accomplished in a very short time. Grant's orders were received on January 14, and Schofield's corps, beginning the next day, was taken by river transports down the Tennessee, and up the Ohio to Cincinnati, and from there by rail to Washington, D.C., and Alexandria. The movement of about 1,400 miles was completed by February 1, the whole journey being made under the direction of the War Department.[8] Schofield had nothing to do with any details of the trip, being only, as he later described it, "a simple passenger on that comfortable journey."[9]

In spite of the remarkably rapid transfer, there was an unavoidable delay at Alexandria. The Potomac was frozen, thus detaining the transports which were to carry the troops to their new area of operations. While waiting for a thaw, Schofield joined Grant at Fort Monroe and accompanied him on the war-steamer *Rhode Island* down the coast to the mouth of Cape Fear River. There the two consulted with General Alfred H. Terry and Admiral David D. Porter in regard to future operations. When Schofield returned to Washington, an order was issued from the War Department creating the Department of North Carolina and assigning Schofield to its command. His ultimate objective was to occupy Goldsboro, North Carolina, open the railroad from there to the coast, accumulate supplies, and form a juction with Sherman, destroying his way northward through the Carolinas.[10] The com-

River to invade the Gulf States, as had been done the year before, just about the time the plans actually adopted resulted in the surrender of all the Confederate armies. To Thomas' mind war seems to have become the normal condition of the country" (*Forty-Six Years*, p. 256).

6. *O.R.*, Ser. 1, XLV, part 2, 474.
7. *Ibid.*, XLVII, part 1, 909.
8. Cox, *Franklin and Nashville*, p. 147.
9. Schofield, *Forty-Six Years*, p. 345.
10. Cox, *Franklin and Nashville*, p. 147. *O.R.*, Ser. 1, XLVII, part 1, 909.

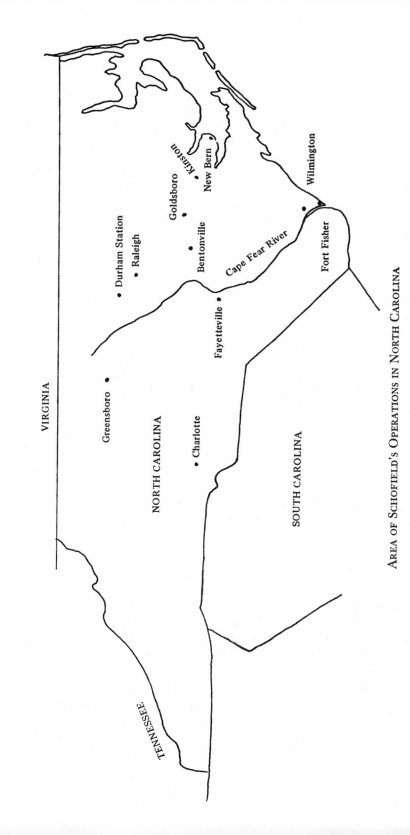

VIRGINIA

TENNESSEE

NORTH CAROLINA

SOUTH CAROLINA

• Greensboro

• Charlotte

• Durham Station
• Raleigh

• Bentonville

• Fayetteville

Goldsboro

Kinston

• New Bern

Cape Fear River

Wilmington

Fort Fisher

AREA OF SCHOFIELD'S OPERATIONS IN NORTH CAROLINA

bined force would then turn upon the woefully depleted "pursuing" Rebel Army of Tennessee or march straight for the rear of Lee's army at Petersburg.

The first objective of the campaign was Wilmington, North Carolina. This would give Schofield a good base from which to operate and secure a possible base for Sherman south of Goldsboro if circumstances necessitated the concentration of his army at an earlier date than anticipated. Schofield embarked from Alexandria with Cox's division on February 4. The rest of the corps was to follow as fast as ships could be obtained. A gale was encountered off Cape Hatteras and the transports were delayed for several hours, but the division landed safely at the mouth of the Cape Fear River, near Fort Fisher, on the ninth.[11] The enemy was then at Fort Anderson, on the west bank of the Cape Fear, just a few miles to the north. General Terry, with about 8,000 men, already held a line across the peninsula about two miles north of Fort Fisher. He also occupied Smithville and Fort Caswell on the west side of the river. The Confederate position stretched southwest from Fort Anderson for about three-fourths of a mile, where the right of the line was anchored at the edge of a large swamp area. The Rebel left extended northeastward from the fort, across the peninsula from the Cape Fear to Masonboro Sound.[12] Since the Cape Fear River flowed more or less through the center of the enemy position, Schofield set up his headquarters on the *Spaulding*, a hospital steamer in the river, and passed from one bank to the other as circumstances required.[13] The enemy position looked impregnable against a direct attack, and Schofield did not like the looks of the swampy country, filled with ponds and lakes, protecting the enemy's right. He decided, with the help of Admiral Porter, to flank the Rebels on their left.

On February 11, Schofield directed Terry to push his line forward, close enough to the Confederates to compel them to hold their works in force. Then, the next night, the navy attempted to convey pontoons up the coast while two infantry divisions marched north along the beach to receive the boats, haul them over the sand, and lay a bridge across Myrtle Sound in the rear of the Rebel line. The dark night was intensely cold, the gale from the

11. Cox, *Franklin and Nashville*, p. 148.
12. *O.R.*, Ser. 1, XLVII, part 1, 910.
13. *Ibid.*, part 2, 545. Cox, *Franklin and Nashville*, p. 149.

ocean chilling the men "to the marrow."[14] When they arrived at
the appointed place, the struggling soldiers found that the stormy
weather had made it impossible for the ships to keep the rendez-
vous. Schofield was not yet ready to give up, and on the night
of February 14, he attempted to have the pontoons moved up the
beach on wagons. But the coast was swept by a severe wind and
the high tide and surf proved too great a hindrance. The sand,
where it was not washed by the water, was too deep and soft for
the horses and mules. The final blow to Schofield's plan came when
the moon rose and revealed the marching troops to the enemy,
who were then on the alert to protect their left flank.[15]

Schofield turned his attention to the Rebel right, where, at
least, he would not have to contend with the sea. On February 16,
troops were ferried to the south bank of the river, and the next
morning two divisions and a brigade advanced along the main
Wilmington road until they encountered the Confederate position
at Fort Anderson. While naval vessels shelled the fort at long range,
two brigades were entrenched to keep up a strong demonstration in
its front. Cox, on the nineteenth, led a division and two brigades
in an intended fifteen-mile sweep around the swamp covering the
enemy's right. He was striking for the Wilmington road in rear
of the fort. The movement was discovered by the Rebel cavalry,
and during the night the Confederates abandoned their works
on both sides of the Cape Fear. They fell back behind Town Creek,
on the west, and a corresponding position covered by swamps on the
east. Schofield then pushed Cox and Terry right up to the enemy's
line once more. While Terry held the Confederates in position east
of the river, Cox began another flanking movement on February 20.
This time he reached the enemy's rear, attacking and routing him,
and capturing some 375 prisoners.

The resistance on the west bank of the river broken, Cox, on
February 21, was threatening to cross the Cape Fear River above
Wilmington. It was impossible for the enemy to hold on to the
town any longer. Setting fire to the steamers, cotton, military and
naval stores, the Confederates abandoned the town on the evening
of February 21. At the same time Schofield, receiving information
that the Confederates in Terry's front were being strongly rein-
forced, ordered Cox back to the east bank of the Cape Fear. But

14. Cox, *Franklin and Nashville*, p. 148.
15. *O.R.*, Ser. 1, XLVII, part 1, 910. Cox, *Franklin and Nashville*, p. 148.

Cox, in a position where he could see columns of smoke ascending from the city, was thoroughly convinced that the enemy was abandoning Wilmington; he started only one brigade back, and, in spite of reiterated orders, continued to try to get a message to Schofield explaining fully the circumstances. It was midnight before a mutual understanding was finally reached. Then Schofield warmly approved Cox's apparent disobedience of orders.[16] The next morning, February 22, Schofield's forces entered Wilmington without opposition. The cost in killed and wounded from the start of operations on the eleventh was about 200 men.[17]

Schofield reported his victory to Grant the same day, and on February 24 Grant sent a brief telegram to the Secretary of War: "I would respectfully recommend the appointment of Schofield as brigadier general in the regular army. He ought to have had it from the battle of Franklin."[18] Stanton responded the next day. Schofield's nomination would be made, as requested, "subject, however, to his obedience to orders." The secretary was disturbed by what he referred to as Schofield's "seizing" the hospital boat *Spaulding* to make it his own quarters in violation of General Orders, Number 18.[19] Grant was more understanding, explaining that Schofield had arrived at the Cape Fear River without his transportation, and as he had to move about on the water, he had "asked the quartermaster if there was a boat he could use temporarily as well as not. He was told the *Spaulding* was doing nothing." Nevertheless, Grant concluded, he himself would have an order made prohibiting the use of boats for headquarters.[20] About two weeks later Schofield wrote Stanton an explanatory letter in which he stated that he had not been aware of the existence of the order which he was violating. "If I had been," he continued, "I hope it is not necessary for me to say that I would not have disobeyed it." He related the circumstances attendant to his use of the steamer in detail, indicating that the situation had been misrepresented to the secretary. His letter is convincing.[21]

Schofield no longer needed the steamer anyway. With a safe base for Sherman assured at Wilmington if required, Schofield was

16. *O.R.*, Ser. 1, XLVII, part 2, 521–23.
17. *Ibid.*, p. 535.
18. *Ibid.*, p. 545.
19. *Ibid.*, p. 562.
20. *Ibid.*
21. *Ibid.*, pp. 827, 833.

planning his next move. After studying the logistics involved, he decided it would be best to shift north and establish his base of supply at Newbern, on the Neuse River. This would enable him to use the harbor at Morehead City which was a better one than that at the mouth of the Cape Fear River. Furthermore, the railway between the harbor and Newbern, about forty miles long, was in operation, with some locomotives and cars already there. No rolling stock was to be had at Wilmington. From Newbern, most of the way to Kinston, the old iron rails could be used again in reconstructing the railroad toward Goldsboro. Thus the task would be easier and more economical.[22] Having made his decision, Schofield sent General Ruger's division by sea to Morehead City, reinforcing about 5,000 convalescents returning to Sherman's army whom he had already ordered to move out from Newbern toward Kinston under General John M. Palmer. On February 25, Schofield ordered Cox to take command at Newbern and push forward at once. Meanwhile, Schofield prepared two divisions at Wilmington to march overland to Kinston. When they started on March 6, Schofield went by sea to Morehead City and joined Cox west of Newbern on the eighth. Cox had advanced to Wise's Forks, reconstructing the railroad as he proceeded. Enemy resistance became stiffer as the Federals neared Kinston. There was heavy skirmishing all day on March 9 as the Confederates felt for the Union flanks. The next day the Rebels made an assault on the left and center but were driven back. That night they retreated across the Neuse, burning the bridge. The next day the two divisions from Wilmington joined up, substantially increasing the strength of Schofield's command. On March 14, with the aid of pontoons brought by rail from Morehead City, Schofield crossed the Neuse and entered Kinston without opposition.

The next few days were spent in rebuilding the wagon bridge over the Neuse and bringing forward supplies. On March 20, Schofield moved out of Kinston, heading west again for Goldsboro. The opposition encountered was slight, and on the evening of March 21 he entered the town, preparatory to his junction with Sherman.[23] The latter's march northward was briefly halted from March 19 to 21, when Joseph E. Johnston, back in command but with few Confederates to lead, attacked at Bentonville. Sherman's numerical

22. *Ibid.*, part 1, 911. Cox, *Franklin and Nashville*, pp. 154–55.
23. *O.R.*, Ser. 1, XLVII, part 1, 912, 913.

strength was too great, and Johnston retreated toward the capital at Raleigh. On March 23, Sherman entered Goldsboro.[24] After Schofield had given him a description of his operations in North Carolina, Sherman on the twenty-fifth turned over his command to Schofield and left for a meeting with Grant at City Point, Virginia. Returning from the conference, Sherman, on April 5, issued orders directing the beginning of a new campaign in seven days. The plans called for a feint on Raleigh and a rapid march across the Virginia line to Burkeville, forty-five miles west of Petersburg. There Sherman's force would be planted between Lee and Johnston, making a junction of their forces impossible.[25]

Events in Virginia brought a change in these plans. Sherman learned on April 6 that Petersburg and Richmond had been captured. He issued new orders that the army would march from Goldsboro on April 10, moving against Johnston at Smithfield. Johnston, with no more than 35,000 men to oppose Sherman's 89,000, retreated, and the Federal columns entered Smithfield the morning of April 11.[26] On the next day word was received that Lee had surrendered. Two days later Johnston asked Sherman for an armistice.

Sherman did not hesitate a moment in arranging for a meeting. On the morning of April 17 he boarded a train in Raleigh for the short ride to Durham's Station. There Sherman and his small party mounted horses and rode toward Hillsboro, the site of the Confederate commander's headquarters. After riding about five miles, they met Johnston and his party. The two generals dismounted, shook hands, introduced the members of their parties, and then conferred in the little farmhouse of Mrs. Daniel Bennett. The discussion went on until sunset, when they agreed to meet again the next day. Confederate General John C. Breckinridge, with Sherman's consent, joined them when negotiations were resumed on the eighteenth.[27]

Sherman presented the Confederate commander with liberal terms of capitulation, so broadly phrased as to cover political reconstruction. He recognized insurgent state governments, seemed to put in question the authority of Union state governments, and

24. Sherman, *Memoirs*, II, 322.
25. John M. Gibson, *Those 163 Days: A Southern Account of Sherman's March From Atlanta to Raleigh* (New York, 1961), p. 237.
26. *Ibid.*, p. 238.
27. *Ibid.*, pp. 259–64.

guaranteed "the people and inhabitants of all States" their political rights and franchises, as well as "their rights of person and
property."[28] Unfortunately, Sherman had not been instructed, as
Grant had, when Lincoln wrote the latter on March 3, "not to
decide, discuss or confer upon any political question; such questions the President holds in his own hands, and will submit them
to no military conference or conventions."[29] Sherman no doubt
thought that he was following the spirit of Lincoln's liberal pro-
gram of reconstruction which had been presented to him at City
Point by the President himself. But the administration did not
intend for the military to deal with political questions. It is not
surprising, therefore, that President Johnson and his cabinet
overruled Sherman, and Secretary Stanton sternly ordered him to
set aside the agreement he had drawn up. Sherman, "outraged
beyond measure" by the way Stanton handled the matter, arranged
another conference with Johnston at the Bennett house on April
26.[30] This time Schofield accompanied his commander.

Sherman and Johnston were as anxious for peace as ever, but
they reached a seeming impasse when they tried to agree on surrender terms. The most disturbing question concerned the status
of surrendered Confederates. Grant's terms at Appomattox had been
generous, but the paroled Confederates had lacked food, transportation, and money. Their passage through Virginia and North
Carolina to their homes had become a trail of thievery. Johnston
intended to prevent such a thing from happening to his men. He
contended that he should receive better terms, in this respect, than
Lee had received. Such terms would be to the advantage of all
concerned. Sherman could see that Johnston had a good point,
but he was equally convinced that since his first terms had been
rejected in Washington, he could consent to no more than Grant
had at Appomattox.[31]

The discussion went on and on, until Sherman decided to call
in Schofield to see if he might help solve the knotty problem.
Schofield offered a solution. After Johnston's surrender, Sherman
planned to take most of his troops to Washington for demobilization. Schofield would be left in command of the small force left to

28. *Ibid.*, pp. 270–71.
29. Lewis, *Sherman*, p. 545.
30. Randall and Donald, *Civil War*, pp. 528, 529.
31. Gibson, *Those 163 Days*, pp. 286, 287.

maintain order. He would have the authority to handle the details of the Confederate demobilization and would do all he could to avoid the condition Johnston feared. He enumerated his plans as follows: Field transportation would be loaned to the troops for their march to their homes and for subsequent use in their industrial pursuits. Artillery-horses might be used, if necessary. Every brigade or separate body of men would retain a number of arms equal to one seventh of its effective strength, which, when the troops reached the capitals of their states, would be disposed of as the general commanding the department might direct. Private horses and other private property of both officers and men would be retained by them. Transportation by water would be furnished from Mobile or New Orleans to the troops from Arkansas and Texas. Naval forces within the limits of Johnston's command would be included in the terms of the convention.[32]

Both Johnston and Sherman were satisfied. Schofield then sat down and wrote the "military convention" of April 26, essentially the same terms as Lee received at Appomattox, except for the supplemental provisions enumerated above. Sherman and Johnston placed their signatures upon the terms, Johnston saying to Sherman, "I believe that is the best we can do."[33] That night in Raleigh, Grant, who had arrived on the twenty-fourth to begin operations against Johnston, approved the terms with his signature. There now seemed no good reason to doubt that Washington would accept them. It was "all over but the shouting."

Doubtless many found it difficult to believe that the great American tragedy had finally ground to its bloody end. Schofield wrote that "it was several years after the war" before he "became fully satisfied," in his dreams at night, "that it was really over."[34] April, 1865, which witnessed both the end of the war and the first assassination of an American President, was a strange mixture of victory, defeat, and sorrow. The South mourned and the North mourned as well. But, at least, four full years of fighting and killing had finally come to an end.

32. *O.R.*, Ser. 1, XLVII, part 3, 482. Schofield, *Forty-Six Years*, pp. 350, 351.
33. Schofield, *Forty-Six Years*, pp. 351, 352.
34. *Ibid.*, pp. 350, 351.

# X. Reconstruction in Virginia

BEING LEFT in command of the Department of North Carolina at the close of the war, Schofield found himself confronted with the problem of restoring civil government. He soon demonstrated a moderate attitude toward the South. His military campaigns had afforded him an opportunity to observe the southern people, blacks and whites, and he had become convinced that moderation was the only sane policy.

Consequently, he was disturbed by a letter of May 7, 1865, from Chief Justice Salmon P. Chase, giving a brief summary of the policy which he and others, "who think as I do," advocated. On the subject of who would enjoy the franchise, Chase proposed to bypass the present constitution of North Carolina—which had been in effect when the war began and which excluded all free men of color from voting—in favor of an older constitution which had recognized all free men, regardless of color, as voters.[1] Schofield considered this both unwise and unconstitutional. The power to determine who should vote had been reserved by the Constitution to the several states. He felt compelled therefore to set forth his views on the policy for restoration of the South that ought to be pursued. They are contained in a letter to General Grant on May 10, 1865. He would place the southern states under military government and declare existing state laws in force, excepting

1. Salmon P. Chase to JMS, May 7, 1865, Schofield MSS.

those which conflicted with Federal laws and the Constitution. Persons who took an amnesty oath would be permitted to elect members to a convention which should repudiate the doctrine of secession, abolish slavery, and restore the state to constitutional relations with the Federal government. He then would allow the people to approve or disapprove the action of the convention and at the same time elect state officers. If the required actions of the convention were approved, the state would be readmitted. He would leave the conditions of suffrage up to the state, as guaranteed in the constitution. He doubted both the wisdom and legality of attempting to force the South to accept Negro suffrage. The Negroes were not prepared for suffrage. They could neither read nor write, had no knowledge of law and government, and needed education before being granted such a responsibilty. He concluded that to "raise the negro, in his present ignorant and degraded condition," to political equality with the whites would be to enslave the latter and would tend to incite them to rebellion.[2]

But Schofield's policy was not to be. First came the appointment of various civilians as provisional governors of the different states and their attempts at reconstruction. Then the Fourteenth Amendment disfranchised most of the southern leadership, the "iron-clad" oath banned them from Congress, and universal enfranchisement of the Negroes was followed by what the Southerners referred to as "carpetbag" government. William W. Holden was soon appointed "provisional" governor of North Carolina, and in June Schofield relinquished command of the department. He was not through, however, with the knotty problems of reconstruction, to which he would eventually return in Virginia. First came a problem of a different kind.

While the government of the United States was occupied with war for the preservation of the Union, Louis Napoleon III, Emperor of the French, had attempted, under the pretense of collecting international debts, to establish a puppet regime in Mexico. By placing the Archduke Maximillian of Austria on the throne, supported by some 20,000 French troops, he had violated the Monroe Doctrine. Protests by Secretary of State William H. Seward were of no avail since Napoleon knew that the United States was in no position to enforce the doctrine while the war lasted. Once

2. Schofield, *Forty-Six Years,* pp. 373–76.

the war was over and the Union intact, steps were soon taken to persuade the French that they must give up their New World ambitions. General Sheridan, with an army of about 50,000 men, was sent to the Rio Grande— whether for immediate military operations in Mexico or as evidence of ultimate military purpose in aid of diplomacy was a question which Napoleon might do well to ponder.

Sheridan's troops were Union volunteers who had been enlisted especially for the Civil War. It was therefore necessary to organize a new army for the sole purpose of acting against the French in Mexico. It was proposed that this army should be enlisted and organized under the Republican government-in-exile of Mexico, thus avoiding the necessity of any political action of the United States government within Mexican territory. And it was Schofield who was selected as the officer to organize and command the proposed army. A letter from Grant in June, 1865, informing Schofield of these plans instructed him, if he were willing to accept the assignment, to report to Washington for consultation.[3]

Schofield seemed ready enough to accept this new responsibility. Journeying to the capital, he conferred with Grant, Seward, Stanton, Señor Romero, the Mexican minister to the United States, and President Johnson. But before plans were completed Secretary Seward approached him with a proposal that, under authority of the State Department, he should go to France and attempt to persuade the Emperor that he must withdraw his army, thus saving the United States the necessity of expelling it by force. Seward was convinced that if Napoleon could be made to understand that the people of the United States would never, under any circumstances, consent to his ambitions in Mexico, he would then withdraw his army. Thus bloodshed would be avoided, and friendly relations between the people of France and the United States would be preserved. Schofield must have been a man who could express himself tactfully and convincingly. Otherwise it appears unlikely that he would have been approached about such a mission.

Seward's reasoning appealed to Schofield. And perhaps the opportunity to tour portions of Europe was not uninviting. It

3. Quoted *ibid.*, p. 379.

did seem most reasonable to try first in every possible manner to accomplish the goal by peaceful means; as Seward, according to Schofield, so aptly put it: "Get your legs under Napoleon's mahogany, and tell him he must get out of Mexico."[4] Force could always be used later if necessary. Thus accompanied by two staff officers, Brigadier General William M. Wherry and his brother, Brevet Brigadier General G. W. Schofield, he sailed from New York on November 15, 1865, on the Cunard Steamer *Java*.

Schofield landed in England at Liverpool and spent several days in London with the United States Minister to England, Charles Francis Adams. Adams, son of former president John Quincy Adams, had been a major factor in keeping United States–British relations on an even keel during the Civil War, despite several incidents of crisis proportions. Schofield explained the purpose of his European visit to Adams, who not surprisingly was in sympathy with the objective of settling the Mexican affair peaceably.[5]

On December 2, Schofield proceeded to Paris. His arrival had been preceded by various rumors of an official mission which was more or less hostile to the interests of France. Writing to his wife on the evening of December 5, Schofield said: "All Paris is in a ferment about my visit here, newspaper editors are beseiging the legation to learn what it means. . . . These French are a most excitable people, but they will boil down pretty soon."[6] Shortly after his arrival, Schofield got an opportunity on December 8 to allay some of the fears of the French. The occasion was a Thanksgiving dinner given by Americans in Paris at the Grand Hotel. Schofield was the principal speaker, and judging from the account by the Paris correspondent of the New York *Herald*, he was received in a most flattering manner. After the band played "Yankee Doodle" and Schofield rose to speak, he was received with "tremendous enthusiasm." "The ladies rose and waved their handkerchiefs, and gentlemen shouted until they were hoarse." Though it was brief, Schofield's speech was several times interrupted with cheers and applause. After heaping praise upon the United States and her armies in the Civil War, Schofield concluded with a pointed toast, which he "knew would be heartily responded to by

4. *Ibid.*, p. 385.
5. *Ibid.*
6. JMS to Mrs. Schofield, December 5, 1865, Schofield MSS.

every true American—'The Old friendship between France and the United States may it be strengthened and perpetuated!' " Schofield took his seat and, again, according to the correspondent, "the applause which followed was deafening."[7]

During the weeks that he spent in Paris Schofield did not actually have a private audience with the Emperor. He was "presented" to the Emperor and Empress on January 19 at a Grand Ball at the Tuilleries.[8] In his autobiography, Schofield said that in their conversation the Emperor was especially interested in knowing something about the American methods of supplying an army at a great distance from its base of operations.[9] The ball, of course, was no occasion to bring up the Mexican question. But Schofield did have several conversations with Prince Napoleon and officers of high rank on the Emperor's staff, especially Admiral de la Graviere, whom Schofield described as "a warm friend of America." These were the men who delivered Schofield's "unofficial" message to the Emperor.

On January 22, 1866, Schofield was present at the opening session of the French legislature, which was addressed by the Emperor. The object of the Mexican expedition, said Napoleon III, had been to found a government resting upon the will of the people. Since this had been accomplished, so the Emperor alleged, the French interests in Mexico were soon to be concluded. Shortly after this, Prince Napoleon inquired pointedly of Schofield whether the Emperor's declaration would be satisfactory to the United States. Though he might have quarreled with the Emperor's premises, Schofield could find no fault with his conclusion, and replied that he believed it would be.[10]

It appeared that Schofield had done all that had been requested of him. On January 24, he prepared a report for Secretary Seward and, while awaiting further instructions, occupied himself by touring southern France, Italy, Switzerland, and England. During the entire period he was in Europe, Schofield wrote his wife almost daily. Since letters to her through the war years are practically nonexistent, the European letters are of special interest. They reveal something of his personality, especially showing his

7. New York *Herald,* quoted in Schofield, *Forty-Six Years,* pp. 386, 387.
8. JMS to Mrs. Schofield, January 19, 1866, Schofield MSS.
9. Schofield, *Forty-Six Years,* p. 392.
10. *Ibid.,* pp. 389, 390.

sense of humor. On December 13, he wrote about his visit to a church fair: "Last night I went with the Bigelows to the fair for the Episcopal church. It was held in a small room which was so much crowded as to make locomotion almost impossible. The display of wares for sale was very fine. . . . Of course as we went the rounds I had to be introduced to them all, and was the subject of observation and remark more than was quite agreeable to so modest a man. But I believe I got through with it all creditably and without any serious damage although terribly squeezed by the crowd of women. Whether they all stood it as well I cannot say."

On January 10, he wrote: "Today I have been engaged in a matrimonial transaction as witness at a Franco-American wedding. A Miss P.—of somewhere in the United States is marrying a young squirt of a French Count. The American minister and myself are the witnesses on the part of Mademoiselle or Madame as the case may be for I do not know which she is now." And concerning the Ball at the Tuilleries: "The Princess Metternich, who is very plain in the face, but tall and queenly in manner, wore a splendid dark dress of grand proportions, which she had the honor of catching upon the end of my sword as she swept by. Our mutual apologies seemed to be entirely satisfactory. The main object of wearing swords seems to be to tear the ladies dresses. All are expected to wear them, civilians as well as military and the destruction of dresses is terrible. Speaking of swords, I believe mine was the finest in the palace. . . . At least it appeared to attract a good deal of attention, whether on its own account or that of its wearer I don't know."[11]

By the spring of 1867 the French were out of Mexico, leaving their puppet, Maximillian I, to face a Mexican firing squad. It is impossible to say how much influence Schofield's mission had on the ultimate decision of the French to leave Mexico. The situation of Napoleon's government was critical. The opposition to him was powerful, and the intervention in Mexican affairs was unpopular in France. But national pride would probably not have permitted the Emperor to yield to open and obvious menace from the United States, nor allow his army to be driven by force from Mexico without an effort to maintain it there. It seems far better

11. JMS to Mrs. Schofield, December 13, 1865, January 10, 1866, January 19, 1866, Schofield MSS.

that Schofield made the decision to go to Paris and talk rather than to go to Mexico to fight.

Seward informed Schofield in early May, 1866, that the object of his mission had been "sufficiently accomplished" and he might return to the United States.[12] The European holiday was over. Schofield was home by early June and soon wrestling once more with the problems of reconstruction. In August he was assigned to command the Department of the Potomac, which included the State of Virginia. Virginia was then governed in part by the Freedman's Bureau and in part by the provisional government which had been organized at Alexandria while the war was still in progress.

Schofield soon showed that he intended to be reasonable and impartial in his dealings with both races. Eleven days after assuming command Schofield reported to the headquarters of the Army that there was a well-founded feeling of insecurity among the whites caused by their being destitute of arms while a considerable portion of the Negro population possessed weapons, many of them of a military nature. Since Negroes were guaranteed the constitutional right to bear arms, the insecurity of the whites could be corrected, Schofield believed, only by organizing volunteer militia companies throughout the state under authority of Governor Francis H. Pierpont. Membership in these companies should be limited to men who were loyal and well disposed toward the freedmen. And the Army should supply the arms and ammunition for these companies.[13]

Neither did Schofield intend to favor whites at the expense of blacks. His impartiality was evident in December, 1866, in the case of a killing of a freedman by Dr. James L. Watson of Rockbridge County. The Negro's wagon had collided with the doctor's carriage, whereupon the doctor shot him. The Rockbridge court acquitted Watson of the charge of murder,[14] but Schofield apparently believed that the evidence did not justify the decision. He had

12. Schofield, *Forty-Six Years*, p. 393.

13. John Schofield to Major George K. Leet, August 27, 1866, Department of the Potomac, in Office of the Adjutant General of the Army, MSS, The National Archives, Washington, D.C. The records of the Department of the Potomac, the Adjutant General's Office, and the First Military District will hereafter be abbreviated respectively as Dept. Potomac, A.G.O., and 1st Mil. Dist.

14. Alrutheus A. Taylor, *The Negro in the Reconstruction of Virginia* (Washington, 1926), p. 26.

Watson arrested and ordered him to be tried by a military commission,[15] citing the 1866 Freedmen's Bureau Act as authority for the trial.

Schofield may have had a dual purpose in doing this: redressing a miscarriage of justice and testing the legality of the new Freedman's Bureau Act.[16] On April 2, 1866, President Johnson had proclaimed that the insurrection was over and that "standing armies, military occupation, martial law, military tribunals, and the suspension of the privilege of the writ of *habeas corpus*" were ended.[17] The proclamation was supplemented by an executive order which forbade trial of citizens by military tribunals where civil courts were in existence which could try them. This order was in harmony with the Supreme Court decision of April 3, 1866, in the case of *ex parte Milligan*. But the Freedmen's Bureau Act gave the bureau "military jurisdiction over all cases and questions" concerning the right of freedmen "to have full and equal benefit of all laws and proceedings, concerning personal liberty, [and] personal security."[18] It was under the provision of this act that Schofield proposed to try Dr. Watson before a military commission. Thus the case would test the constitutionality of the Freedmen's Bureau Bill in light of the presidential order and the Supreme Court decision in *ex parte Milligan*.

When the military commission assembled on December 19, it was served with a writ of *habeas corpus* from the circuit court of Richmond. Schofield refused to comply with the writ. Then President Johnson, upon the advice of Attorney General Henry Stanberry, concluded the case by dissolving the commission and discharging Watson from custody.[19] Schofield's efforts to bring the murderer to justice were thus nullified.

When the state legislature convened on December 2, 1866, Schofield's interest, like that of most Virginians, turned to its proceedings. The most important question up for consideration was the ratification of the Fourteenth Amendment. Schofield believed the amendment was unjust and unwise. He prepared a written

15. Special Order 186, December 14, 1866, Schofield MSS.

16. Oliver O. Howard to JMS, December 10, 1866, Schofield MSS.

17. James D. Richardson, comp., *A Compilation of the Messages and Papers of the Presidents, 1789–1902*, 10 vols. (New York, 1903), VI, 429–32.

18. General Order 61, August 9, 1866, A.G.O.

19. Hamilton J. Eckenrode, *The Political History of Virginia During the Reconstruction* (Baltimore, 1904), pp. 50, 51.

argument on the subject which shows that he was especially opposed to section three. This section, he said, disqualified from office nearly everyone "whose social position, intellectual attainments and known moral character entitle him to the confidence of the people." He argued that it was "folly to attempt to bring back a revolted people by disfranchising all leaders in whom they trust and confide. These leaders if they will act in good faith [and Schofield believed a sufficient number would] can bring their people back to their allegiance. Without them it can not be done during the existing generation."[20]

Schofield also objected to the national government prescribing qualifications for state officers or for voting in state elections. Section three was also unfair to Negroes, he said, since its effect would be to allow more of the "poor whites" to hold local office, thus putting the Negroes in the hands of their only real enemies in the South. Any thought of universal suffrage, without regard to intelligence or other qualifications, was absurd. Northern politicians might "theorize as much as [they] pleased about the criminality of the late rebellion," but Schofield contended, it was "folly to suppose that the present generation of Southerners can be made to acknowledge or believe that it was anything more than a legitimate war for the settlement of a great political question left unsettled by the framers of the constitution. . . ." Therefore, looking at the matter in "a practical common sense light," the Federal government should not demand "repentance in sack cloth and ashes" when any show of such repentance would be "the purest hypocrisy."[21]

In spite of these objections, Schofield strongly urged that Virginia should ratify the amendment. He believed that it offered the best terms on which the state could be restored. He warned that failure to ratify probably would cause Congress to impose harsher conditions. In addition, he claimed that Congress could hardly refuse to recognize the existing state government if the amendment were ratified. In fact, Schofield visited Washington and received assurances to that effect from leading Republicans in Congress.[22] His advice was not heeded. The state Senate voted unan-

20. Schofield, "Reconstruction," Schofield MSS. William M. Wherry, in an attached statement, says the essay was written in the winter of 1866–67.
21. *Ibid.*
22. Schofield, *Forty-Six Years*, pp. 394, 395.

imously against the Fourteenth Amendment and the margin in the House of Delegates was 74 to 1.[23] Schofield said in his autobiography that the amendment would have been ratified except for other influences from Washington, probably exerted by Johnson.[24]

When the Virginia legislature began its extra session on March 4, 1867, the accuracy of Schofield's prediction had become apparent. Two days earlier the United States Congress had passed over Johnson's veto the first of a series of measures prescribing the mode of action which southern states must follow to be readmitted to the Union. The Reconstruction Act of March 2, 1867, declared that except for Tennessee no legal governments existed in the former Confederate states. These states were to be apportioned into military districts until good order and "loyal and republican" governments could be established in them. The act established five military districts, each under a general officer of the army who was to be the supreme authority in each state under his command in accordance with the laws of the United States. Each state was to hold a constitutional convention, with delegates to be elected by all male citizens of the state of voting age, regardless of color, except those disfranchised for participation in the rebellion. This convention should frame and the voters should ratify a constitution extending the franchise to those persons entitled to vote for delegates to the convention. The state legislature elected under the constitution then should ratify the Fourteenth Amendment. The state might be readmitted to the Union after the Fourteenth Amendment had become law, and after Congress had approved those actions and had declared the state entitled to representation in Congress.[25]

On March 23, 1867, Congress passed a supplementary Reconstruction Act ordering the district commander to direct the entire process of state action in carrying out the provisions of the first act of March 2. He was to establish voting districts, supervise registration of voters, conduct an election on the question of calling a

23. William T. Alderson, "The Influence of Military Rule and the Freedmen's Bureau on Reconstruction in Virginia, 1865–1870," (Ph.D. dissertation, Vanderbilt University, 1952), pp. 133, 134.

24. Schofield, *Forty-Six Years*, p. 395.

25. *The Statutes at Large of the United States . . . 1789–1873*, 17 vols. (Boston, 1846–73), XIV, 428–29. Act of March 2, 1867. Hereafter cited as *U.S. Statutes at Large*.

constitutional convention and choosing delegates to it, and submit the proposed constitution to the voters for ratification or rejection.[26]

President Johnson vetoed both bills, attacking the infringement upon state powers and the establishment of military government as unconstitutional and dangerous. He denied the right of Congress to impose Negro suffrage on the South and claimed that the nature of the acts indicated that such was their true intent and purpose. He also denied the constitutionality of imposing military government on the southern states in time of peace and warned that the relatively unlimited authority entrusted to the military commanders would be a real danger to the people of these states. Johnson asserted that this authority made the military commander "an absolute monarch."[27] Congress passed both bills over the President's veto.

As Johnson indicated, the far-reaching authority entrusted to military commanders meant that mildness or harshness, justice or injustice, would largely depend on the character of the commander. Virginia was fortunate to have Schofield as her commander. He regarded the reconstruction acts as a terrible oppression which was not "appreciated by even the most enlightened and conservative people of the North," and could only be realized by "those who actually suffered the baneful effects of the unrestrained working of those laws."[28] Schofield's moderate attitude and just treatment of the citizens had already made a favorable impression on Virginians who only a few months before had complained bitterly about the actions of his predecessor General Alfred H. Terry. In fact, the Virginia state legislature petitioned the President to appoint Schofield to the position of district commander because of the "great impartiality" with which he had "discharged his duties . . . toward all classes."[29]

Schofield officially assumed command of the First Military District on March 13, 1867.[30] His first general order, issued on the same day, did much to gain the respect and confidence of the people. Officers of the existing provisional government were directed

26. *Ibid.*, XV, 2–5. Act of March 23, 1867.

27. Richardson, *Messages and Papers*, VI, 498–511, 531–35.

28. Schofield, *Forty-Six Years*, pp. 395–96.

29. Francis Pierpont to Andrew Johnson, forwarding a petition of Virginia General Assembly, March 8, 1867, Johnson MSS, Library of Congress.

30. General Order 10, March 11, 1867, A.G.O.; General Order 1, March 13, 1867, 1st Mil. Dist.

to continue performing their duties unless otherwise directed in individual cases, until their successors were duly elected and qualified under the Reconstruction Act of March 2, 1867. The order further stated: "It is desirable that the military power conferred by the before mentioned act [of March 2, 1867] be exercised only so far as may be necessary to accomplish the objects for which that power was conferred, and the undersigned appeals to the people of Virginia, and especially to Magistrates and other civil officers, to render the necessity for the exercise of this power as slight as possible, by strict obedience to the laws, and by impartial administration of justice to all classes."[31]

"In common with the public journals in every portion of the State," responded the Lexington *Gazette*, "we express our decided gratification that if we are to be subjected to military rule, we are at least to have the consolation of being governed by a gentleman. . . ."[32] Similar statements were expressed by the Lynchburg *Virginian*, the Norfolk *Journal*, the Richmond *Whig*, and the Abingdon *Virginian*. Available evidence seems to indicate that these sentiments were shared by most conservatives in the state.[33]

But the satisfaction over Schofield's appointment did not remove the outraged feelings of most white Virginians over the Reconstruction Acts. The Lynchburg *Virginian* declared that it preferred a military dictator over the entire country rather than rule "by that mob at Washington." The Staunton *Spectator* considered Congress' action with respect to Virginia parallel to rape, and it advocated that Virginia should resist the outrage and retain her honor rather than submit and become party to the act. And the Charlottesville *Chronicle* said that the South, now that the war was over, was asked "to love, to kiss the hand that wielded the lash," and the penalty for not doing so was "to be ruled by the blacks."[34] Many newspapers advised conforming to the Reconstruction Acts, however, as there seemed no reasonable alternative. Negro suffrage was an outrageous measure for many to accept, and conservative whites feared that the freedmen's vote would be controlled by radicals and adventurers. But suffrage for the former slaves was regarded as a fixed fact.[35]

31. General Order 1, March 13, 1867, 1st Mil. Dist.
32. Quoted in Alderson, "Military Rule in Virginia," p. 151.
33. *Ibid.*, pp. 150, 151.
34. *Ibid.*, p. 152.
35. *Ibid.*, p. 153.

Several times Schofield invoked his authority as commanding general to preserve the peace or to insure against violations of the Reconstruction Acts. When Negro votes were rejected at a city election in Alexandria on March 5, he issued orders prohibiting any further elections under the provisional government until registration was completed.[36]

Schofield also sought to prevent inciting disorder through speeches or newspaper editorials. He warned the Richmond *Times* that he would not tolerate any more of its articles which fostered enmity, created disorder, and led to violence. He sustained the action of General O. B. Wilcox, subdistrict commander at Lynchburg, who forbade a public lecture by H. Rives Pollard, a man who had openly declared his hostility to the United States government. But he also told Wilcox that he would prefer not to interfere with freedom of speech or the press. He desired rather to wait until an offense was committed and then to punish the offender.[37]

A riot occurred in Richmond in May which was quelled only by intervention of the military. When the Richmond *Dispatch* reported that a Massachusetts man named Jedekiah K. Hayward had delivered incendiary speeches tending to incite the Negroes to riot, Schofield summoned the reporter, ascertained the truth of the report, and arrested and turned Hayward over to Mayor Mayo for trial and punishment. As an additional preventive measure he ordered the Negro "Lincoln Mounted Guard" to cease parading or drilling under arms. A detachment of Federal cavalry was assigned to patrol the city night and day.[38]

Meanwhile, Schofield was busy preparing for the approaching registration and election. Existing state office-holders continued to exercise the duties of those offices unless removed for disloyalty or misdemeanor. When vacancies did occur, Schofield appointed someone to fill the position temporarily. He left control of civil affairs to the people, if at all possible, by selecting replacements on the recommendations of county courts or city councils and the president of the board of registration of the county or city. These appointees had to swear that they had not been disfranchised for

36. JMS to John C. Underwood, March 16, 1867, 1st Mil. Dist. Eckenrode, *Virginia During Reconstruction*, pp. 65–66.
37. Alderson, "Military Rule in Virginia," p. 154.
38. *Ibid.*, p. 155.

participating in the war and would not be denied the right to hold office by the proposed Fourteenth Amendment.[39] Such appointees were to be replaced as soon as new office holders were elected under the provisions of the Reconstruction Acts.

On April 2, 1867, Schofield began the process of appointing three-man boards of registration for Virginia's counties and cities. He designated a five-man panel of army officers to select and recommend persons for appointment to the boards. An officer of the army or bureau was to be selected as a member of each board, wherever possible, and the remaining two members were to be selected in order of preference from the following groups: honorably discharged United States Army officers, loyal citizens of the county or city for which they were selected, or other loyal citizens having the proper qualifications. Schofield insisted that the men appointed must be of unwavering loyalty to the Union, of high character and impartial judgment, and that they possess the confidence of the people.[40] This order is important because it gave preference for appointment first to officers, past and present, of the Union Army, second to the native loyal whites, and last of all to those who might be "carpetbaggers." All but twenty-seven who were appointed presidents of the boards of registration in the ninety-nine counties, and the cities of Richmond, Petersburg, and Norfolk, were army officers. And three of the non-Army appointees were civilian agents or former agents of the Freedmen's Bureau.[41] The presidents, aided by their two subordinates, directed the registration at the county seat and exercised supervisory jurisdiction over subordinate boards of registration in each magisterial district.

Registration began in late June, 1867. In an effort to insure a fair and just registration Schofield provided that three white and three Negro voters in each election district might serve as challengers for the purpose of detecting any person who fraudulently attempted to register. The names of voters, white and Negro, were entered on separate lists, as were the names of persons registered after challenge and persons denied the right to register. In the latter two cases Schofield required that the cause of challenge and

39. General Order 9, April 5, 1867, 1st Mil. Dist.; General Order 16, April 20, 1867, 1st Mil. Dist.
40. Special Order 16, April 2, 1867, 1st Mil. Dist.
41. General Order 15, April 20, 1867, 1st Mil. Dist.

the grounds for refusal of registration should also be entered on the lists.[42]

In compliance with the Reconstruction Act of March 23, 1867, Schofield declared that all male citizens of the United States twenty-one years of age or older who were residents of the state for at least one year were entitled to vote unless they were disfranchised for felony or for participation in the rebellion. All persons were disfranchised who at any time had served as members of Congress, as civil or military officers of the United States, or in any official capacity which had required taking an oath to support the Constitution of the United States, as legislative, executive, or judicial officers of a state, and afterwards had participated in the rebellion. Schofield drew up a specific list of executive and judicial officers who would be disfranchised by the law.[43]

Great political excitement was expected as Negroes and whites, radicals and conservatives, campaigned and voted on the heated issues. Schofield therefore took measures to preserve peace and maintain order if the necessity arose. He issued an order designed to protect the personal and property rights of all persons "in cases where the civil authorities may fail, from whatever cause, to give such protection, and to insure the prompt suppression of insurrection, disorder and violence." The order provided for the appointment of army officers and Freedmen's Bureau officials as military commissioners in the state's seven subdistricts. To ensure that the commissioner's orders would be complied with, police officers, sheriffs, constables, and other law enforcement officials were required to obey their orders. The commissioners were also given judicial powers in the counties and cities. Civil trials were to be preferred, but if the commissioner believed these would result in a miscarriage of justice, he was empowered, subject to Schofield's approval, to call upon a military commission. Civil officers were ordered to continue to discharge the functions of their offices and were assured that they would not be superseded except in cases of necessity.[44]

Thus, when Schofield began the registration process, he possessed almost absolute control over the State of Virginia. For

42. General Order 28, March [sic. May] 13, 1867, 1st Mil. Dist.
43. U. S. Statutes at Large, XV, 14–16. Act of July 19, 1867. General Order 7, July 26, 1867, 1st Mil. Dist.
44. General Order 31, May 28, 1867, 1st Mil. Dist.

purposes of Army administration and command, he had the state divided into seven subdistricts, each of which had seven or eight military commissioners, with each commissioner responsible for one or more counties.[45] Through the military commissioners and bureau agents he exercised supreme judicial power, while his right to remove from office any state officers and replace them with men of his choice, gave him complete executive power. He also exercised supreme legislative power through his right to suspend any law and issue any new regulations which he considered necessary for the accomplishment of his work. Fortunately for Virginia, Schofield exercised his power as little as possible and in the best interests of the state. He permitted the civil authorities to continue to function with little hindrance, appointed men to office who, in most cases, were recommended by state officials and who could, at the same time, take the iron-clad oath.[46] And he reported that "no case arose in Virginia in which it was found necessary, in my opinion, to supersede the civil authorities in the administration of justice. Not a single citizen of that state was tried by military commission."[47]

The registration seems to have been conducted in an impartial and orderly manner. Relatively few complaints of injustices to either whites or blacks were received by the registration boards.[48] The official returns listed 227,376 voters in the state, 121,271 of whom were whites and 106,105 Negroes.[49] Comparing these figures with the tax list for 1867, Schofield reported that 17,649 more Negroes had registered than were contained on the tax list. This fact prompted him to order a census conducted by a board of army officers in a Richmond Ward where the disparity was greatest. The registration was found to be "very nearly correct" while the tax list was "quite erroneous."[50] Schofield was convinced that nearly all the people who were entitled to register had done so. The Freedmen's Bureau helped get out a large Negro registration, since its agents were considered negligent in their duties if any

45. General Order 33, June 3, 1867, 1st Mil. Dist.
46. General Order 9, April 5, 1867, 1st Mil. Dist.; General Order 48, July 26, 1867, 1st Mil. Dist.
47. Schofield, *Forty-Six Years*, p. 399.
48. Alderson, "Military Rule in Virginia," p. 168.
49. Memorandum, May 10, 1869, 1st Mil. Dist.
50. Schofield to Adjutant General of the army, December 13, 1867, 1st Mil. Dist.

freedman, through ignorance, failed to register.[51] And the press had made a strong effort to secure a complete white registration.[52]

Attention was soon focused on election day (designated by Schofield for October 22) when the voters would decide for or against holding a constitutional convention and elect delegates to the convention if it was approved. Voting was to be by ballot and conducted at the same places and by the same army officers, bureau agents, and civilians who had conducted the registration.[53] Separate ballot boxes were to be maintained for whites and Negroes. All sales of liquor were to be suspended on election day, and civil police officers were required to maintain good order. Any person who attempted to prevent any qualified voter from casting his ballot, whether by fraud, force, or intimidation, was to be tried for the offense by a military commissioner, and registering officers were authorized to exercise all the powers of a military commissioner during the time of election and counting of ballots. Registering officers and their assistants were to count the returns, certify the results of the election, and turn over all books, papers, and ballots to the president of the board of registration for the county or city. Having tallied the reports, the latter would deposit the ballots in a safe place and forward his tally, along with all rejected ballots, to the commanding general. Schofield warned the people that if ballot boxes or poll books should be lost or destroyed a new election would be held in the district or ward affected, but he expressed the hope that there would be "full and free exercise of the elective franchise."[54]

Schofield provided that 105 delegates should be elected to the Constitutional Convention, or one for every 2,061 electors. His apportionment gave 47 delegates to election districts with white majorities and 58 to districts having Negro majorities. Since there was a white majority in the state, this action led to charges that he had gerrymandered the state in favor of the radicals. But his explanation for this apportionment disproves such an assertion. There were 52 counties and cities with white majorities, Schofield said, and 50 with Negro majorities. In the former there were only 90,555 voters, both white and colored, while in the latter

51. Alderson, "Military Rule in Virginia," p. 168.
52. *Ibid.*
53. General Order 65, September 12, 1867, 1st Mil. Dist.
54. General Order 68, October 4, 1867, 1st Mil. Dist.

there were 125,895. On that basis, since the number of electors entitled to elect one delegate was 2,061, the white counties would have elected 44 delegates and the Negro counties would have elected 61.[55] Apportionment by the congressional districts of 1860 would have resulted in 34 delegates from white counties and 71 from Negro counties. By congressional districts of the provisional government the numbers would have been 32 and 73 respectively. By following the state senatorial districts as a basis for apportionment, the number of delegates from Negro and white districts would have been the same as by Schofield's apportionment, but many large factions would have been unrepresented and many districts would have had greater representation than they were strictly entitled to. Therefore, Schofield apportioned delegates on a county or city basis, and when necessary, combined several counties and cities into election districts when each individually was entitled to fractional representation but lacked a large enough fraction to justify its having another delegate.[56] Schofield's plan of apportionment seems to have been as fair as any that could have been worked out and was at least as favorable to the whites as any existing method of apportionment—obviously more favorable than some.

On October 22, the radicals registered a decisive victory, approving the holding of the convention by a vote of 107,342 to 61,887, and electing 73 delegates to the conservatives' 32.[57] Whites could hardly blame the result upon Schofield's reapportionment. Of 121,271 registered white voters, more than one-third, or 44,017, failed to vote, while only 12,687 of 106,105 registered Negroes neglected to vote. And only 638 freedmen in the entire state voted against the convention.[58]

Charming the Negroes with glowing promises of social equality, confiscation, and free land, the extreme radicals had forged a tightly knit, compact party of Negroes, carpetbaggers, and radical white Virginians. The extent and thoroughness of the organization was not realized by most conservatives, and they had no single political leader or any fixed political policy—except opposition to

55. This was due to the fact that the western counties had large white majorities while the more heavily populated eastern counties had very small Negro majorities.

56. Alderson, "Military Rule in Virginia," p. 183.

57. *Ibid.*, p. 184.

58. Schofield, Personnel of the Virginia Convention, Schofield MSS.

radicalism. The conservatives were divided over whether to vote for the convention, whether to ally with political parties of the North, and whether to oppose or submit to the congressional plan of Reconstruction.[59] That the radicals won is hardly surprising.

Feelings ran high in Richmond where Schofield allowed the polls in certain wards to reopen an extra day in order to poll a complete vote.[60] He was accused of doing so in order to insure a radical victory. The Richmond *Southern Opinion*, perhaps the most "unreconstructed" paper in Virginia, denounced him for this "marvellous, stupendous and utterly unparalleled atrocity," and thanked him for "yet another lesson in that intricate infinite maze of confounded villainy with stealth—the Yankee character."[61] The defeated conservative candidates also protested against keeping the polls open and charged voting frauds.

Schofield defended himself well, saying that the purpose of keeping the polls open was to record the fullest possible vote. His critics' position, he continued, seemed to be taken on the erroneous premise that the "party is entitled to the victory which can poll the greatest number of votes in a given number of hours." He also denied that any voting frauds had taken place.[62] It is highly unlikely that Schofield's action was motivated by a desire to secure a radical victory. The men elected in Richmond were extreme radicals while Schofield's views were moderate. The Richmond *Whig* stated that Schofield "personally strongly desired the defeat of the Hunnicutt [extreme radical] ticket."[63] And Schofield also kept the polls open an extra day in Norfolk, which gave the whites an additional opportunity to poll their votes.[64]

The Negroes and radical leaders were jubilant over the victory. They had defeated several moderate Republicans as well as conservative whites. Their triumph seemed to be a heady wine, as some of the radical leaders were soon delivering incendiary speeches. James W. Hunnicutt was arrested on a warrant of the Charles City county court for inciting Negroes to insurrection against whites

59. Alderson, "Military Rule in Virginia," pp. 169–80.
60. General Order 65, September 12, 1867, 1st Mil. Dist.; Special Order 154, October 23, 1867, 1st Mil. Dist.; Richmond *Whig*, October 25, 1867.
61. Richmond *Southern Opinion*, October 26, November 2, 1867, quoted in Alderson, "Military Rule in Virginia," pp. 184, 185.
62. JMS to Thomas J. Evans and others, November 7, 1867, 1st Mil. Dist.
63. Richmond *Whig*, November 1, 1867, quoted in Alderson, "Military Rule in Virginia," p. 185.
64. Alderson, "Military Rule in Virginia," p. 186.

and charged with having advised Negroes to burn the homes of their enemies.[65] Also arrested for incendiary language was Lewis Lindsay, Negro delegate to the convention from Richmond. He proclaimed that the streets of Richmond would "run knee-deep in blood" before any of his children would suffer for food. He also thanked the Almighty "that the Negroes had learned to use guns, pistols and ram rods."[66] Negro military organizations again were formed, in violation of Schofield's orders, and he used troops to disarm them.[67]

Moderate Republicans were unhappy over the radical victory and conservative whites were appalled as they thought about the constitution which this convention might adopt. Now aroused from relative apathy, they issued a call for a convention of conservative white men from throughout Virginia, to be held on December 11, 1867.[68] This convention would be an instrument working to unite all whites before the expected radical constitution was submitted to the electorate for ratification. It was hoped that it might be defeated.

The constitutional convention assembled in Richmond on December 3, 1867. In order to be as fully informed as possible about what to expect from it, Schofield investigated the political background of its members. His description of them is interesting and enlightening. He characterized Charles H. Porter and John Hawxhurst as political adventurers. David S. White was a Methodist minister and political adventurer who associated "entirely with Negroes." James H. Platt was a speculator and former Union army officer. The outstanding Republican leader was Judge Edward Snead, a native of Virginia and a consistent Unionist. The leading conservatives were James C. Southall, editor of the Charlottesville *Chronicle*; Jacob W. Liggett, member of the recent House of Delegates; and James M. French, former colonel in the Confederate Army. The outstanding "unreconstructed" delegates (Schofield used the term "unreconstructed" to refer to those unalterably opposed to the Reconstruction Acts, and determined to retain political

65. Richmond *Enquirer*, December 3, 1867, quoted in Alderson, "Military Rule in Virginia," p. 191.

66. Richmond *Whig*, November 15, 1867; Richmond *Enquirer*, November 15, 1867, quoted in Alderson, "Military Rule in Virginia," p. 191.

67. JMS to George Stoneman, December 16, 1867, 1st Mil. Dist.

68. Richmond *Whig*, November 11, 1867, Alderson, "Military Rule in Virginia," p. 112.

power exclusively in the hands of whites) were John L. Marye, Jr., of Fredericksburg; Norval Wilson, a Methodist minister and former abolitionist who became a violent secessionist during the course of the war; J. C. Gibson, who had killed a man in a street fight; and Eustace Gibson, a former Confederate Army officer. The most influential Negro delegates were "Dr." Thomas Bayne of Norfolk, who was illiterate; William A. Hodges of Princess Anne County, who irritated radicals by denying that Negroes were indebted to the North for their freedom; and Lewis Lindsay, previously mentioned, who had thanked God that Negroes had learned how to use firearms.

Other important delegates were William James, a radical from England who had been dismissed from his post as collector of internal revenue in Richmond for alleged malpractices; James C. Toy, recently acquitted on a charge of stealing hogs (Schofield thought he was guilty); Edgar Allan, a radical who later joined the moderate Republican ranks; Edward W. Massey, a former Confederate, but now a bitter radical; Daniel M. Norton, a self-styled Negro physician whom Schofield described as a "sharp trickster and schemer"; Sanford M. Dodge, adventurer from the North who was employed in a distillery; John Robinson, Negro and former slavetrader; and C. L. Thompson, illiterate tobacconist from Albermarle County who received only three white votes in his native town but still won the election as a delegate to the convention. Altogether there were, he wrote, 51 radicals, 22 Republicans, 13 conservatives, and 19 unreconstructed.[69] Not only was Schofield an astute observer of the convention's personnel, but he must have had "connections" in order to gain this information.

The convention lasted until April 7, 1868, with the exception of a Christmas recess, and the resulting constitution, as had been expected, was highly objectionable to most whites. All persons were disfranchised who had ever held any state or Federal office, had taken an oath of such office, and afterward had participated in the rebellion.[70] No person could hold office unless he first took the iron-clad oath. Sections concerning ownership of church property, provisions for local government, and homestead exemptions,

69. Schofield, Personnel of the Virginia Convention, Schofield MSS.
70. The list of such officers included all those disfranchised by the congressional reconstruction act of July 19, 1867, with the addition of members of the city council.

also created considerable dissatisfaction.[71] The Constitution provided, significantly, for a statewide system of free public schools—the first such provision in Virginia's history—for equal and uniform taxation on property, and for an income tax on incomes exceeding $600 per year.[72]

The commendable provisions of the Constitution do not negate the fact that it represented an attempt to establish Negro and radical supremacy in the state. Its office-holding and disfranchisement provisions would make it very difficult in many places to carry on the government efficiently. Negro enfranchisement, coupled with disfranchisement of many whites and restrictions of office-holding to persons who could take the iron-clad oath, would mean that most state offices would be filled by carpetbaggers, unqualified Negroes, and scalawags. Well aware of the difficulties which the new constitution could create, Schofield addressed the convention and warned the delegates that if the proscriptive measures were carried out, many counties would be without a sufficient number of men eligible for and capable of filling the offices. They would probably result in the defeat of the constitution when submitted for ratification.[73] Schofield's words were in vain. In a letter to Grant he reported that his speech "seemed not to have the slightest influence. . . . The same baneful influence that secured the election of a majority of ignorant blacks and equally ignorant or unprincipled whites to the convention, has proved sufficient to hold them firmly to their original purpose. They could only hope to obtain office by disqualifying everybody in the state who is capable of discharging official duties, and all else . . . was of comparatively slight importance."[74] Thus, "villifying General Schofield for giving them good advice and driving them from the treasury which they wished to empty," said the Richmond *Enquirer,* "the Negroes and carpetbaggers . . . adjourned."[75]

71. The section on church property stated that title to such property was not affected by the late war, by an antecedent or subsequent event, or by any legislative enactment, but was to be vested in the parties originally holding the title, or their assignees. The title of northern church organizations to much property that had been taken by southern churches was thus confirmed.

72. *Senate Executive Documents,* 40 Cong., 2 sess., no. 54 (Serial 1317), 1–26.

73. Richmond *Whig,* April 21, 1868, quoted in Alderson, "Military Rule in Virginia," p. 204.

74. JMS to U. S. Grant, April 18, 1868, Schofield MSS.

75. Richmond *Enquirer,* April 23, 1868, quoted in Alderson, "Military Rule in Virginia," p. 204.

Schofield's efforts in the latter case probably saved the state a large sum of money. The Constitutional Convention soon used up the $100,000 which had been appropriated for its expenses by the state legislature back in March, 1867. It then passed an ordinance to levy a tax on the people for another $100,000. Since the Reconstruction Act of March 23, 1867, placed no limit on the amount to be collected in taxes levied by the convention, Schofield feared an endless taxation process for as long as the convention stayed in session. Determined to prevent such a drain on the state treasury, he told General Grant: "The sum already expended ought to have been ample—more than was necessary— to defray all their expenses. . . . They ought in my opinion to be debarred from the exercise of the authority given them by Congress to levy and collect a special tax."[76]

With Grant's approval, Schofield negotiated a loan to pay the convention expenses up to April 6, 1868. It seems likely that Schofield's actions helped bring the convention to a conclusion sooner than would have been the case otherwise.

Besides the proscriptive measures of the Constitution, Schofield also objected to the county organization section which provided for the election of city, town, and county officers. In more than half of these places Negroes were in the majority. In view of "their present temper," he said, they could be expected to elect "persons of their race who can neither read nor write to fill the majority of those offices."[77]

If Schofield could not persuade the convention to modify the Constitution, perhaps he could prevent it from going into effect. The wisest course, he believed, was not to submit it to the people for ratification at all, thus letting "the thing fall and die where it is." Then, he wrote Grant, he could go on putting Union men in office and reorganize the provisional government upon a loyal basis, "until the friends of reconstruction get control of the state." Then a convention could be called which would frame a constitution fit to be ratified by the people and approved by Congress and the country at large. The Republican party, he continued, could only be damaged by endorsing such a constitution as that framed by the recent convention. It would be necessary, however, for Congress to modify the iron-clad oath and provide greater latitude

76. JMS to Grant, March 21, 1868, 1st Mil. Dist.
77. JMS to Grant, April 19, 1868, Schofield MSS.

for the selection of officers before another constitution could be framed.[78]

Since neither Congress nor the Constitutional Convention had appropriated money to pay the expenses of an election on the proposed Constitution, Schofield told Grant that he intended to postpone the election until Congress made an appropriation. As Congress knew the contents of the Constitution, Schofield said he would regard Congressional action in appropriating money, or failure to act, as indicating his duty in the matter.[79] Apparently Grant and the Republican leaders approved his plan to circumvent the Constitution. At any rate, on April 24, 1868, Schofield issued an order suspending the election until further notice.[80]

A number of newspaper editors believed that the Constitution would have been defeated if submitted to a vote, while Schofield feared it would have been adopted. However, his motives were misinterpreted. The editors charged that he had acted so that separate votes could be taken on the objectionable provisions and the Constitution would thus be approved.[81] He did later recommend that the Constitution be submitted to the electorate with provisions for a separate vote on the section requiring office-holders to take the iron-clad oath. But his correspondence indicates that this action was primarily designed to defeat the iron-clad oath and save the state from the results of adopting the Constitution in an unexpurgated condition, rather than to ensure that the Constitution would be adopted. He himself said that he would have preferred drawing up a new Constitution. He recommended a separate vote on the test oath provision because it was the maximum concession which friends of the Constitution would accept, while further concessions would "produce discord among the friends of reconstruction."[82]

It should be remembered that Schofield's primary responsibility as district commander was to enforce the Congressional Recon-

78. JMS to Grant, April 18, 1868, Schofield MSS.
79. *Ibid.*
80. Schofield to the people of Virginia, April 24, 1868, 1st Mil. Dist.
81. Richmond *Enquirer,* April 30, 1868; Harrisonburg *Rockingham Register,* April 30, 1868; Charlottesville *Chronicle,* May 2, 1868; Lexington *Gazette,* May 6, 1868; Harrisonburg *Old Commonwealth,* April 29, May 6, 1868; Richmond *Whig,* April 28, 1868; Norfolk *Journal,* April 27, 1868. Cited in Alderson, "Military Rule in Virginia," p. 211.
82. JMS to Grant, May 6, 1868, Schofield MSS.

struction Acts. These acts directed that "loyal and Republican" state governments must be established, and Congress, of course, was to decide when such governments existed. Schofield realized that to an overwhelming Republican Congress Republicanism was as much criterion for readmission as loyalty to the Union. Therefore if he were going to secure Virginia's re-admission to the Union, he would have to sacrifice his own wishes in order to secure the greatest possible support from the friends of Reconstruction. He personally disliked the Reconstruction Acts and would have liked to expurgate other provisions of the Constitution, but this was not within his power.

Meanwhile he was facing another difficult problem—what to do about elections for state, city, and municipal offices. On April 2, 1867, he had issued an order suspending all elections for these offices until the registration had been completed.[83] These offices were greatly desired by the radicals, and now pressure was being exerted to get Schofield to remove the incumbents and replace them with "loyal" men. But Schofield was convinced that most of these offices could not be filled by competent persons. The men who were most zealous for Negro suffrage and most clamorous for offices, he wrote to Grant, were in many cases "entirely unfit for the offices they aspire to." Schofield decided to appoint Republicans to the vacant offices in "all cases where respectable and competent persons of that party could be found. If by this course I incidentally give strength and influence to the respectable Republicans as against the lower class of men who have acquired control over the mass of colored voters," he continued, "I am sure I shall thereby render the county an important service and not be justly subject to the charge of partisanship."[84] He then asked Grant's opinion on whether he should remove from office the disfranchised persons whose terms had not expired. Grant approved Schofield's plans and suggested that no removals be made "except for cause" until the vacant offices had been filled. It would then be possible to better judge the wisdom of further removals and appointments, "and also as to whether they are required to a proper administration of the reconstruction acts."[85]

On the basis of this ruling, Schofield, on April 4, 1868, made

83. General Order 33, March 30, 1868, 1st Mil. Dist.
84. JMS to Grant, April 2, 1868, Schofield MSS.
85. Grant to JMS, April 3, 1868, Schofield MSS.

what was probably his most important appointment to office. He declared the office of governor vacant by reason of the expiration of Francis Pierpont's term of office, and appointed Henry H. Wells, a native of New York, former member of the Michigan legislature and recent general in the Union Army, as governor of Virginia.[86] Schofield had been considering removing Pierpont for several months. He advised Grant that by his official conduct and influence, Pierpont had done more "to prevent the proper execution of the acts of Congress than all the disfranchised office-holders in Virginia combined."[87] Recently the governor had made extensive use of his pardoning powers in freeing Negroes who had been convicted by state courts—and this while Schofield's military commissioners were supervising the actions of the civil courts.

Pierpont's term of office had expired on January 1, 1868, and under the state constitution he was ineligible to succeed himself. Schofield had recommended that Grant issue an order appointing Schofield to discharge the duties of governor. This would relieve the state of the burden of the governor's salary and relieve Schofield of the necessity of making an appointment to the office of governor that likely would not "be acceptable to any considerable proportion of any party."[88] Schofield's recommendation was not followed, and Pierpont continued to hold office after the expiration of his term. By April, 1868, Schofield was convinced that Pierpont was using his official position "for no other apparent purpose than to secure his renomination and election" to the office of governor in spite of the constitutional prohibition against successive terms. Therefore Schofield wrote Grant that he believed it was his duty "to appoint a successor who is eligible under the laws of the state . . . who will be more acceptable to the people and who can and will aid us instead of being a dead weight or worse in the work of reconstruction."[89]

The appointment was first offered to Judge Alexander Rives, a native Virginian and prominent Republican who, Schofield said, "would have been invaluable to the Union cause." But Rives preferred to retain his judgeship.[90] Therefore, after consulting with

86. *Ibid.;* General Order 36, April 4, 1868, 1st Mil. Dist.
87. JMS to Grant, April 2, 1868, Schofield MSS.
88. JMS to Grant, December 1867, Schofield MSS.
89. JMS to Grant, April 2, 1868, Schofield MSS.
90. JMS to Grant, April 24, 1868, Schofield MSS.

leading Republicans, Schofield proposed to Grant that Wells be appointed.[91] Grant approved and Wells became governor.

Pierpont did not give up without a struggle, however. Charging that Schofield's action was made "in the interest of the rebels" to defeat the adoption of the constitution, the ex-governor tried to get Grant to countermand Schofield's order.[92] Grant refused, but Pierpont continued his efforts to reclaim the office. He accused Schofield of subverting the reconstruction laws to give state offices to Confederates and outsiders. This was especially true, claimed Pierpont, in Schofield's appointment of tobacco inspectors. There were to be two inspectors at each warehouse, and these inspectors could nominate deputy inspectors. Inspectors were required to take the test oath and therefore Schofield had appointed only one inspector at each warehouse, allowing this inspector to appoint deputies who would do the work of the second inspector but would not be required, as subordinate officers, to take the test oath.[93]

Schofield did make appointments just as Pierpont stated,[94] but it hardly seems likely that he was acting to aid the "rebels." It seems much more reasonable to conclude that he did so in the interest of good government and to keep such offices from falling into the hands of extreme radicals. Besides, Grant ordered an investigation made of accusations, presented by a radical committee, that Schofield was selling out to conservatives, and Schofield was exonerated.[95]

Pierpont also charged that Schofield, with his conservative friends, was discriminating against Virginia Unionists and placing "strangers [carpetbaggers] in all the important offices, state and Federal."[96] These charges were repeated by extreme radicals who, though pleased by Pierpont's removal, were displeased that a man of their own persuasion was not appointed in his place.

Pierpont's charge that Schofield's action was a deliberate attempt to favor carpetbaggers over Virginia Republicans has persisted in several accounts of the Reconstruction period in Virginia.[97]

91. JMS to Grant, April 2, 1868, Schofield MSS.
92. Grant to JMS, April 6, 1868, Schofield MSS.
93. Francis Pierpont to Grant, April 23, 1868, Schofield MSS.
94. General Order 15, February 14, 1868, 1st Mil. Dist.
95. Alderson, "Military Rule in Virginia," 220.
96. Francis Pierpont to Grant, April 23, 1868, Schofield MSS.
97. Eckenrode, *Virginia During Reconstruction*, p. 105; W. Asbury Christian,

But such a conclusion is not adequately supported by the facts. While it is true that Governor Wells was not a Virginian and that many of Schofield's appointments did go to so-called carpetbaggers, it is equally true that Schofield's correspondence with Grant about appointments to office, particularly Wells' appointment, makes it clear that the basic consideration was "respectable" or moderate Republicanism plus the ability to take the test oath and perform the duties of office. The fact that the governor's office was first offered to Judge Rives—who was preferred by Schofield—and that it was only after Rives refused the position that it was awarded to Wells, seems to disprove the charge that Wells' appointment was part of Schofield's "carpetbagging" plans. And, of course, the fact that Wells later came to uphold the extreme radical position does not negate the fact that at the time of his appointment he was widely recognized as a moderate Republican.[98]

The appointment of Wells was the first of a long list of military appointments to replace incumbent state officials. By May 15, 1868, Schofield reported that he had already appointed nearly five hundred officers and would have appointed more if qualified persons could have been found. But now the Fourteenth Amendment was about to become law. All office holders disqualified under its provisions were to be immediately removed from office, and all men appointed to fill the vacated offices would have to take the iron-clad oath. Schofield wrote Grant that he already had appointed nearly all available men who were competent to fill these offices, and the Fourteenth Amendment would create several thousand more vacancies. It appeared to Schofield that these offices would have to remain vacant unless Congress made some special provision to avert the situation.[99]

But Schofield was spared solving this problem because of the acquital of President Johnson on May 26, 1868, in the impeachment proceedings. During the course of the trial several Republican senators, among whom, it was intimated, were William Fessenden, Lyman Trumbull, and John Sherman, became fearful that Johnson, against whom there was not sufficient evidence, would be convicted

---

*Richmond: Her Past and Present* (L. H. Jenkins, 1912), p. 300. Nelson M. Blake, *William Mahone of Virginia, Soldier and Political Insurgent* (Richmond, 1935), p. 99.

98. Alderson, "Military Rule in Virginia," p. 222.

99. JMS to Grant, May 15, 1868, 1st Mil. Dist.

on grounds of simple party necessity. They were convinced that this would completely discredit the Republican party. But if the President would nominate to succeed Edwin Stanton as Secretary of War, a man whom the moderate Republicans were confident would enforce the acts of Congress, they could then vote for acquittal. These senators allegedly effected a compromise with Johnson through the agency of William M. Evarts, one of Johnson's counsel. Upon their suggestion, Evarts approached Schofield and received his consent to be nominated for the post. The President then nominated Schofield for Secretary of War, and when Johnson was acquitted the Senate confirmed the nomination.[100] On June 1, 1868, Schofield was relieved as commander of the First Military District and assumed the office of Secretary of War.[101]

100. Schofield, Memorandum of an interview between Schofield and Mr. William Evarts relative to Schofield's Nomination as Sec. of War, May, 1868, Schofield MSS. The memorandum is subsequently reprinted in Schofield's autobiography, pp. 413–18, although the paragraph which intimates that Fessenden, Trumbull, and Sherman were behind the scheme is omitted.
101. General Order 24, June 1, 1868, A.G.O.

# XI. An Appreciation

JOHN SCHOFIELD was only thirty-six years old when he became Secretary of War. Many of the Union officers of high rank were by then approaching their declining years. In less than five years Thomas and Meade were dead. Within twenty years Grant, Sheridan, McClellan, Burnside, and McDowell were deceased. Sherman died in 1891 and Pope in 1892. For Schofield, however, more than half of his years were still ahead of him. Before his retirement he would hold several prominent positions, such as commander of the Divisions of the Pacific, the Missouri, and the Atlantic, Superintendent of the United States Military Academy at West Point, and, finally, commanding general of the army from 1888 to 1895, with the rank of Lieutenant General conferred upon him in the latter year. He lived until 1906.

While these positions, his military record, and his friends in high places (both politicians and military figures) enabled him to move in select company, Schofield's most important service to the United States of America was rendered during the Civil War and Reconstruction. In the following paragraphs are summarized some conclusions about Schofield's personality, character, and ability during those years.

In spite of his West Point training Schofield might have spent his life as a professor if the Civil War had not occurred. He was a man of scholarly interest and temperament. He also might have

189

been fairly successful as a politician if he had chosen such a course. Contemporary accounts indicate that he was an adequate speaker, although far from an orator in the stamp of a Webster or Bryan. A moderate Republican, Schofield undoubtedly understood politics and developed friendships with a number of important figures such as the Blairs, Henderson, Fessenden, John Sherman, and others. But the Civil War turned Schofield irrevocably to a military career which he pursued successfully.

He was a good department commander. He did, especially in the early part of the war, show tendencies to be petty and jealous of fellow officers—not uncommon faults among officers in both the Union and Confederate armies. These tendencies were overshadowed, however, by his ability as an organizer and administrator. While commanding the Department of the Missouri he was sometimes subjected to bitter criticism. There were difficulties inherent in that situation which would have made it impossible for anyone to have avoided considerable criticism. In a difficult position he performed well. When commanding in Virginia after the war Schofield, perhaps because of lessons learned in Missouri, seemed more cautious in his handling of newspapers and generally acted with a greater degree of understanding.

Schofield's record as commander of the Army of the Ohio in Sherman's Atlanta campaign shows that he was a dependable subordinate field commander. When contesting Hood's advance into Tennessee he risked too much in staying at Columbia as long as he did, but he was not in the desperate, almost hopeless, plight at Spring Hill which has come down in Confederate legend. He did not have the opportunity, except upon rare occasions, to conduct independent campaigns. Even when commanding prior to the Battle of Franklin, he was basically following the instructions of Thomas. Although he obviously does not rank with the foremost Union generals such as Grant and Sherman, he was a reasonably successful corps commander whose ability compared favorably with that of generals like McPherson who exercised commands similar to his own.

Schofield did not possess the kind of personality which inspired fighting men as Thomas, the "Rock of Chickamauga," did, or in a somewhat different way, as the fiery and brilliant Rebel Forrest did. Yet he was efficient and cool—in his own way building a feeling of confidence in many of the soldiers.

During Reconstruction in Virginia, as earlier in Missouri, Schofield demonstrated an outstanding administrative ability as district commander, creating a systematic and well-developed administrative plan. He had matured a great deal since his days in Missouri. He no longer allowed himself to become involved in petty matters. And he had brought his ambition under control or at least learned to conceal it somewhat. Like many ambitious men, once having gained a certain measure of power and success as well as more experience, Schofield seemed to mellow, becoming less "touchy" about matters involving him personally—with the notable exception of General Thomas.

Schofield was not a brilliant man, but he possessed a good mind and did his "homework" well. His letters, reports, and even memoranda were consistently precise and thorough. He was careful to try to avoid mistakes.

He was motivated by an understanding and sympathy for the defeated southern people. He desired to prepare Virginia for readmission to the Union as soon as possible, on the best terms possible and with a minimum of hardship. There is no evidence that he was vindictive. He believed that many former Confederate civil and military officials would faithfully serve the Union (and if some of them did not, the United States Army would be present to deal with them). Without the services of such men Schofield thought that many offices would inevitably be filled by the untrained, incapable, or self-seeking.

While it is true that Schofield opposed universal male Negro suffrage, there is no evidence (unless it be the fact that he was white) that would warrant the conclusion that he was a racist. His opposition was partially on Constitutional grounds—and this does not appear to have been a subterfuge with Schofield. Also, he thought that most Negroes, being illiterate, were not prepared to accept the responsibility of suffrage. He believed that granting immediate, unqualified Negro suffrage could only be detrimental. In his opinion, the Negroes would be incapable of exercising the new privilege wisely, and the disfranchised whites, observing their failures, would develop a bitterness which, in the long run, would create a more difficult situation in race relations.

Though convinced that the civil authorities in Washington were pursuing an unfortunate course in these matters, Schofield also believed that the military should be subordinate to civil authority. He would use such influence as he possessed to change what he considered an unwise policy, or soften its blow, but as a soldier it was his duty to carry out the national policy defined by the civilian heads of government.

As a military commander Schofield was industrious and reasonable. He was never adequately tested as a field commander beyond the level of corps command. As an administrator the key to his success was realistic good sense, attention to avoiding mistakes, and an ability, in most cases, to remain above personal prejudices.

# Bibliography

## PRIMARY MATERIALS

### Documents, Records, Reports

*Annual Report of the Adjutant General of the State of Missouri, for the Year of 1863*. Paper C. Roster and History of Regiments, etc., Missouri State Militia, Accompanying Adjutant General's Report for 1863.

*Annual Report of the Superintendent of the United States Military Academy, Department of West Point, for the Years 1877–1880*. Washington: Government Printing Office.

*Atlas to Accompany the Official Records of the Union and Confederate Armies*. Washington: Government Printing Office, 1891–95.

Cullum, G. W. *Biographical Register of Officers and Cadets of the United States Military Academy*. 3 vols. New York: James Miller, Publisher, 1879.

*Delinquency Record of Cadet John M. Schofield*, West Point Library. West Point, New York.

*Official Register of the Officers and Cadets of the United States Military Academy*. Edited by B. J. D. Irwin. New York, 3 pamphlets, 1819–40, 1841–60, 1861–78.

*Record of Books Borrowed from USMA Library by Cadet John M. Schofield*, 1849–53.

*Regulations Established for the Organization and Government of the Military Academy at West Point, New York*. New York, n.p., 1839.

Report of Commandant Bradford R. Alden, enclosed with letter of Superintendent Henry Brewerton to General Joseph G. Totten, July 8, 1852, Letter Sent File, 175, West Point Library.

Richardson, James D., comp. *A Compilation of the Messages and Papers of the Presidents, 1789–1902*. 10 Vols. New York: Bureau of National Literature and Art, 1903.

*Senate Executive Documents*, 40 Cong., 2 Sess., No. 54 (Serial 1317). The Constitution Framed by the Virginia Convention.

*The Statutes at Large of the United States, 1789–1873.* 17 vols. Boston: Little and Brown, 1846–73.

U.S. *Congressional Record.* 53rd Congress, 3rd Session, 1895. Vol. 27.

United States War Department
   Adjutant General's Office, Records, January 1, 1865 to July 30, 1870. The National Archives, Washington, D.C.
   Department of the Potomac, Records, August 16, 1866 to March 12, 1867. The National Archives, Washington, D.C.
   First Military District, Records, March 13, 1867 to January 29, 1870. The National Archives, Washington.

*War of the Rebellion: A Compilation of the Official Records of the Union and Confederate Armies.* 129 vols. Washington: Government Printing Office, 1880–1901.

## MEMOIRS AND REMINISCENCES

Buel, Clarence C., and Robert U. Johnson, eds. *Battles and Leaders of the Civil War.* 4 vols. New York: The Century Co., 1887–88.

Cox, Jacob D. *Atlanta.* New York: Charles Scribner's Sons, 1882.

⸺⸺. *The Battle of Franklin, Tennessee, November 30, 1864.* New York: Charles Scribner's Sons, 1897.

⸺⸺. *The March to the Sea, Franklin and Nashville.* New York: Charles Scribner's Sons, 1882.

⸺⸺. *Military Reminiscences of the Civil War.* 2 vols. New York: Charles Scribner's Sons, 1900.

Dodge, Grenville M. *The Battle of Atlanta and Other Campaigns, Addresses, etc.* Council Bluffs, Iowa: The Monarch Printing Co., 1910.

⸺⸺. *Personal Recollections of General William T. Sherman.* Des Moines: n.p., 1902.

Fremont, John Charles. *Memoirs of My Life.* Chicago: Belford, Clarke, 1887.

Grant, Ulysses S. *Personal Memoirs of U. S. Grant.* 2 vols. New York: Webster Co., 1885.

Green, Wharton J. *Recollections and Reflections.* Raleigh, N.C.: Presses of Edwards and Broughton Printing Co., 1906.

Hayes, Rutherford B. *Diary and Letters.* Edited by Charles R. Williams. 4 vols. Columbus, Ohio: Ohio State Archaeological Society, 1925.

Hitchcock, Henry. *Marching with Sherman.* Edited by M. A. DeWolfe Howe. New Haven: Yale University Press, 1927.

Hood, John B. *Advance and Retreat.* New Orleans: Published for the Hood Orphan Memorial, 1880.

Howard, Oliver Otis. *The Autobiography of Oliver Otis Howard.* 2 vols. New York: The Baker and Taylor Co., 1941.

Joyce, John A. *A Checkered Life.* Chicago: S. P. Rounds, Jr., 1883.

McIntyre, Benjamin F. *Federals on the Frontier: The Diary of Benjamin F. McIntyre, 1862–1864.* Edited by Nannie M. Tilley. Austin: University of Texas Press, 1963.

Nichols, George W. *The Story of the Great March.* New York: Harper and Brothers, 1865.

Palmer, John M. *Personal Recollections of John M. Palmer.* Cincinnati: R. Clarke Co., 1901.

Rusling, James F. *Men and Things I Saw in Civil War Days.* New York: Eaton and Mains, 1899.

Schaff, Morris. *The Spirit of Old West Point.* Boston and New York: Houghton Mifflin and Co., 1907.

Schofield, John M. *Forty-Six Years in the Army.* New York: The Century Co., 1897.

Sheridan, Philip H. *Personal Memoirs.* 2 vols. New York: Charles L. Webster and Co., 1888.

Sherman, William T. *Home Letters of General Sherman.* Edited by M. A. DeWolfe Howe. New York: Charles Scribner's Sons, 1909.

_____. *Memoirs of General W. T. Sherman.* 2 vols. New York: D. Appleton and Co., 1875.

Sherwood, Isaac R. *Memories of the War.* Toledo, Ohio: H. J. Chittenden Co., 1923.

Stanley, David Sloane. *Personal Memoirs of Major General D. S. Stanley, U.S.A.* Cambridge: Harvard University Press, 1917.

Wilson, James H. *Under the Old Flag.* 2 vols. New York and London: D. Appleton and Co., 1912.

## REGIMENTAL HISTORIES

Bennett, L. G., and W. M. Haigh. *History of the 36th Regiment of Illinois Volunteers.* Aurora, Illinois: Knickerbocker and Hodder, 1876.

Benton, Charles Edward. *As Seen from the Ranks.* New York: G. P. Putnam's Sons, 1902.

Clarke, Charles T. *125th Ohio Volunteer Infantry: Opdycke Tigers.* Columbus, Ohio: Spahr and Glenn, 1895.

Hutchins, M. C. *16th Kentucky Infantry: The Battle of Franklin, Tennessee.* Cincinnati: n.p., 1903.

Lawler, D. F. et al. *73rd Illinois Infantry Volunteers.* Springfield, Illinois: The Regimental Association of Survivors of the 73rd Ill. Inf. Vols., 1890.

Pinney, N. A. *History of the 104th Ohio Volunteer Infantry from 1862 to 1865.* Akron, Ohio: Werner and Lohmann, 1886.

Redway, George. "A Bloodless Victory," *National Tribune,* September 18, 1902.

Romeyn, Henry. "Hood's Campaign," *National Tribune,* June 27, 1889.

Scofield, Levi T. "The Retreat from Pulaski to Nashville." A paper read before the Ohio Commandery of the Military Order of the Loyal Legion of the United States, December 1, 1886. Cincinnati: H. C. Sherick and Co., 1886.

_____. *The Retreat from Pulaski to Nashville, Tennessee: Battle of Franklin, Tennessee, November 30, 1864.* Cleveland, Ohio: Press of the Caxton Co., 1909.

Shellenberger, John K. *The Battle of Franklin.* Cleveland, Ohio: Arthur H. Clark Co., 1916.

_____. *The Battle of Springhill, Tennessee, November 29, 1864.* A refutation of the erroneous statements made by Captain Scofield in his paper entitled "The Retreat from Pulaski to Nashville." Cleveland: Arthur H. Clark Co., 1913.

Sherratt, H. P. et al. *74th Illinois Volunteer Infantry.* Rockford, Illinois: W. P. Lamb, 1903.

Stone, Henry. "The Battle of Franklin." *Papers of the Military Historical Society of Massachusetts, Campaigns in Kentucky and Tennessee.* Boston, 1908.

Thompson, B. F. *History of the 112th Regiment of Illinois Volunteer Infantry.* Toulon, Illinois: Stark County News Office, 1885.

Ware, E. F. *The Lyon Campaign in Missouri: A History of the First Iowa Infantry*. Topeka, Kansas: Crane and Co., 1907.

Watkins, Samuel R. *"Co. Aytch," Maury Grays, 1st Tennessee Regiment*. Jackson, Tennessee: McCowat-Mercer Press, 1952.

Wherry, William M. "The Campaign in Missouri and the Battle of Wilson's Creek, 1861." A paper read before the Missouri Historical Society of St. Louis, March, 1880.

————. "The Battle of Prairie Grove, Arkansas, December 7, 1862," *Journal of the Military Service Institute of the United States*, 33 (1903), 177–89.

————. "The Franklin Campaign," Schofield MSS, Library of Congress, Container 74.

Williams, John H. "44th Missouri Infantry, Battle of Franklin," *National Tribune*, July 4, 1889.

Young, B. F. "The Charge at Franklin," *National Tribune*, April 7, 1892.

## Manuscripts

Francis Preston Blair, Jr. Papers. Library of Congress, Washington, D.C.

Samuel R. Curtis Papers. State Historical Library, Springfield, Illinois.

Thomas Ewing, Jr. Papers. Library of Congress.

Ulysses S. Grant Papers. Library of Congress.

Henry W. Halleck Papers. Library of Congress.

Andrew Johnson Papers. Library of Congress.

Abraham Lincoln Papers. Library of Congress.

John M. Palmer Papers. State Historical Library, Springfield, Illinois.

John M. Schofield Papers. Library of Congress.

Edwin M. Stanton Papers. Library of Congress.

Richard Yates Papers. State Historical Library, Springfield, Illinois.

## Newspapers

Cincinnati, *Enquirer*.

Leavenworth, *Daily Times*.

New York, *Tribune*.

New York, *Times*.

San Diego, *Union*.

St. Augustine, *Evening Record*.

St. Louis, *Daily Missouri Democrat*.

St. Louis, *Missouri Republican*.

Washington, D.C., *National Tribune*.

Washington, D.C., *Post*.

# SECONDARY MATERIALS

## Books

Adamson, Hans Christian. *Rebellion in Missouri: 1861; Nathaniel Lyon and His Army of the West*. Philadelphia and New York: Chilton Co., 1961.

Alderson, William T. "The Influence of Military Rule and the Freedmen's Bureau on Reconstruction in Virginia, 1865–1870." Ph.D. dissertation, Vanderbilt University, 1952.

Ambler, Charles H. *Francis H. Pierpont: Union War Governor of Virginia and Father of West Virginia.* Chapel Hill: University of North Carolina Press, 1937.

Ambrose, Stephen E. *Halleck: Lincoln's Chief of Staff.* Baton Rouge: Louisiana State University Press, 1962.

Andrews, J. Cutler. *The North Reports the Civil War.* Pittsburgh: University of Pittsburgh Press, 1955.

Banks, Robert W. *The Battle of Franklin.* New York and Washington: The Neale Publishing Co., 1908.

Beale, Howard K. "What Historians Have Said about the Causes of the Civil War," *Theory and Practice in Historical Study: A Report of the Committee on Historiography.* New York: Social Science Research Council, Bulletin No. 54, 1946.

Belser, Thomas A., Jr. "Military Operations in Missouri and Arkansas, 1861–1865." Ph.D. dissertation, Vanderbilt University, 1958.

Blake, Nelson M. *William Mahone of Virginia, Soldier and Political Insurgent.* Richmond: Garrett and Massie, 1935.

Boney, F. N. *John Letcher of Virginia: The Story of Virginia's Civil War Governor.* Tuscaloosa: University of Alabama Press, 1966.

Britton, Wiley. *The Civil War on the Border.* New York: G. P. Putnam's Sons, 1899.

Brownlee, Richard S. *Gray Ghosts of the Confederacy: Guerrilla Warfare in the West, 1861–1865.* Baton Rouge: Louisiana State University Press, 1958.

Cadwallader, Sylvanus. *Three Years with Grant.* Edited by Benjamin P. Thomas. New York: Alfred Knopf, 1956.

Catton, Bruce. *This Hallowed Ground: The Story of the Union Side of the Civil War.* New York: Doubleday and Co., Inc., 1956.

————. *Never Call Retreat.* New York: Doubleday and Co., Inc., 1965.

Christian, W. Asbury. *Richmond: Her Past and Present.* L. H. Jenkins, 1912.

Cleaves, Freeman. *Rock of Chickamauga: Life of General George H. Thomas.* Norman: University of Oklahoma Press, 1948.

Connelley, William E. *Quantrill and the Border Wars.* New York: The Pageant Book Co., 1956.

Conyngham, David P. *Sherman's March Through the South.* New York: Sheldon and Co., 1865.

Crawford, Samuel J. *Kansas in the Sixties.* Chicago: A. C. McClurg and Co., 1911.

Dana, Charles A., and James H. Wilson. *The Life of Ulysses S. Grant, General of the Armies of the United States.* Springfield, Mass.: Bill Co., 1868.

Dyer, John P. *The Gallant Hood.* Indianapolis and New York: The Bobbs-Merrill Co., Inc., 1950.

Eckenrode, Hamilton J. *The Political History of Virginia During Reconstruction.* Baltimore: The Johns Hopkins Press, 1904.

Edwards, John N. *Shelby and His Men, or the War in the West.* Cincinnati: Miami Printing and Publishing Co., 1867.

Freeman, Douglas S. *Robert E. Lee: A Biography.* 4 vols. New York: Charles Scribner's Sons, 1934–35.

Fulwider, Addison L. *History of Stephenson County, Illinois.* 2 vols. Chicago: The S. J. Clarke Co., 1910.

Gibson, John M. *Those 163 Days: A Southern Account of Sherman's March from Atlanta to Raleigh.* New York: Coward-McCann, Inc., 1961.

Hay, Thomas Robson. *Hood's Tennessee Campaign.* New York: W. Neale, 1929.

Hebert, Walter H. *Fighting Joe Hooker.* Indianapolis and New York: The Bobbs-Merrill Co., 1944.

Henry, Robert Selph. *First with the Most Forrest*. Indianapolis and New York: The Bobbs-Merrill Co., 1944.

Holcombe, R. I., and F. W. Adams. *An Account of the Battle of Wilson's Creek, or Oak Hills, Compiled and Written from Authentic Sources*. Springfield, Missouri: Dow and Adams, Publishers, 1883.

Horn, Stanley F. *The Army of Tennessee: A Military History*. Indianapolis and New York: The Bobbs-Merrill Co., 1941.

————. *The Decisive Battle of Nashville*. Baton Rouge: Louisiana State University Press, 1956.

*In the Footprints of the Pioneers of Stephenson County, Illinois*. Freeport: The Pioneer Publishing Co., 1900.

Jackson, Luther P. *Negro Office-Holders in Virginia, 1865–1895*. Norfolk, 1945.

Johnson, Allen, and Dumas Malone, eds. *Dictionary of American Biography*. 21 vols. New York: Charles Scribner's Sons, 1928–37.

Lewis, Lloyd. *Sherman, Fighting Prophet*. New York: Harcourt, Brace, Co., 1932.

Liddell-Hart, Basil Henry. *Sherman, Soldier, Realist, American*. New York: Dodd, Mead Co., 1929.

Livermore, Thomas L. *Numbers and Losses in the Civil War in America, 1861–1865*. Boston: Houghton, Mifflin, Co., 1900.

Mayer, George H. *The Republican Party 1854–1966*. New York: Oxford University Press, 1967.

Macartney, Clarence Edward. *Grant and His Generals*. New York: The McBride Co., 1953.

McKinney, Francis. *Education in Violence: The Life of George H. Thomas*. Detroit: Wayne State University Press, 1961.

Miers, Earl Schenck. *The General Who Marched to Hell: William Tecumseh Sherman and His March to Fame and Infamy*. New York: Alfred Knopf, 1951.

Monaghan, Jay. *Civil War on the Western Border, 1854–1865*. Boston: Little, Brown and Co., 1955.

Nevins, Allan. *Fremont: Pathmaker of the West*. New York and London: D. Appleton-Century Co., 1939.

Nicolay, John G., and John Hay. *Abraham Lincoln*. 10 vols. New York: The Century Co., 1886.

O'Conner, Richard. *Hood: Cavalier General*. New York: Prentice-Hall, 1949.

————. *Sheridan the Inevitable*. Indianapolis and New York: The Bobbs-Merrill Co., 1953.

————. *Thomas: Rock of Chickamauga*. New York: Prentice-Hall, 1958.

O'Flaherty, Daniel. *General Jo Shelby: Undefeated Rebel*. Chapel Hill: University of North Carolina Press, 1954.

Palmer, George T. *A Conscientious Turncoat: The Story of John M. Palmer, 1817–1900*. New Haven: Yale University Press, 1941.

Peckham, James. *General Nathaniel Lyon and Missouri in 1861*. New York: American News Co., 1886.

*Portrait and Biographical Album of Stephenson County, Illinois*. N.p., 1888.

Pratt, Fletcher. *Ordeal by Fire: An Informal History of the Civil War*. New York: William Sloane, 1935.

Pressly, Thomas J. *Americans Interpret Their Civil War*. Princeton: Princeton University Press 1954.

Quarles, Benjamin. *The Negro in the Civil War*. Boston: Little, Brown, 1953.

Randall, James G., and David Donald. *The Civil War and Reconstruction*. New York: D. C. Heath Co., 1953.

Sefton, James. *The United States Army and Reconstruction, 1865–1877.* Baton Rouge: Louisiana State University Press, 1967.

Shoemaker, Floyd C. *Missouri and Missourians, Land of Contrasts and People of Achievements.* Chicago: Lewis, 1943.

Smith, Edward C. *The Borderland in the Civil War.* New York: Macmillan, 1927.

Smith, James D. "The Virginia Constitutional Convention of 1867–1868." M. A. Thesis, University of Virginia, 1956.

————. "Virginia During Reconstruction, 1865–1870—A Political, Economic and Social Study." Ph.D. dissertation, University of Virginia, 1960.

Sneed, Thomas L. *The Fight for Missouri from the Election of Lincoln to the Death of Lyon.* New York: C. Scribner's Sons, 1888.

Taylor, Alrutheus A. *The Negro in the Reconstruction of Virginia.* Washington: The Association for the Study of Negro Life and History, 1926.

Thatcher, Marshall P. *A Hundred Battles in the West, St. Louis to Atlanta, 1861–1865.* Detroit: the Author, 1884.

Thomas, Benjamin P. *Abraham Lincoln.* New York: Alfred A. Knopf, 1952.

Van Horn, Thomas B. *The Life of Major General George H. Thomas.* New York: Charles Scribner's Sons, 1882.

Vance, Joseph C. "The Negro in the Reconstruction of Albemarle County, Virginia." M.A. Thesis, University of Virginia, 1953.

Wiley, Bell I. *The Life of Johnny Reb.* Indianapolis: Bobbs-Merrill, 1951.

Williams, Kenneth P. *Lincoln Finds a General.* 5 vols. New York: Macmillan, 1949–59.

Williams, Walter, ed. *A History of Northeast Missouri.* Chicago: Lewis, 1913.

Wilson, Theodore B. *The Black Codes of the South.* Tuscaloosa: University of Alabama Press, 1966.

### PERIODICALS

Blunt, James G. "General Blunt's Account of His Civil War Experiences." *Kansas Historical Quarterly,* 18 (May, 1932), 211–65.

Cain, Marvin R. "Edward Bates and Hamilton R. Gamble: A Wartime Partnership." *Missouri Historical Review,* 56 (January, 1962), 146–55.

Castel, Albert. "Kansas Jayhawking Raids into Western Missouri in 1861." *Missouri Historical Review,* 54 (October, 1959), 1–11.

————. "Order No. 11 and the Civil War on the Border." *Missouri Historical Review,* 57 (July, 1963), 357–68.

Crownover, Sims. "The Battle of Franklin." *Tennessee Historical Quarterly,* 14 (December, 1955), 291–322.

Gist, W. W. "The Battle of Franklin." *Tennessee Historical Magazine,* 6 (October, 1920), 213–65.

Grover, George S. "The Shelby Raid, 1863." *Missouri Historical Review,* 6 (April, 1912), 107–26.

Horn, Stanley F. "Nashville During the Civil War." *Tennessee Historical Quarterly,* 4 (March, 1945), 2–22.

Hulston, John K. "West Point and Wilson's Creek." *Civil War History,* 1 (December, 1955), 333–54.

Laughlin, Sceva Bright. "Missouri Politics During the Civil War." *Missouri Historical Review,* 14 (October, 1929), 87–113.

Lee, Bill R. "Missouri's Fight over Emancipation in 1863." *Missouri Historical Review,* 45 (April, 1951), 256–74.

Lewis, Lloyd. "Propaganda and the Kansas-Missouri War." *Missouri Historical Review,* 34 (October, 1939), 3–17.

McDougal, H. C. "A Decade of Missouri Politics—1860 to 1870—From a Republican Viewpoint." *Missouri Historical Review,* 3 (January, 1909), 126–53.

Moger, Allen W. "Railroad Practices and Policies in Virginia after the Civil War." *Virginia Magazine of History and Biography,* 59 (October, 1951), 423–57.

Morton, Richard L. "Life in Virginia by a 'Yankee Teacher,' Margaret Newbold Thorpe." *Virginia Magazine of History and Biography,* 31 (1926), 266–84.

Mudd, Joseph A. "What I Saw at Wilson's Creek." *Missouri Historical Review,* 7 (January, 1913), 89–105.

Nelson, Earl J. "Missouri Slavery, 1861–1865." *Missouri Historical Review,* 28 (July, 1934), 260–74.

O'Connor, Henry. "With the First Iowa Infantry." *The Palimpset,* 3 (1922), 53–61.

Olsen, Otto H. "Reconsidering the Scalawags." *Civil War History,* 12 (December, 1966), 304–20.

Parrish, William E. "General Nathaniel Lyon: A Portrait." *Missouri Historical Review,* 49 (October, 1954), 1–18.

Philips, John E. "Hamilton R. Gamble and the Provisional Government of Missouri." *Missouri Historical Review,* 5 (October, 1910), 1–4.

Potter, Marguerite. "Hamilton R. Gamble, Missouri's War Governor." *Missouri Historical Review,* 35 (October, 1940), 25–71.

Robinett, Paul M. "Marmaduke's Expedition into Missouri: The Battles of Springfield and Hartville, January, 1863." *Missouri Historical Review,* 58 (January, 1964), 151–73.

Robison, Dan M. "The Carter House: Focus of the Battle of Franklin." *Tennessee Historical Quarterly,* 22 (March, 1963), 3–21.

Scroggs, Jack B. "Southern Reconstruction—A Radical View." *Journal of Southern History,* 24 (November, 1958), 407–29.

Shoemaker, Floyd C. "The Story of the Civil War in Northeast Missouri." *Missouri Historical Review,* 7 (January and April, 1913), 63–75, 113–31.

Trelease, Allen W. "Who Were the Scalawags." *Journal of Southern History,* 29 (November, 1963), 445–68.

Walker, Hugh. "Bloody Franklin." Civil War Times *Illustrated* (December, 1964), 16–24.

Weigley, Russell F. "The Military Thought of John M. Schofield." *Military Affairs,* 22–23 (1958–59), 77–84.

# Index

## DATE DUE

| FEB 17 | | | |
|--------|---|---|---|
| JUL 17 AUG 0 1 | | | |
| FEB 18 | | | |
| | | | |
| | | | |
| | | | |
| | | | |
| | | | |
| | | | |
| | | | |
| | | | |
| | | | |
| | | | |
| | | | |

Demco, Inc. 38-293